PRINCIPLES AND PRACTICE OF CONSUMER CREDIT RISK MANAGEMENT

Helen McNab   and   Anthea Wynn

FINANCIAL WORLD Publishing

Financial World Publishing
IFS House
4-9 Burgate Lane
Canterbury
Kent
CT1 2XJ
United Kingdom

Telephone: 01227 818687
e-mail: editorial@ifslearning.com

Financial World Publishing publications are published by The Chartered Institute of Bankers, a non-profit making registered educational charity.

The Chartered Institute of Bankers believes that the sources of information upon which the book is based are reliable and has made every effort to ensure the complete accuracy of the text. However, neither CIB, the author nor any contributor can accept any legal responsibility whatsoever for consequences that may arise from errors or omissions or any opinion or advice given.

Trademarks

Many words in this publication in which the authors and publisher believe trademarks or other proprietary rights may exist have been designated as such by use of Initial Capital Letters. However, in so designating or failing to designate such words, neither the authors nor the publisher intends to express any judgment on the validity or legal status of any proprietary right that may be claimed in the words.

Typeset by Kevin O'Connor
Printed by Selwood Printing, Burgess Hill
© Helen McNab and Anthea Wynn 2000
Reprinted 2001
ISBN 0-85297-519-8

Fair, Isaac is very proud to be associated with The Chartered Institute of Bankers for this prestigious publication, which represents an industry we have been associated with for over 40 years.

About Fair, Isaac

Fair, Isaac (NYSE: FIC) is a global provider of customer analytics and decision technology. Widely recognized for its pioneering work in credit scoring, Fair, Isaac revolutionized the way lending decisions are made. Today the company helps clients in multiple industries increase the value of customer relationships. With headquarters in San Rafael, California, Fair, Isaac has 20 offices worldwide, including offices in the UK, France, Spain, Italy, Germany, Austria, South Africa, Canada, Mexico, Brazil and Japan.

For more information about Fair, Isaac email *emeainfo@fairisaac.com*

Acknowledgments

We have received an enormous amount of help from many people while compiling this book. We should particularly like to thank Gerard Scallan of ScorePlus Ltd and Anthony Sharp of Anthony Sharp Associates for their support and their significant contributions to many of the chapters.

Andrew Churchill and Robert Sleight of Halifax plc, Roger Williams of Nationwide Building Society, Chris Sykes of The Royal Bank of Scotland plc, Graham Prosser of GUS Home Shopping Ltd, David Cavell, Industry Advisor, Stephen Pratt of Clandon Associates Ltd and Tony Masters of WWAV Rapp Collins have all contributed in various ways we could not have managed without.

We also formally acknowledge the support of Peter Madge of *Adviser* journal for permission to reproduce the diagram and much of the material used in Chapter 15.

Unfortunately but understandably, we are unable to acknowledge a large number of other people for reasons of corporate anonymity but we are equally grateful to all of them for their contributions. We hope they will know who we mean.

Helen McNab and Anthea Wynn

January 2000

CONTENTS

Contents

PREFACE

This book has been specifically written to complement The Chartered Institute of Bankers' Diploma in Financial Services Management subject Principles and Practice of Consumer Credit Risk Management. We have placed limitations on its content so that it does not overlap excessively with other subjects in the Diploma. We have confined the content specifically to products that would usually be operated on a centralized basis, namely credit (or option) cards, charge cards, budget cards and personal loans.

The underlying theme throughout this book has been to represent what we see as best practice in the industry. This means that you, the reader, may encounter ideas and/or practices that you do not see in your own workplace. You will almost definitely encounter areas of expertise or specific functions that, so far, are outside your own professional experience. This is deliberate. The whole objective of any professional course is to learn about these wider activities so that when the career opportunities arise in the future, you will have some basic knowledge for the new job.

For sections on legislation, we have highlighted *principles* rather than specific details or the enactment of the law. These principles should transcend geographic boundaries, whereas the specifics may not. However we have based the content of the book largely on UK practices, environment and legal requirements.

Areas of exclusion

We have excluded any details about taking or processing securities, credit hire or hire purchase, guarantees or indemnities, or land transactions. However, where the credit process interacts with retailers then the relevant detail is included. Any details specific to current accounts and debit cards are also excluded.

Marketing as a function is also specifically excluded. However, there are references to marketing where other functions interact with it, e.g. the acquisition of new business. Similar references are made as appropriate to the other excluded functions of IT/systems, customer database/management information, finance/planning/treasury and support areas.

Areas covered in the book

Chapters 1 and 2 set the scene by looking at the social framework for a credit operation as well as the internal functions required to successfully run a modern credit company.

Chapters 3 to 9 examine risk management and decision-making theory, with their associated monitoring and control techniques.

Chapters 10 to 16 deal with the practicalities of credit risk operations and consider best practices within applications processing, account management, fraud, collections/recoveries, and litigation.

The final chapters look at the legal and regulatory framework within which the credit organization must operate. These details will inevitably change over time.

To decode the industry jargon, there is a Glossary of Terms at the back of the book.

1

CONSUMER CREDIT ENVIRONMENT

In order to understand any operation or function, it is important to be able to grasp the context within which it operates. For consumer credit grantors, there is the external world that governs the legal and operating boundaries and the marketing opportunities. There is also the internal company, with its own structures and policies.

1.1   Legal Framework and Compliance

Every organization operates within a number of universal parameters, the main ones of which are political, economic, social, ethical, technological and legal. Political and economic drivers are outside the scope of this course and the extent to which modern technology is used will govern the degree of competitive edge and overall success that a company enjoys.

The legal framework varies in detail from one country to another, but the basic concepts are generally consistent. At the top level there will be some form of Companies Act that determines the corporate structure, shareholding and accounting/reporting methods. There will be a wide variety of employment laws, health and safety criteria, registration requirements and any number of other constraints.

In the UK a consumer credit lender must be licensed under the Consumer Credit Act and under the Data Protection Act. Every stage of its lending procedures must comply with the details spelt out in both these Acts together with the Money Laundering Regulations and various voluntary codes of practice. The lender is likely to belong to a trade association (e.g. British Bankers Association, Finance and Leasing Association, Building Societies Association), which may also lay down guidelines for some aspects of professional behaviour for their members. If it is a credit card issuer affiliated with Visa or MasterCard, then these two umbrella organizations will also impose operating constraints in areas that include authorizations and plastic card design and content. If it is a bank or a subsidiary of a bank, then specific banking regulations will also apply.

With this increasing degree of complexity, it has become common in recent years for lenders to establish a job/function to ensure that the requirements of all this legislation are met on a day-to-day basis. This function is called compliance, and the Compliance Manager is usually a senior role. This role will also include being aware of forthcoming changes in legislation or voluntary codes of practice, anticipating the impact of these on the company and setting in motion the necessary new practices and procedures. The Compliance Manager may also be the nominated Money Laundering Officer as required under the Money Laundering Regulations.

1.2   Composition of the Organization

A typical credit grantor has all of the following functions:

- marketing;
- application processing;
- account management including customer service and authorizations;
- collections;
- recoveries;
- risk management (credit strategy);
- fraud;
- legal/compliance;
- IT/systems;
- management information (MI);
- accounts/finance/planning/audit; and
- support resources – human resources, premises, etc.

The organizational structure of these functions will vary by company. Some will be managed centrally and others from within a branch network. Some functions may be outsourced to third-party suppliers whereas others may be provided from another part of the organization. All except support resources influence the account life of the customer.

1.3   Organizational Functions and the Credit Cycle

Any open account follows a life or credit cycle pattern that starts with the customer applying for the credit and ends when the account is closed for whatever reason. Figure 1.1 illustrates the different phases of the credit cycle. These phases also relate to different organizational functions and departments.

Figure 1.1: Credit cycle

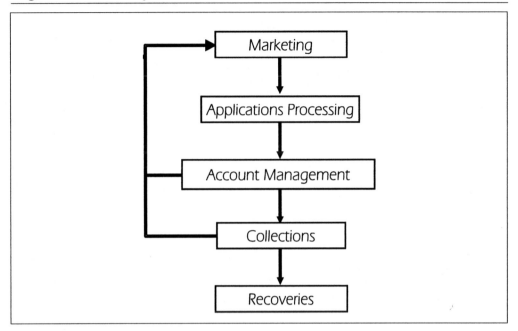

The marketing through to the recoveries functions are all directly involved with customers and accounts through the credit cycle.

Marketing is responsible for business development – initially for attracting new customers and subsequently for maintaining and extending relationships with 'good' existing customers.

Application processing is accountable for the efficient and responsible administration of customer applications.

Account management is a wide-ranging function dealing with customers during the active life of their account(s).

Collections, also a customer service unit, is responsible for rehabilitating delinquent customers into the normal credit cycle.

Recoveries manages those accounts no longer considered 'customers' – where the key objective is recovery of the outstanding debt, in the most cost-effective fashion.

Fraud cuts across all these areas, with processes in place for fraud avoidance and detection at any point in the credit cycle.

Risk management (sometimes called credit strategy) also has influence across this credit cycle, with the responsibility for optimizing credit losses against business development (see Figure 1.2).

Figure 1.2: Credit cycle with risk management function

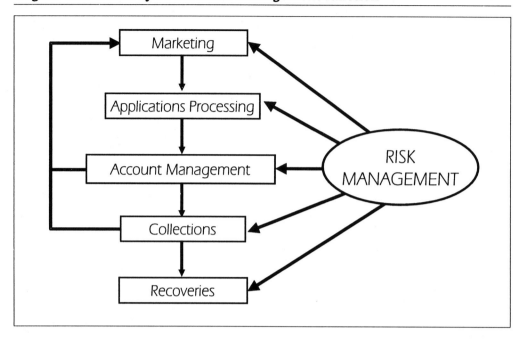

All the decisions made throughout the credit cycle have bad debt risk implications. The role of the risk management unit is to:

● agree with marketing about prospect identification, eligibility, and pre-approval selections;

● determine risk parameters for product pricing, facilities and 'packages';

● create and audit credit/risk strategies and policies for new application underwriting, fraud avoidance, limit setting, and overlimit authorizations; and

● develop risk-based collections and recoveries strategies.

To support these business areas, the risk management function provides decision tools, (typically score-based models), and develops strategies and policy rules around these tools. Thereafter, it monitors the effectiveness of these decision tools and the outcome of their associated strategies.

In most organizations, risk management has a key management information role, specifically forecasting bad debt levels and developing provision methodologies. It is also responsible for the specification and management of systems for the delivery of their strategies to the business areas.

Other departments with widespread influence include:

Legal/compliance – ensures that all product offerings and business practices conform to regulatory requirements; and

IT/systems – responsible for delivering/maintaining operational and management systems across the credit cycle, with appropriate flexibility and functionality to meet user requirements.

Historically IT services have been supplied and maintained centrally. With the advent of PC-based systems, this responsibility has largely devolved to users. For example, risk management functions within many organizations have parameterized 'strategy manager' systems that allow the user to set up and change credit policy criteria.

Management information – the key to understanding customer behaviour and managing customers across the credit cycle in a cohesive manner. Traditionally, MI would have been within the control of IT, but is now generally managed as a distinct function with flexible user access.

Accounts, finance, planning and audit – responsible for understanding product and customer profitability and determining overall pricing strategies, as well as accountancy, budgeting and compliance roles. To be effective in their task, close ties are required with the operational areas, marketing and risk management.

1.4 Why Organizations use Credit Scoring – a Brief History

Credit granting organizations use many different tools and systems to make day-to-day decisions. From a risk management perspective, the most important tool has become credit scoring, which is now often complemented by behavioural scoring.

What is credit scoring?

Credit scoring is a statistically derived decision-making tool comprising a scorecard and a set of associated statistics. The first scorecards were built to predict application risk and this was given the title 'credit scoring'.

A scorecard (see example in Figure 1.3) is a set of questions, called characteristics, with a set of answers, called attributes. Each attribute has a different score value. In Figure 1.3 the characteristic 'telephone number given' has four attributes, namely 'none', 'work', 'home' and 'both'. (It should be noted that this scorecard and its components are illustrative only.)

For any given customer, the attribute scores are summed to give a total score that is interpreted using the scorecard statistics. For an application risk scorecard these statistics tell the decision maker the likely risk of non-payment in the future.

Figure 1.3: Example scorecard

Accommodation type	Home owner 50	With parents 38	Tenant 30	Other 30
Time with bank	<1 year 20	1-3 years 28	4-9 years 35	10+ years 48
Telephone number given	None 18	Work 28	Home 32	Both 35
Years at current address	<3 years 25	4-8 years 30	9-14 years 32	15+ years 35
Worst status of other credit accounts	All good 40	Arrears 1-2 15	Arrears 3+ -10	Write-off -30
No. CCJs found at bureau	None 32	1 -50	2+ -100	

Although scoring is most commonly used for risk assessment, scores can also be developed to predict any dimension of behaviour – response, propensity, attrition, fraud, churn – at the point of application and throughout the life of the account/customer.

A score is therefore a one-dimensional summary of a particular aspect of customer behaviour, based on the information known about that customer at a specific point in time.

Credit organizations without scoring

Before the 1980s, credit organizations had relatively simple organizational structures, with standard products and little competition. The operational staff were generally dispersed in branches and were the customer contact point. As illustrated in Figure 1.4, their line managers were there to oversee the operations staff and handle complex cases, and the general managers at the top of the organization were the policy makers.

Figure 1.4: Simple organizational structure

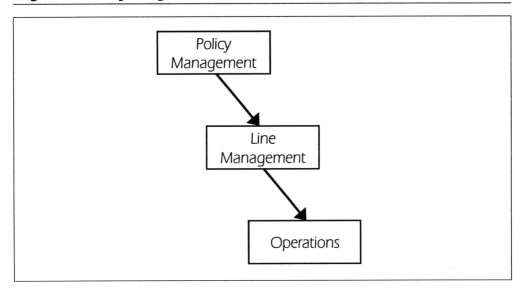

For these organizations, there was often little need for a feedback loop between operations and policy makers. This was because the policy makers graduated through, and therefore had experience of, each level within the organization.

From the 1980s, these organizations began to change in response to increasing competition from new products and credit providers, fuelled in the UK, by the deregulation of the credit industry.

Main reasons for using scoring

The primary reason for introducing credit scoring was to improve the trade-off between acquisition volumes and bad debt. The secondary reason was to improve operational efficiency. When the process is also automated, scores are easy to compute and they remove the lengthy task of manual credit assessment. The third reason for using scoring was to obtain better portfolio control, through the monitoring of the scoring process and the subsequent portfolio performance.

Integration of credit scoring

The first users of credit scoring were mail order organizations, followed by bank credit card and private label card issuers. The characteristics of their products and their organizational set-up were ideal for scoring:

● large volume of applications;

● low-value transactions;

- centralized operations;

- little customer contact; and

- good management information systems.

In addition, credit was peripheral to these organizations. For mail order and private label operators, credit was a mechanism for supporting sales. Bank credit card issuers set up centralized units, outside the scope of their mainstream, dispersed banking operations. This left the decision makers free from any legacy of traditional credit granting.

The introduction of scoring was slower in banks and building societies, where the opposite product and organizational characteristics existed:

- small volumes of applications;

- higher-value transactions/loan amounts;

- network/branch based; and

- much personal contact.

In the UK over the last 15 years, scoring has gradually become an established decision-making tool for branch banking, mortgages and small business risk assessment.

For many organizations the introduction of scoring coincided with/facilitated the automation of the new applications assessment process. Many branch-based organizations have also undergone fundamental structural changes in order to capitalize on further efficiency gains, through the centralization of the new application process.

Credit organizations with scoring

Scores simplify decision making because they summarize all available knowledge about a customer into an easily calculated, easy to use, numerical value.

Using scoring has required organizational change. The operations people remain the customer contact point but are more likely to be located in a central unit rather than dispersed in branches. Increasingly their role is to process customer information and relay score-based decisions to the customer. They are supported by their traditional line managers, and by referral operators who deal with cases outside the scope of the scoring system.

Now, general managers control policy through effective management information feedback loops as shown in Figure 1.5.

Figure 1.5: Organizational structure with feedback loops

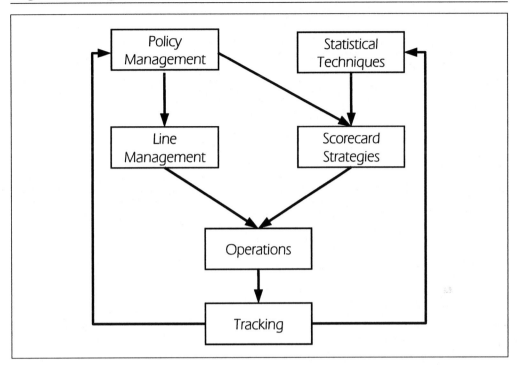

Scoring has become an internal communication channel, creating a mechanism for management to translate policy into action and control the decisions made by operational areas. It allows them to improve decisions through the monitoring of scores, decisions and associated strategies.

2

Data, Its Sources and Importance

Without data modern commercial opportunities would be very limited. Data and information (and they are different from each other) are fundamental to the success of any business today and they increasingly provide a commercial competitive edge. Without data it is impossible to build a scorecard, to provide management information, to take a debtor to court or provide almost all the other credit control functions.

For the credit grantor, data comes from a number of different sources both internal and external to the company. Some data is a matter of public record but other sources are available for purchase from external agencies. However, most of it comes from internal accounts files and the original application forms.

2.1   The Nature of Data

Quality and quantity are fundamental requirements when collecting raw data of any sort, and quality is the more important.

Quality

There are two aspects to quality, namely consistency and accuracy.

Consistency

This requires that, within a small tolerance:

● every new record (customer or account) created on the database, each field is (nearly) always filled in; and

● over time, any field on an input screen or database will be used to collect data for the purpose for which it was originally designed and only that purpose, i.e. its usage is not modified.

Accuracy

This is required from both parties:

- transcription, spelling, keying and data items with absolute values (e.g. dates or postcodes) are all correct in the absolute sense; and

- the customer, when providing information by any means, supplies truthful data.

When data is being used collectively for any purpose (e.g. developing a scorecard) then all these issues directly affect the end result. If there is just one data field which is of mediocre quality, then the final product (in this case the scorecard) will be reduced in quality accordingly. No amount of sophisticated computer programs or statistical techniques can overcome the inherent limitations of the raw data that goes into them.

Implications of inaccuracies

Poor data capture and quality control can lead to many problems. These can result in additional operational and bad debt costs, and low levels of customer service. Examples include:

- fraud detection – inconsistencies on an application form need to be highlighted to investigate genuine errors versus potential fraud;

- payment processing – delays occur where direct debit details are incorrectly recorded/set up;

- collections effectiveness – if an account defaults then an accurate name and address is fundamental to a successful collections process;

- likewise, if the account is subsequently passed to an external collections or tracing agency; and

- recording of judgments – if an account goes to litigation, and the lender obtains a judgment against the customer, then these details are recorded at the court. In due course this data is transferred from the court back to the credit bureaux to be added to their files. However, the law prohibits any alteration or correction to the data throughout this process, including any obvious misspellings of name or address details. Thus any inaccuracies occurring in the data before and during litigation could end up on the bureau records in such a manner that it will not match up with existing records, and never be found in a future search, i.e. vital information is lost to any subsequent enquirer.

Quantity

This is of particular importance when it comes to developing scorecards. Without a sufficiently large sample of accounts (both good and bad) it becomes statistically impossible to build a robust and long-lasting model. This sample size was traditionally held to be 1,500 goods, 1,500 bads and 1,500 rejects. This is still a valid guideline.

Data is always and only historic

All account data is historic by definition; it only accumulates retrospectively. The files of existing customers reflect only their past, i.e. historic, behaviour and when using data there is no choice about accepting this limitation. Therefore when data is used for purposes that will affect the future (particularly developing scorecards) the assumption that 'the future will be like the past' is implicit.

Common sense suggests that this assumption is unlikely to hold true for very long – particularly in today's rapidly changing environment. Many external influences will have an impact on the future behaviour of customers and their accounts – including the way that lenders manage them.

Generic data sources

There are two generic sources of data, namely 'free' data and data that incurs a cost to acquire. (Neither is free when it comes to data capture however.)

Free data

This is anything that an applicant willingly reveals. It usually comes in the form of answers to questions on the application form, but it can be supplemented with items like a driver's licence, or information gleaned from a telephone conversation. However, to be of benefit, all the information gained from an interview must be recorded in a usable form (preferably on a computerized database) and it must be held consistently for every person interviewed.

However, there is a downside. Just how reliable and truthful are the facts quoted? Equally, to what lengths should a lender go to check them? The question of reliability depends to some extent on the method by which the information was obtained. Generally speaking, if an applicant has had personal contact (by interview or telephone) then there is a better chance that his or her responses are largely truthful. If an application form is posted to a remote company (with no personal contact), then the applicant may be more tempted to 'enhance' the answers. This is not to suggest that applicants are inherently dishonest. It is human nature to dislike being rejected, even for credit, so some people may embellish their responses in order to maximize their chances of being accepted.

Having identified that this is the reality, is data reliability really a problem? Firstly this type of enhancement is not a new phenomenon nor has it materialized with the advent of modern systems or application scoring. Secondly, the percentage of applicants who seriously embellish their answers is very small. (In terms of scoring, if you accept that this is what some of your customers have always done, and that they are likely to continue to do it, then this is one instance where the future will be like the past.)

Cost data

This is data that:

- has a direct monetary cost associated with it, e.g. credit references; and
- costs in terms of time or other resource, e.g. internal files.

Current best practice is to take credit references for new applications regardless of cost, and both internal and external files are sources of independent, factual data that can usefully verify the information originally given by the applicant.

2.2   Application Form Data

A typical application form is shown in Figure 2.1. It contains most of the questions that most lenders ask.

All application forms contain a considerable number of similarities in both design and content. The similarities, on the whole, reflect legal requirements whereas the differences arise from the variety of questions asked. Not all questions are aimed at assessing creditworthiness – many companies also take the opportunity to ask security and marketing questions. The form must be well designed to make it easy to complete – and complete *fully* – and to encourage applicant honesty (see Chapter 4).

The application form has to satisfy a number of immediate requirements for credit assessment (see Chapters 4 and 10). It also becomes the basis for the account files and the legally binding contract between the lender and the customer.

2.3   Credit Reference Data

A credit reference agency (CRA) is an independent, commercial organization whose primary function is to collect, store and make available personal data about consumers. This data is derived primarily from the voters roll each year but is supplemented by financial records submitted by other lenders and County Court Judgments (CCJs) handed down by the courts. (Credit bureaux also operate in the same way by providing information about the financial status of companies, but that is outside the scope of this book.) They also offer many other, computer- and data-related services including application scoring, bureau processing of applications, credit systems and software, and marketing data, databases and services. In more recent times various legislation has come into effect which imposes a large degree of control over the activities of the bureaux (see Chapter 16).

The UK bureaux provide four basic types of information:

● public domain information, i.e. electoral or voters roll (VR) and CCJs;

● previous searches made by enquiring credit grantors in the last six months;

● subscriber or shared-information databases for various purposes including non-competitive, industry-wide systems for fraud and gone-aways; and

● geo-demographic files.

Voters' roll
This information is publicly available and the bureau files are corrected and updated annually.

Figure 2.1: Typical application form

APPLICATION FORM FOR A CREDIT CARD FROM XYZ BANK

1. PERSONAL DETAILS

Mr ❑   Mrs ❑   Ms ❑   Other _____

First Names: _____

Surname: _____

Address:_____

_____

_____Post Code: _____

Home Phone: _____

Date of Birth: ___/____/____

Marital Status:

Single ❑   Married ❑   Divorced / Widowed ❑

Are You: A homeowner ❑   A tenant ❑

Living with parents ❑   Other ❑

Are You: Employed ❑   Self-employed ❑

Retired ❑   Other ❑

Mother's Maiden Name (for security purposes):

_____

_____

2. EMPLOYMENT DETAILS:

Name & Address of Employer/Company:

_____

_____

Nature of Business: _____

Business Phone Number:

_____

Time in Present Job: _____ (years)

3. FINANCIAL DETAILS

Gross Annual Income: £ _____

Monthly Outgoing:

Mortgage/Rent: £ _____

MasterCard &/or Visa   £ _____

Other Cards   £ _____

Other borrowings/loans   £ _____

4. BANK DETAILS

Bank: _____

City/Town: _____

Sort Code: ____ - ____ - ____

Account Number: _____

Years with this Bank: _____

5. ADDITIONAL CARDHOLDER

Mr ❑   Mrs ❑   Ms ❑   Other _____

First Names: _____

Surname: _____

Date of Birth: ____/____/____

6. PAYMENT PROTECTION INSURANCE

Details of offer ... including

Please tick the box if you would like to take advantage of this offer   **Yes** ❑   **No** ❑

Your Right to Cancel:

Once you have signed this agreement you will have, for a short time, the right to cancel it. Exact details of how and when you can do this will be sent to you by post by the Bank.

Signature of Customer

Date of Signature: ____ / ____ / ____

Data Protection Act:

Any information provided by you may be held on the Bank's computers. One of the ways in which the Bank may use it, is to identify other products and services which may be of interest to you. If you do not wish to receive such details from us, please tick this box ❑

Figure 2.2 is a genuine extract from one of the UK's voters roll files for a specific UK address, although the names and address have been changed. It shows both the current resident (Mary Wright – the only resident in 1999) and all the previously registered voters at the same address over the previous 15 years. This latter data is called third-party data and there is a view in the UK that this information should not be supplied when a search is done on a named individual at a specific address.

Figure 2.2: Electoral roll data[1]

> ELECTORAL ROLL INFORMATION
> AT 1 SNATCH LANE, CREDITSVILLE, COUNTY, XY9 9AB
>
> JENNIFER P KNIGHT 1985-1986
> CLIVE C WHITWORTH 1986-1989
> JANE F WHITWORTH 1986-1989
> JAMES RICHARDS 1989-1990
> EILEEN RICHARDS 1989-1990
> MARY WRIGHT 1989-1999
> GRAHAM T KNIGHT 1985-1986
> MRS JENNIFER KNIGHT 1983-1985
> MR GRAHAM KNIGHT 1983-1985

County Court Judgments

This is also publicly available information. CCJs are the result of a County Court handing down a decision against a debtor that requires him or her to pay the debt to the claimant (usually a lender). The debtor has 28 days in which to pay, and if this is not done, a CCJ is registered against him or her (see Chapter 15). Each court holds registers of these unfulfilled judgments that are subsequently data captured and the files are sold onto the credit bureaux. If the debtor subsequently pays the debt, then the records can be amended and the bureaux will, in due course, hold the amended files. Figure 2.3 illustrates the details provided.

Figure 2.3: Typical court information[1]

COURT INFORMATION AT 1 SNATCH LANE, CREDITSVILLE, COUNTY, XY9 9AB	
Court Date	: 25/02/97
Case Number	: 0012345
Court Name	: Coventry
Judgement Value	: £345.00
Defendant	: MARY WRIGHT
Satisfied	: 14/11/98

[1] Equifax (1999)

Search information

Figure 2.4 is an example of the information that is registered on the bureaux files when a lender makes an enquiry. It is limited to the date of the enquiry, the type (i.e. credit enquiry) and the names of the enquirer and the applicant.

Figure 2.4: Typical search information[2]

SEARCH INFORMATION
AT 1 SNATCH LANE, CREDITSVILLE, XY9 9AB

Record Date	: 25/02/99
Search Type	: Credit Enquiry
Client Name	: BANK OF BINGO CARD SERVICES
1st Applicant Details -	
Name	: MARY WRIGHT
Date Of Birth	:
Date Moved In	:
Date Moved Out	:
Spouse/Cohabitee/2nd Applicant Details - NO 2ND APPLICANT	
Name	:
Date Of Birth	:
Date Moved In	:
Date Moved Out	:

Shared information schemes

This concept is one of sharing information for mutual benefit and the original schemes were based solely on financial records. With the growth in fraudulent activity, schemes for fraud identification and for tracing gone-aways have also become successful. Lenders who participate in such schemes agree to contribute a copy of their own records periodically to the bureaux. In return they have access to every other contributor's data in addition to their own but *only* for the purpose for which the data was originally given, i.e. credit control or fraud/trace. The schemes currently available in the UK are for:

● account information – CAIS (pronounced keys) and Insight;

● fraud identification – CIFAS (pronounced sigh-fass); and

● gone-aways – GAIN.

The first two systems provide data about an individual's financial commitments and are

[2] Equifax (1999)

competitive schemes, whereas the other two schemes are industry-wide, non-competitive and operated equally by both bureaux. The greater the range and numbers of contributors to such schemes, the greater the quantity of data available to all and the stronger are the benefits for everyone – including protection for the consumer.

Financial shared-information schemes

The value of collective credit data comes from using it to determine whether an applicant has defaulted in the recent past with other creditors, and whether he or she is already overburdened with existing credit commitments. Figure 2.5 is again a genuine entry and has been included to illustrate several points.

A typical entry gives:

●	the name of the contributing organization (i.e. the organization to which the individual has applied for the credit);

●	the type of credit facility (e.g. credit card or personal loan);

●	various financials and their related dates (which vary with the type of credit);

●	when the records were last updated; and

●	a summary of the payment history.

In the above case, the following abbreviations apply:

●	Any number from 0-6: the number of months in arrears;

●	N: facility not used this month;

●	S: Settled or satisfied account;

●	U: No payment due – new account; and

●	.: No information supplied by the lender.

Other codes are used to indicate the various stages of decay right through to repossession, and the left-hand entry in the list is the most recent.

To illustrate an earlier point about data accuracy, the first three records (i.e. Bank ABC, Retailer PQR, Retailer XYZ) show a different date of birth. Another lender, searching and retrieving this information, would not know which (if any) of these is correct.

In the last entry (Comms Company JKL) the account was closed many months earlier, but the company has not entered an S code, hence the row of dots continues.

CIFAS[3]

The Credit Industry Fraud Avoidance System (CIFAS) is an on-line information-sharing scheme whose data covers both application and transaction fraud, or suspected fraud. It is

[3] CIFAS (1999) *Credit Industry Fraud Avoidance System,* CIFAS, London

Figure 2.5: Typical data from a shared information database[4]

INSIGHT INFORMATION		
AT 1 SNATCH LANE, CREDITSVILLE, COUNTY, XY9 9AB		

BANK ABC VISA CREDIT CARD MS M WRIGHT

Balances	Limit	£4500
	Outstanding	£65
	Written Off	£0
Effective Dates	Start	01/12/91
	Birth	26/07/49
Insight Last Updated		28/04/99
Monthly Status	0000000000000000000000000000000000000 .0000000	

RETAILER PQR CHARGE CARD MS M WRIGHT

Balances	Limit	£1250
	Outstanding	£111
	Written Off	£0
Effective Dates	Start	31/10/85
	Birth	06/07/47
Insight Last Updated		12/04/99
Monthly Status	000000000000000000000000000000000000000000000	

RETAILER XYZ INSIGHT BUDGET MS M WRIGHT

Balances	Limit	£2500
	Outstanding	£0
	Written Off	£0
Effective Dates	Start	11/06/98
	Birth	26/07/47
Insight Last Updated		27/04/99
Monthly Status	N00000000UU	

COMMS COMPANY JKL :CELL COMMUNICATION SUPPLIER MS MARY WRIGHT

Balances	Limit	N/A
	Outstanding	£0
	Written Off	£0
Effective Dates	Start	15/02/96
Insight Last Updated		14/04/98
Monthly Status	............000.00000000000000000000000U	

[4] Equifax (1999)

available only for fraud identification and prevention purposes. There are seven categories of fraud data and members are responsible for contributing information by identifying, categorizing and filing fraudulent, or suspicious, cases:

- empty house fraud;

- impersonation;

- successful massaging of information to obtain credit;

- attempted fraud: not accepted by a lender;

- conversion: selling on of assets to which the seller has no title;

- criminal first-party fraud of all types; and

- aiding and abetting.

CIFAS is augmenting its files by encouraging organizations with credit-related fraud problems to become members, e.g. BT, telecommunications companies and the DVLC. This expansion will continue to strengthen and enhance the industry's fraud identification capabilities to everyone's benefit.

GAIN[5]

The Gone Away Information Network (GAIN) is a non-competitive, on-line information exchange network that stores up-to-date information about consumers who are in arrears and have moved without leaving a forwarding address. The database contains the name and address(es) of those listed as having gone away. The information is useful in:

- application processing – prevents lending to someone who has defaulted with another lender or who has returned mail pretending not to be at the address;

- collections and recoveries – traces addresses and shares all new addresses found; and

- customer management – provides a forewarning of customers who may still be performing well with one lender but have absconded from another.

Geo-demographic systems

Geo-demographic systems are lifestyle classification systems that are, at a minimum, derived from public domain data (e.g. census, CCJs) and financial data and sometimes from market surveys. Each postcode (not each house) in the UK is defined in terms of geo-demographic codes.

This is another source of data, which is more commonly used in marketing activities. A recent, and effective, trend is to include this type of data in application scoring systems, occasionally in behavioural scoring and it is particularly effective in customer scoring and attrition models.

[5] GAIN (1997) *Gone Away Information Network*, GAIN, London

2.4   Databases Used in Credit Management

All the databases discussed below are internal to the company. (External sources of data are discussed in Section 2.3 above.) They are overlayed with their corresponding operations systems and each has its own management information/reporting facility to monitor operational and financial activity.

Some of these databases and systems (e.g. authorizations) are not applicable to personal loan products.

Accounts database

This is the key internal database for any lending product. It is the most extensive, and the most directly relevant, source of data about account performance. This is true both for developing application and behavioural scorecards, as well as applying and monitoring customer-specific strategies for account management purposes.

Accounts databases are likely to contain at least the data shown in the tables in Figures 2.6 and 2.7 *in addition to* most (or possibly all) of the data acquired from the application form, the application and behavioural scores and the credit bureau information. This data will comprise:

● Static data (Figure 2.6), which is fixed from the outset of the agreement or varies only infrequently; and

● Dynamic data (Figure 2.7), which is collected each month. In some systems, some of these items may be calculated on demand as distinct from being held explicitly as fields on the database, e.g. amount over-limit or amount of interest due at any point.

Application database

Regardless of whether the application is finally approved or declined, virtually all of the data from the application process is collected on this database. This includes:

● personal identifiers, i.e. name, address, phone number, age, marital status;

● personal details, i.e. number of children, employment, bank details;

● credit reference details; and

● application scoring details, i.e. scorecard identifier, application and final score, characteristics scores, final decision, and any overides and their reasons.

Figure 2.6: Static account data

	Credit/Charge Cards	**Personal Loans**
Start of agreement	Date loan/card agreed & issued	
Amount	Declared credit limit, shadow limit & date set	Loan amount & date agreed
Annual fee	Amount and date due if applicable	N/A
Arrangement fee	N/A	Amount
Time	N/A	Length of loan (in months)
Billing cycle	Date for statement creation and payment-due date – will vary slightly each month	Fixed date for monthly instalments
Special customer	Marker to indicate a VIP, staff or other significant-customer category	
Interest free period	Days if applicable	N/A
Payment method	Direct debit details if offered	Direct debit details
Interest rate & date set	Rate (%p.a.) – fixed until next variation	Rate (%p.a.) for the full term of the loan
Plastic reissue	Month/year of reissue	N/A
Lost/stolen	Markers to indicate card gone missing, & date & account closed. New account number for replacement account	N/A
Fraud	Markers to indicate if account subject to fraud investigation	
Correspondence	Codes & dates to indicate standard letters & contact history	
Extension	N/A	Top-up loan offered – date & amount
Settlement value	N/A	Early settlement amount
Agreement terminated	Date – either by customer request or by charge-off – and reason codes	Agreed completion date
Additional cardholders	Details	N/A

Figure 2.7: Dynamic account performance data

	Credit/Charge Cards	Personal Loans
Authorizations	Usually automatic via electronic terminals. Transient data held only until the transaction is agreed.	N/A
Outstanding balance	Updated daily with transactions	Updated monthly after payment
Available credit	Amount and date	N/A
Over-limit	Amount and date	N/A
Payments due	Minimum amount and date	Monthly amount and date
Payment received	Amount and date received – might be minimum, part or full payment	Amount and date received
Purchases	Date of purchase, merchant number, authorization code, amount. May also include date posted to account.	N/A
Interest due	Calculated regularly (often daily) and added to account monthly	Usually calculated at outset of loan and added into monthly payments
Arrears	Number of months and total amount overdue	
Behavioural scores	May be multiple scores that are recalculated periodically depending on their purpose	
Reward Schemes	Date, amount of points/credits awarded, amount of points/ credits redeemed	N/A

Authorizations database

This database is designed as a short-term repository for holding the accepted authorizations until the confirmed transactions can be posted to the cardholders' accounts. The declines may also be stored.

Some credit card companies may choose to operate without an in-house authorizations system and use the Visa or MasterCard authorizations facilities instead.

Transactions and payments

This includes all details about both payments and purchases. It includes the date, amount and account number and possibly name for all incoming payments. Transaction details include date of purchase (and possibly date the details are posted to the account), merchant number, authorization code, and the amount.

This data may be held on a separate database(s) or may be posted directly to the accounts database.

Collections/recoveries database

Once an account is past a certain point of delinquency, it is copied onto a collections database. This is used with a specialist collections system that has prioritizing and queuing features, enabling the collections staff to work the account, hopefully to bring it back into order. The database will include personal identifiers and all the account payment and spending history. If the account continues to deteriorate, at some later point it is either marked as a recoveries case or moved to a recoveries database. Eventually, if the account is deemed irrecoverable, it is closed on the account database.

Fraud database

This contains personal identifiers, the date and details of the type of fraud, whether it is suspected or confirmed, and it links into the CIFAS database and the fraud system of which it is part.

Behavioural strategy manager database

This is part of the behavioural scoring system and it is used for designing, testing and evaluating alternative strategies. It contains a representative subset of accounts (with the full account details and history) copied from the main accounts database and it may be enhanced with credit bureaux data and geo-demographic data.

2.5   Management Information Requirements

Every operational and application assessment system needs to be monitored regularly to ensure objectives and targets are being met as well as ensuring that legal and operational efficiency requirements are in hand. The data is likely to be extracted from the operational systems and downloaded into an MI database for manipulation and analysis. It is important to recognize that personal identification data (usually account number, name and address) are not used for these purposes and the data becomes anonymous.

The data required depends to some extent on the function being monitored and it is not necessarily all downloaded in one pass. If the accounts database is particularly large (e.g. millions of accounts) a representative sample of accounts might be used for MI purposes. In general at least the following items are necessary:

- date of the data extraction;
- all credit and behavioural scores;
- scorecard identifiers if multiple scorecards are in use;
- some demographic data;
- any special markers, e.g. fraud account;
- declared and shadow limits;
- loan amounts and terms for personal loans;
- monthly payment history for the past x months;
- monthly arrears and over-limit history for the same period;
- monthly spending patterns for credit cards; and
- if delinquency status codes are used, the history for the same period.

3

MARKETING'S ROLE IN NEW BUSINESS GENERATION

This chapter is intended to give an overview of the marketing processes that precede the risk management functions. Marketing is a complex subject with many approaches and methods, and what follows here is intended to only illustrate the underlying principles.

A large proportion of all applications for new accounts are the consequence of pro-active efforts by the marketing department. Traditionally marketing operated independently from any risk management or operational departments, with a resultant antagonism between the two functions. In many organizations the conflict still persists, despite a variety of means available for resolving it.

3.1   Credit and Marketing Conflict

This problem arises when there is a lack of communication and understanding between the two functions, and both perceive that the other is working against its objectives. In these circumstances, typical points of view include:

From the risk management or application processing department's perspective:

– The marketing department uses the most appropriate means (e.g. direct mail, advertising) to solicit new customers, or offer new products to existing customers.

– Marketing's success is measured by the volumes of applications received. Therefore it optimizes its campaign budget by attracting the maximum number of applications seemingly with little regard for quality.

From marketing's perspective:

– The risk management acceptance parameters are too rigid, leading to excessive decline levels and therefore wasted marketing spend.

– The application processing department is alert to the longer-term consequences of opening accounts that are a potential bad risk which has a direct impact on the decline rates.

The nature and source of this conflict occurs at two levels, one being an operational, day-to-day level and the other being more strategic. At a strategic level, marketing might plan campaigns targeted at new sectors not previously approached. It might also change the specification of the product (e.g. interest rates or terms for loans) or offer consolidation loans. When any of these situations occur without prior consultation with risk management or application processing departments, there are hidden risk consequences that will be reflected in the decline rates and the longer-term bad debt levels.

At a practical day-to-day level, where there is limited communication between marketing and operations, the application processing department is not forewarned about impending volumes resulting from a campaign, and therefore it does not have sufficient resources available to meet the turnaround targets. Marketing is then dissatisfied with the slowness of the response as well as the decline levels.

Ways of resolving this conflict

There are a number of ways of improving this situation. The most important factor is communication. There must be frequent meetings where everyone involved in new business activities communicates future plans and the results of recent past activities.

Sophisticated strategy manager systems, which can be used by both credit and marketing for common objectives and targets, can form the basis for working together to mutually plan and devise new campaigns that take into account all the necessary risk and marketing requirements.

Finally, both credit and marketing should work to a common, measurable target. Instead of separating out the two components (i.e. volumes versus bad rates), they could be combined into a financial measure of success that caters for the responsibilities of both functions. For example, a goal of 'amount of total spend per £1,000 of good-quality credit written' combines all the costs (from both marketing and operations) required to write the new business. It takes into account the cost of future bad debt and the volumes of business actually written, as well as the direct costs of both parties.

There are other ways of resolving this conflict which are largely outside the scope of this book.

3.2   Pre-screening Techniques

Despite the perception of some credit people that marketing uses random-selection techniques without any regard for quality, marketing has always been constrained, at a minimum, by a budget for each campaign. Statistical tools have been used in direct marketing equally as long as credit scoring. Like credit scoring, marketing's use of these tools to improve efficiencies and reduce costs has increased significantly over the years.

Screening and cleaning

At a minimum, lists purchased for direct marketing campaigns targeted at new customers are screened and cleaned before delivery to the purchaser. This entails:

- de-duplicating – removing names that are repeated within the list (this can occur when a list is compiled from multiple sources);

- removing the names of existing customers who already have the product being offered;

- removing names with any adverse or unwanted criteria that the purchaser might specify, e.g. certain lifestyle qualities; and

- screening the resultant list against credit bureau files and removing all entries with bad credit histories, e.g. with existing CCJs. This is the first step towards improving the quality of the list.

The same process (except the first step) should apply when lists of existing customers are being compiled for cross-selling additional products.

These steps can then be complemented, either in-house or by the supplier, with a range of scoring activities that aim to further increase the quality of the resultant list, thereby reducing the costs of the campaign.

Response scoring

This was probably the first use of credit scoring techniques to predict an outcome other than risk. A scorecard(s) is used to screen a list by predicting the likelihood of a person responding to a mailshot. If the chances are too low, then those names are removed from the list and the corresponding cost is saved. Conversely, if marketing knows that it wishes to achieve a specific response rate overall, it can select that percentage of the list it needs to mail in order to achieve that target figure.

Figure 3.1: Response rates by score

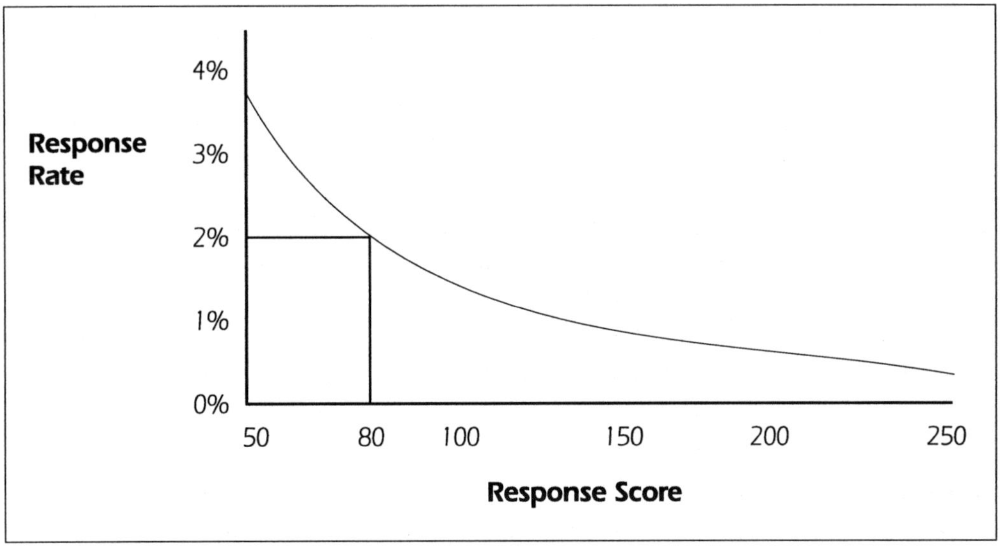

In Figure 3.1, a minimum response rate of 2% is required, and this should be achieved by mailing only those prospects with a score of 80 or lower.

Response scorecards are developed and used in the same way as credit scorecards. Customer marketing data (including data on previous campaigns and responses) is used together with geo-demographic and lifestyle data in the development process.

Risk scoring

Before a mailing is sent out, it is also possible to predict the likely risk corresponding to any name. Again, if the risk is too high, those names are deleted from the list. These risk scorecards are not quite as precise as application-scoring models because they have been developed from less-focused data. If the list has been derived from a database of existing customers where much more data is available, then this is less likely to be a problem.

Risk-response screening

It is possible to use these two models either sequentially or together in a two-dimensional approach.

When used sequentially, the response scorecard is applied to the list first, and the names with the lowest likelihood of responding are eliminated. The resultant list is then screened against the risk model, and again the highest risk names are removed. The remainder of the list is then ready for use.

Using the two scorecards together in a matrix can provide a different perspective.

Figure 3.2: Risk-response matrix

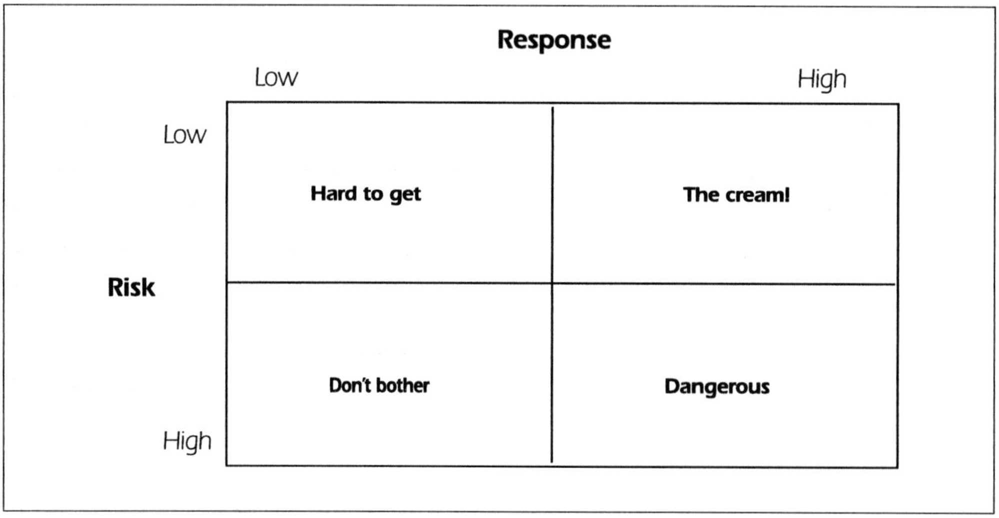

	Response	
	Low	High
Risk Low	Hard to get	The cream!
High	Don't bother	Dangerous

In Figure 3.2 the low risk-low response group is hard to get and may not be cost effective to mail. The low risk-high response sector is the cream – responding easily and generally good customers thereafter. The high risk-low response group is the segment to avoid, while the high risk-high response set pose a challenge. Candidates from this set will respond very well, but have a much greater chance of becoming tomorrow's bad debts.

Sophisticated strategies

Developing and using risk and response models together illustrates both the principles and the historic position of bringing the marketing and risk management functions together. In more recent years, the advent of sophisticated strategy manager systems has provided the basis for far more elaborate variations to be designed and implemented. Instead of adopting a 'mail/don't mail' choice, further options can be introduced by creating more segments. In Figure 3.1, several scorebands could be defined with different offers being made to each segment. In Figure 3.2 multiple subdivisions within both the risk and response dimensions would allow each cell to be treated in a different way that reflects the likely future risk and returns.

It is also realistic to develop scorecards that model other outcomes, e.g. revenue, propensity, or attrition (see Chapter 4). If revenue scorecards are used, they can be coupled with the response models in the same way as shown in Figure 3.2. Other combinations are limited in the end, only by the budget, the available systems and the imagination.

3.3   Marketing-risk Scoring or Application-risk Scoring

If risk scoring is undertaken before a list is mailed, why is risk scoring also applied when the applications are returned, given that an indication of the likely risk is already known? In reality, there are a number of reasons for doing this:

- several months can elapse between the compilation of a list and the mailshot finally reaching the targets, and individual circumstances could have changed in the interim;

- many months may have elapsed between the offer being received and the application being returned to the lender, and again the applicant's circumstances may have changed;

- the application may be returned by someone other than the person to whom it was originally sent, e.g. another member of the household or neighbour;

- because the application form contains more specific and up-to-date information about the applicant, the applications scorecard and the score in each case will be more accurate; and

- the data from credit bureaux files will also be more up-to-date at the time of application scoring, which will be a significant contribution the accuracy of the application risk score.

4

APPLICATION-RISK ASSESSMENT

All credit applications are subject to an underwriting process that assesses the creditworthiness of each application. In broad terms, the process aims to identify and accept potential good payers. Conversely it aims to identify and decline potential bad payers. This chapter examines industry techniques used for application-risk assessment, how they are used, and how they are monitored in order to meet company objectives.

4.1   Principles of Scoring

Marketing is largely responsible for the quality of credit applications received by an organization for any given product (see Chapter 3). In general, the more 'up market' the target audience, the lower the overall risk and the higher the acceptance levels are likely to be, and vice versa. The marketing effort therefore sets the context for all risk management decisions.

Application scoring is the most commonly used method for underwriting consumer credit products within lending organizations today. It is a statistical model for predicting the likelihood of good future repayment, based on the organization's own previous experience. A scoring model comprises a scorecard and a set of statistics for interpreting scores in terms of risk.

Scoring models take into account all the information known about a customer or applicant at the point of application. For an application scoring model, information comes from the application form and the credit bureau. For existing customers applying for an additional product, information about the way in which the applicant has run his or her other accounts should also be included in the model.

The scorecard comprises a set of characteristics (i.e. questions from the application form) broken into attributes (answers). Each answer has a statistically derived score or 'weight'. A typical scorecard has 10-15 characteristics, each with 2-10 attributes (see Chapter 1, Figure 1.3).

Not all the available characteristics are included in the scorecard directly, because there are overlaps between the characteristics. For example, long time with bank, long time with employer and older age all individually predict low applicant risk. However, the older the applicant, the longer their time with their bank or employer is likely to be. The scorecard development process statistically balances overlapping information and in this way all characteristics are implicitly included in the scorecard.

The score is calculated for each applicant by using the scorecard to look up the attribute scores that correspond to the answers given by the applicant, and from the information found at the credit bureau or from existing customer account records. For example, a home owner may get 50 points and a tenant 30 points for the characteristic accommodation.

The individual attribute scores are added together to give a total score which is then compared against a cut-off, at or above which the applicant is accepted. Below the cut-off, applicants are declined.

The score predicts the likely risk of non-repayment in the future. This is typically quantified as the likely bad rate – the number of bad payers as a percentage of those accepted. It is the probability that the applicant will be a future bad payer (a 'bad').

Figure 4.1: Bad rate by score

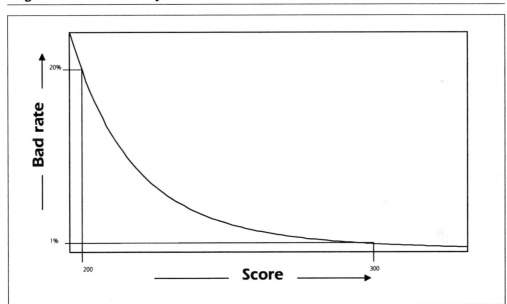

Figure 4.1 gives an illustration of the score-to-risk relationship. In this example a score of 300 equates to a bad rate of 1%. This means that out of every 100 applicants scoring 300, 99 should turn out to be good payers ('goods') and 1 should turn out to be a bad. A score of 200 equates to a bad rate of 20%, so, out of every 5 applicants scoring 200, 1 should turn out to be bad.

The score therefore rank orders risk. The higher the score, the lower the risk; the lower the score, the higher the risk.

The cut-off point sets the highest level of risk at which the company is willing to do business. This is the level of risk predicted by the model for applicants achieving the cut-off score.

Note that if the cut-off was set at the lowest possible score (found by adding together the lowest attribute scores across the scorecard characteristics), all applicants would be accepted. The resulting risk, or bad rate, would define the quality of applications for the portfolio overall.

If the cut-off score was set at the highest possible score, all applicants would be declined and the resulting risk would be nil.

In reality the cut-off score is set somewhere between these extremes. The cut-off determines the trade-off between the volumes of applicants accepted and the overall risk of those accepted, within the context of the quality of the available applications.

4.2   Application Scorecard Development

The basic steps in building an application scorecard are:

- feasibility study;
- sample definitions;
- data assembly;
- analysis of characteristics;
- reject inference;
- scorecard build;
- validation;
- strategy selection and documentation; and
- implementation.

Feasibility study

The purpose of the feasibility stage is to determine the business need and viability of building the scorecard. It seeks to define:

- the costs and benefits of the project;
- the objectives of the scorecard;
- resource requirement for each stage; and
- responsibilities for each stage.

In addition, the feasibility should consider operational and implementation issues.

At this point, organizations choose whether the development is to be undertaken in-house or outsourced to a third-party scorecard development specialist. Invitations to tender are good business practice in selecting the developer.

Sample definitions

The sample is the set of applications used to build the scorecard. Defining this sample is a fundamental stage in the project. The final scorecard will only be as good as the data and definitions used to develop it (see Chapter 2).

A time line model is valuable for understanding all the definition decisions that are required:

Figure 4.2: Time line model for application scorecard development

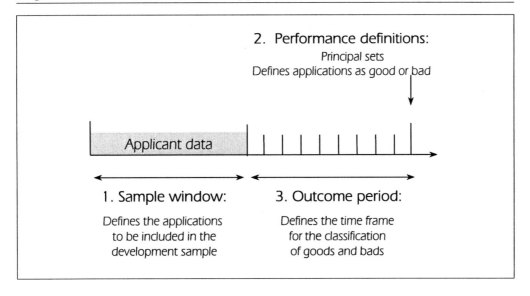

Sample window

The sample window defines the applications that are to be included in the development sample. The sample window selected depends on a range of factors and reflects the company's own experience. For example, a 12-month sample of past applications might be selected, to allow for seasonality and variations in marketing strategies.

Performance definitions

Each application in the sample is given a performance definition, i.e. one of good, bad, indeterminate, inactive or reject.

Goods and bads

A scorecard is built primarily on an analysis of good payers versus bad payers. These two groups are known as the principal sets.

In general terms, a bad should be an account which, given the known performance, would not be accepted in the future. It should equate to a loss-making account, either because of its potential as a bad debt or because of the additional expenses incurred by the collections process in handling the account.

In general terms, a good should be an account that the company is happy to continue doing business with.

The most practical way to define goods and bads is by their arrears status. A typical definition for a card or personal loan product might be:

- good = never delinquent or worst delinquency is one payment down; and

- bad = three or more payments down.

The definition of good and bad should reflect company experience and the product. The definitions need to determine the number of payments in arrears. They also need to consider whether this level of arrears relates to the outcome point, i.e. a 'currently delinquent' type definition, or to any point during the outcome period, i.e. a 'worst delinquency' definition.

Indeterminates

In the example definitions above, a group of accounts are missing – those that are two payments down. This group, called indeterminates, is not included in the scorecard modelling process for statistical purposes; it should be kept to a minimum, and as a guideline it should represent no more than 3% of the accepted sample of applications. Although indeterminates are excluded from the scorecard build, they do need to be included in the output statistics and must be included in the sample.

Inactives

For some portfolios, typically card products, the good group may include a proportion of dormant or credit-inactive accounts. To isolate the credit-active goods, and create a more effective scorecard, dormant and inactive goods may be excluded from the scorecard build. As with the indeterminates, these accounts are still included in the output statistics.

Rejects

The sample must also include rejected applications even though their performance is not known. These must be included because the scorecard needs to address all future applicants, not just those that were previously accepted. Each of these sample records is assigned good/bad performance indicators during the 'reject inference' phase of the scorecard development (see page 38). They are then included in the final scorecard build and output statistics.

Outcome period

The outcome period defines the point in time where the accepted applications are to be classified as good or bad payers. Setting the outcome period requires data analysis to understand the pattern of delinquency of accounts over time.

Figure 4.3: Bad rate over time

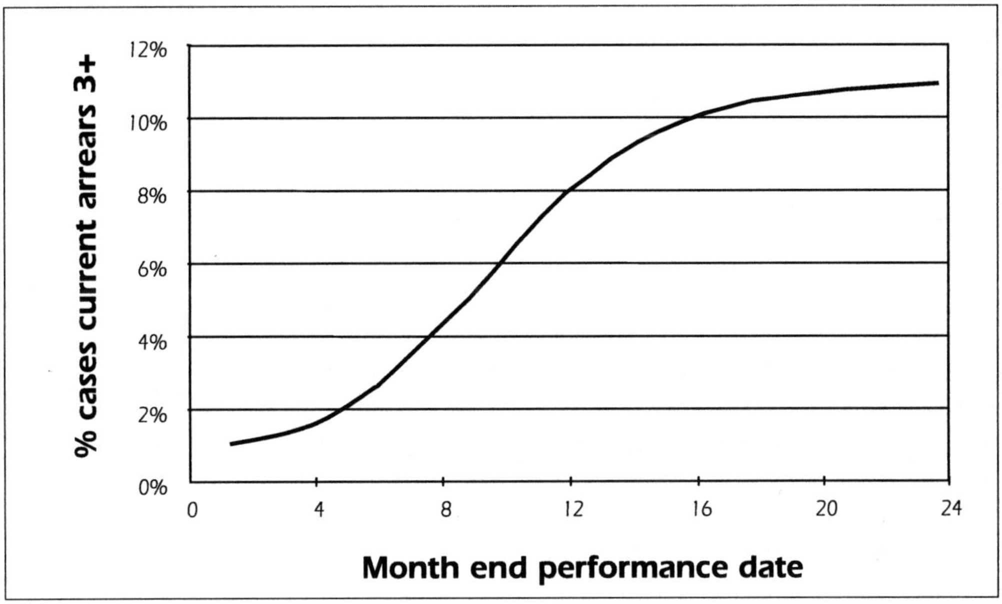

One method, illustrated in Figure 4.3, is to track bad rate over time. In this example 'bad' is defined as three or more payments in arrears.

There is no delinquency immediately following acceptance. All accounts are 'good' because there has been no opportunity for missed payments. The bad rate then rises rapidly for a time and then reaches a plateau. This is known as the life cycle pattern of delinquency.

If the outcome period is too short then bads will be mis-classified as goods. If the outcome period is too long then the sample will become out of date. There is no specific formula – the outcome period definition has to balance these two factors.

In the Figure 4.3 example, an appropriate outcome period might be defined as 16-18 months. This is the point at which the increase in bad rate has slowed. Although further bads emerge after this point, these 'mistakes' might be regarded as less important than the age of the sample. The 'older' the sample, the less likely it is to apply to the future applicants for which the scorecard is to be used.

Exclusions

Certain types of applications are excluded from the scorecard development sample. These are applications that fall outside the scope of the normal underwriting process or that do not have full or accurately recorded performance. Examples include:

- applications that are accepted regardless of score, e.g. V.I.P.s;

- applications that are rejected regardless of score, e.g. bankrupt, under age, with high level of previous default;

- fraudulent/suspect fraudulent applications (an application score predicts risk – not whether the applicant is genuine); and

- accepts which for various reasons do not have a true recording of their performance, e.g. lost, stolen, deceased.

Sample size

Scorecards can be built successfully on relatively small sample sizes, for example 1,500 goods, 1,500 bads and 1,500 rejects. Smaller samples can be used, but fewer than 500 sample points for any group will cause statistical problems. In general, organizations have more problems finding sufficient bads than goods and may be forced to use smaller sample sizes in these cases. Here, the smaller group will determine the accuracy of the scorecard.

It is more common today for organizations to take all applications from the sample window into the development sample. This has become practical because of the availability of good data management and storage systems. However, there is little statistical benefit to be gained from using sample groups of more than 5,000 records.

Data assembly

For an application scorecard, data is gathered from:

- the application form;
- the individual's credit bureau record;
- geo-demographic files (generally available from the credit bureau); and
- existing account records held by the organization (for additional product applications only).

Application forms

The application form should provide basic demographic data such at age, time at address, time with bank, telephone numbers, type of accommodation, bank and other product holdings. All information from the application form should be captured for analysis (see Chapter 2, Figure 2.1 for an example).

The range and quality of data available will be a consequence of the application form design, the way data is captured during the new application process and the way it is stored for analysis. Pitfalls to watch out for include:

- incomplete recording of information during the new application process leading to 'missing information' fields – this can be avoided by auditing and validation routines within the process;

- capturing 'grouped' rather than raw data during the new application process, e.g. time at address banded into years rather than the actual number of years at the address – the raw data gives the scorecard developer more precision;

- incomplete capture of information for rejected applications – often this is missing for operational efficiency reasons but is key to the successful development of a scorecard; and

- changes to the application form that can degrade the performance of a scorecard. For example:

  - changing the question 'do you have a home phone?' with tick box yes/no responses to 'give your home telephone number' will significantly change the applicant's interpretation and response; or

  - reducing the number of data items captured because of pressure from other areas of the business to make the account opening process quicker.

In addition, the scorecard developer should be aware of any weaknesses within the application processing system that may affect the correct recording of applications. For example, some systems allow applications to be cancelled. If these are then re-entered, potentially with slight changes to details to ensure the applicant passes the cut-off, applicant details will not have been recorded properly. This is more problematic in a branch environment.

Credit bureau data

The range of bureau information available varies nationally, reflecting ownership, national culture, legislation, and maturity of the credit markets. All available information should be captured for scorecard analysis (see Chapter 2).

Many organizations capture only a small proportion of all the bureau information available at the time of application for sound operational and economic reasons. Generally only the information required for decision making is passed from the bureau to the credit grantor.

In these circumstances, a retrospective credit bureau report is sought for applications in the development sample. This will capture all information held at the bureau, as it was at the time the applicant applied for credit.

Creating characteristics and attributes

For each characteristic, e.g. time at address, valid attributes are defined, e.g. 'yymm' for years and months. Ideally the finest level of attribute should be recorded. If the application form has requested date of birth then the age in years should be recorded. If the application form has asked 'what is your age?' with 'age range' tick boxes, then this grouped level data will have to suffice.

Part of the data assembly process is to check the range of attributes recorded for each characteristic. This is to validate the recorded data and investigate the incidence of 'null values'.

Analysis of characteristics

The purpose of analysing the characteristics is to identify those that can separate out the goods from the bads. A 'predictive characteristic' contains attributes that display very different levels of risk for the different attributes.

Figure 4.4: Cross tabulation example

Age	Total	Good	Bad	Bad rate
18-21	1,619	1,158	244	15.1%
22-33	8,084	6,050	849	10.5%
34+	28,317	22,144	1,285	4.5%
Total	**38,020**	**29,352**	**2,378**	**6.3%**

Figure 4.4 demonstrates a common method of analysing characteristics. In this case, bad rate is used to quantify the predictive power of each attribute. It demonstrates a clear relationship between age and risk – the older the applicant the lower the risk. This characteristic is therefore likely to be included in the final scorecard.

Each characteristic is analysed first by the finest breakdown of attributes. Where the predictive pattern of these attributes is similar, the attributes are then grouped for further analysis. This process is traditionally known as classing.

Statistical tests are applied to determine the overall power of each characteristic. The most powerful are taken forward into the scorecard build.

Reject inference

Reject inference is the process of estimating how rejected applications would have performed had they been accepted, and scorecard developers employ various methods of doing this. The starting point for one method involves extrapolating the observed performance of the accepted applications across the rejected applications. A safety margin is built into the estimation because it cannot be assumed that rejected accounts would have performed in exactly the same way as their accepted counterparts, had they been taken on.

This estimation approach relies on the rejected applications having some attributes in common with the accepted group. However, scorecard developers often find that some rejected applications have no attributes in common with the accepted group. The more systematic the underwriting process has been in the past, the less the two groups will have in common. This makes the extrapolation process problematic. Solutions to this problem include buying information, for example:

● looking at how the applicant ran accounts with other lenders – using information from an account information sharing database held at the credit bureau (see Chapter 2); and

- running a test period, and accepting all or most applications that would be rejected under normal circumstances.

The viability of the second option depends on the product. Mail order companies, with their 'high volume, low ticket' business combined with close control of sales, find the cost of acquiring this information (additional bad debt) is out-weighed by the value of the additional information obtained. For bank, loan and card products, the higher transaction values and lower volumes make this second option less viable.

At the end of the reject inference process, every rejected application will have been assigned a probability of being good or bad. For example, if a reject is assigned a probability of being bad of 0.2, this means it had a 20% chance of being bad, had it had been taken on. This same reject would have had a 0.8 probability of being good, i.e. an 80% chance of being good, if it had been taken on.

Scorecard modelling

The scorecard model is built on both the accepted applications with the actual, known performance (good or bad) and the rejected applications with their inferred or estimated performance classification.

The strength of each characteristic in discriminating between goods and bads is considered either in its entirety or by the individual attributes. The sequence with which these characteristics/attributes are brought into the model is controlled in part by the analyst building the scorecard and in part by the statistical technique employed.

Traditionally this sequence is controlled to reflect characteristic qualities, such as:

- operational ease of use, e.g. home owner/renter or time at address is introduced early into the model;

- reliability of the data, e.g. those characteristics with previous data capture problems may be introduced towards the end;

- data items that may be influenced by operational or marketing policy change, e.g. incentives to encourage payment by direct debit or take up of credit insurance, will change applicant response to payment method/insurance questions; and

- cost of acquiring the data, e.g. credit bureau characteristics may be introduced after the application form characteristics. This allows lenders to apply cut-off policies that will save on future bureau costs (see Section 4.3).

Within this framework, the most powerful characteristics/attributes are generally brought into the model first. The remaining characteristics/attributes are introduced in a sequence corresponding to their strength. This has the effect of giving the widest spread of attribute scores to the most predictive characteristics.

Other methods introduce all characteristics/attributes into the model at the start. The statistical technique determines which characteristics are included in the final scorecard.

An alternative approach is to introduce credit bureau characteristics first and application form characteristics second. This increases operational efficiency by allowing lenders to make a proportion of acceptance decisions based only on name and address. The decision for the remaining applications requires data capture and scoring of the full applicant data (see page 49-50).

During this process, the statistical technique used to build the model takes into account the overlap of information contained in the characteristics. For example, the older the applicant, the longer their time with bank or employer is likely to be. This overlap is called correlation.

At the end of the scorecard build, all characteristics will have been considered. Only those that add sufficient value in discriminating between goods and bads are included. It will be a statistically balanced combination of all the information available in the development sample.

There are a number of statistical techniques available for building a scorecard:

● linear regression;

● logistic regression;

● discriminant analysis;

● divergence maximization; and

● neural networks.

Each method has merits and limitations, although the overall ideas are similar.

Scorecard validation

Once the scorecard is completed, all applications in the development sample are scored using the new scorecard. Tables are produced for validation and decision making, showing the total number of applications by score, broken down by goods, bads and any other performance definitions used in the development sample. These tables are called score distributions; they become the benchmark against which to measure future expectations of performance.

A new scorecard should be validated to ensure that it is statistically robust and to verify how well the scorecard will fit the current applications. It is also desirable to run a set of scorecard diagnostics to determine the power of the scorecard and check the ability of the scorecard to discriminate between goods and bads, particularly around the cut-off point.

Figure 4.5: Scorecard development score distributions

Scoreband	Total	Goods	Bads	Bad rate	Odds
Up to 170	351	161	131	37.3%	1.2
170 to 194	2,205	1,345	545	24.7%	2.5
195 to 201	1,404	938	270	19.2%	3.5
202 to 211	2,682	1,894	420	15.7%	4.5
212 to 221	3,663	2,729	444	12.1%	6.1
222 to 239	7,866	6,111	583	7.4%	10.5
240 to 264	11,466	9,120	471	4.1%	19.4
265 to 279	5,573	4,415	113	2.0%	39.1
280 and up	6,845	5,275	71	1.0%	74.3
Total	**42,055**	**31,988**	**3,048**	**7.25%**	**10.5**

Notes:

The difference between the total figures and the good+bad figures are inactives and indeterminates

Bad rate = number bads/total number of applications

Odds = number of goods/number of bads

Some example summary score distributions are given in Figure 4.5. The scorecard developer should provide similar tables, but in greater detail – using one point scorebands around the potential cut-off area. The statistics in Figure 4.5 have been used to illustrate each of the scorecard measures in the rest of this chapter.

Statistical validation

The traditional way of validating the scorecard is to set aside part of the development sample. This set-aside group is excluded from the scorecard build. At the end of the development it is scored using the new scorecard and the distributions are compared with the distributions of the scorecard-build sample. Significant variations are followed up and parts of the scorecard development stages are repeated if necessary. This validation is particularly important where the development sample is small. With very large sample sizes, this test is less important.

Compatibility with current applications

Any development sample is likely to be at least two years old at the time an application scorecard is implemented. For example, a development sample with a 12-month sample window, an average outcome period of 15 months, and a swift development/implementation lead-time of 6 months, will be approaching an average of two years old at implementation.

Over time, the composition and quality of applications will change. It is necessary therefore to validate how well the current applicant profile matches that of the development sample. This is achieved by scoring out a set of recent applications using the new scorecard and comparing their distributions with the distributions of the benchmark. Any changes between the two distributions can then be taken into account when determining the cut-off score.

Scorecard diagnostics: odds-to-score relationship

Before accepting a new scorecard, the user should examine the ability of the scorecard to discriminate between goods and bads, particularly around the cut-off point.

In Figure 4.1 the risk-to-score relationship was illustrated by showing the bad rate by score. (The figures for this graph came from the scorecard distribution tables in Figure 4.5).

An alternative way to illustrate this relationship is to examine the odds-to-score relationship. The odds are calculated by dividing the number of goods at any given score by the number of bads at that score. Figure 4.6 shows this odds-to-score relationship, using the same base statistics as for Figure 4.1. The higher the score, the higher the odds, the lower the risk.

Figure 4.6: Odds:score relationship – normal scale

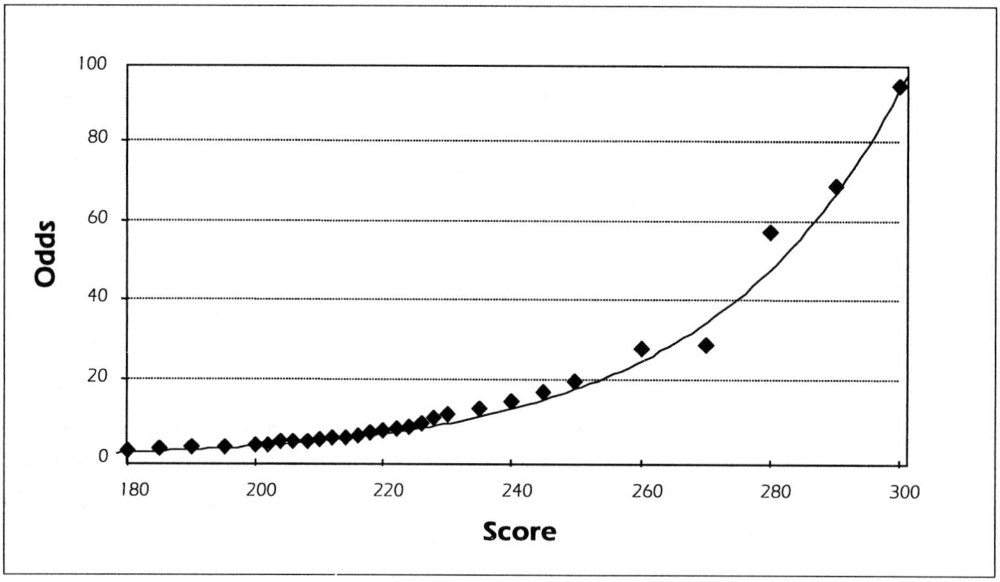

Figure 4.7: Odds:score relationship – natural log scale

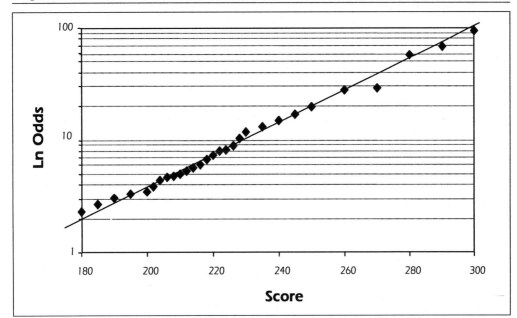

Figure 4.7 is the same graph again, using a natural logarithmic scale for the y-axis (odds axis). The log scale is a useful and effective mathematical tool which allows the odds-to-score relationship to be presented as a straight line. The log odds scale has been found to be the best way to measure the risk-to-score relationship, regardless of the method used for building the scorecard. It shows the risk-to-score relationship around the cut-off more clearly than the normal scale graph.

The slope or angle of this line demonstrates how well the scorecard will work. The steeper the slope, the more effective the scorecard. The slope itself is the line of best fit through data points from the model. These data points need to be included on the graph. The more clustered these data points are around the line of best fit, the better the scorecard will work. This is particularly important in the cut-off area. The overall slope of the line may be acceptable, but if the data points around the cut-off form a relatively lower angle, fine cut-off adjustments may be relatively ineffective. Problems of this nature need to be addressed with the developer, before the final scorecard is accepted.

Scorecard diagnostics: scorecard performance

Most organizations wish to quantify the efficiency of a new scorecard. Care should be taken in making comparisons across different portfolios. This is because differences in good/bad definitions and overall portfolio quality may influence the resulting statistics.

Four methods are used regularly and all these measures require both accepts and rejects to be included. If they are used to monitor the performance of the scorecard after implementation, i.e. applied only to future accepts, the measures will be distorted, because the highest risk applicants will be missing (rejected).

Strategy quote

The strategy quote (see Figure 4.8) gives the bad rate at any given level of acceptance. It depends on the acceptance rate chosen and on the overall quality of the portfolio. In this example, for a 90% acceptance rate, a bad rate of 5.4% is expected. Alternatively, for an 80% acceptance rate, a bad rate of 4.4% is expected. The overall quality of the portfolio is given by the bad rate if all applicants were accepted, i.e. 7.3% bad rate for 100% acceptance.

Figure 4.8: Strategy quote graph

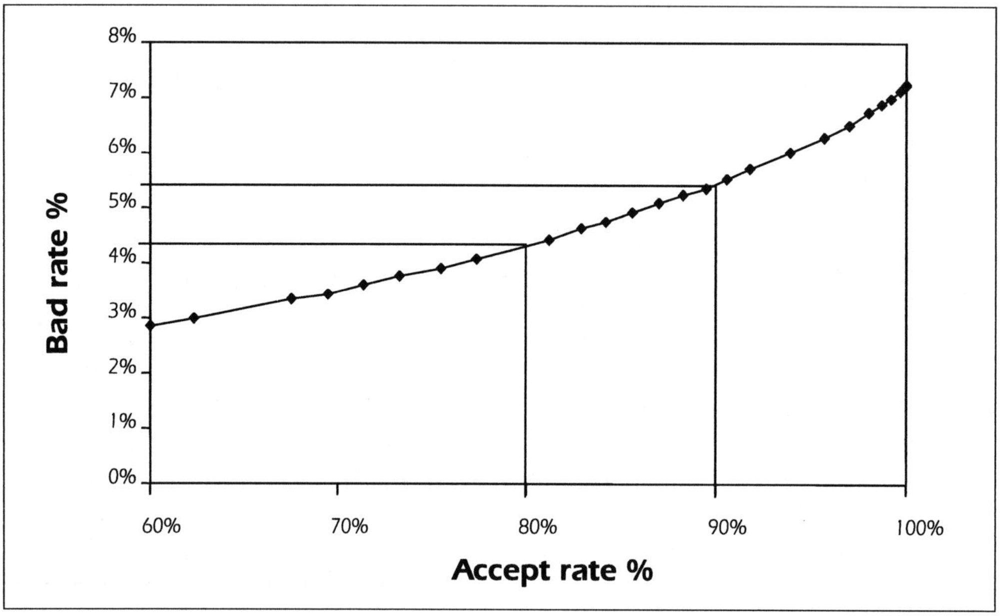

Cross-portfolio comparisons cannot be made using this measure, but it is useful for testing different scorecards for the same portfolio.

Divergence

Divergence is the difference in the average score of the goods and average score of the bads, taking into account the variance of each group around its mean (average).

A limitation of the divergence measure is that it depends on the assumption of normal distributions, which does not tend to apply to typical score distributions, as illustrated in Figure 4.9.

Figure 4.9: Divergence graph

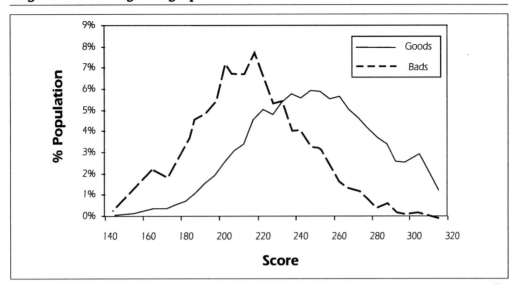

However, divergence does not depend on the overall quality of the portfolio and therefore cross-portfolio comparisons can be made using this measure.

Efficiency – Gini curve and coefficient

The Gini coefficient measures the distance between the distributions of the goods and bads. Graphically, it shows the percentage of bads that will be accepted and the corresponding percentage of goods accepted at any given cut-off. In Figure 4.10, taking on 85% of the goods would also mean taking on 53% of the bads.

Figure 4.10: Efficiency curve

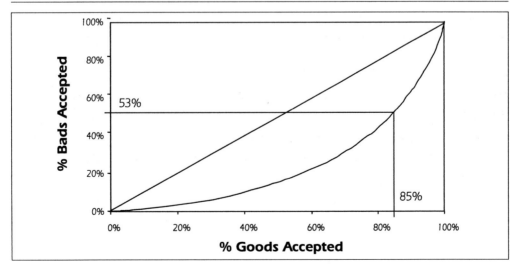

A perfect scorecard would accept 100% of the goods and no bads – 100% efficient – and the efficiency curve would be located in the bottom right-hand corner of the graph. A completely useless scorecard – 0% efficient – would accept the same proportion of goods and bads at any score; its efficiency curve would run along the diagonal of the graph, from the bottom left-hand to top right-hand corner.

The efficiency coefficient of any scorecard is then the area between the diagonal and the curve representing the mix of goods-to-bads across the scores. In this example the Gini co-efficient is just less than 60%, which is a good index for an application scorecard.

As with divergence, this measure does not depend on the overall quality of the portfolio and therefore cross-portfolio comparisons can be made. The measure is also known as the Lorenz curve or Somers D statistic.

Efficiency – Kolmogorov-Smirnov curve and statistic
The Kolmogorov-Smirnov (K-S) statistic is similar to the Gini coefficient because it measures the distance between the distributions of goods and bads (Figure 4.11).

Figure 4.11:K-S Curve

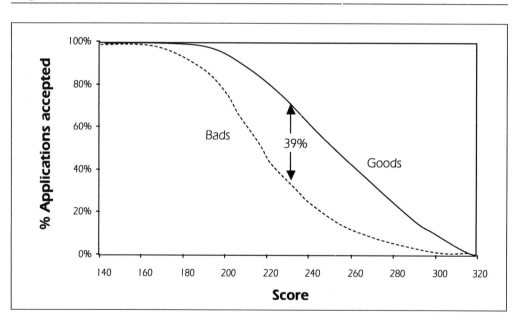

The Kolmogorov-Smirnov curve shows the percentages of goods and bads that would be accepted at any given cut-off score. The K-S statistic is the maximum distance between the goods and bads curves. In this example the statistic is 39%.

Again, this measure does not depend on the overall quality of the portfolio and therefore cross-portfolio comparisons can be made. Also, the measure does not depend on a score-to-risk probability relationship – it works on the rank ordering of the data (non-parametric measure). It can therefore be used to measure the strength of decision models built using other techniques, such as expert systems and neural networks.

Strategy setting and documentation

Once the scorecard has been accepted, the user is ready to set strategies using the score distribution tables. Although this is covered in detail in Section 4.3, the key decisions include the acceptance cut-off, limits or loan amounts, and account condition parameters.

This is also the point where policy and referral rules should be defined in relation to the score (see Section 4.5).

All this needs to be clearly documented with rationale for decisions, followed up with a diary of events which catalogues any subsequent parameter changes.

Implementation

There are four key areas to consider when implementing a scorecard. The first is the programming of the scorecard, acceptance cut-offs, credit limit cut-offs and other decision parameters. Many organizations now have decision delivery systems that allow user control over this process. Where this is not the case, a mechanism for changing score-related decision parameters needs to be found. Small but significant changes to these parameters are frequently required soon after implementation, as experience of using the scorecard increases.

The second area is user acceptance testing, to ensure that the scorecard and associated parameters have been coded correctly in the application processing system.

The third process is to ensure scores, credit limits, other decision parameters and decision reason codes can be captured for future analysis.

The final area is effective communication with the applications processing department and marketing. This needs to focus most on the reasons why applications may be referred and the decision process that should be followed (see Chapter 10).

For example, if the application is above the cut-off, but requires an address confirmation check, the operator should fulfil this check only. Where positive confirmation is found the application is accepted, and vice versa. The operator in these circumstances will not undertake a credit review of the application. Where the application falls outside the scope of the scorecard, then clear rules for application review need to be established. Many organizations have a separate 'referrals' section to handle these cases (see Section 4.5 and Chapter 10).

4.3   Strategy Setting

Setting acceptance cut-offs

The role of the underwriting decision process has already been established. It is to identify and take on future good-paying, profitable customers, from the prospects attracted by the marketing effort. Similarly, the process aims to identify future loss-generating, bad payers and refuse them credit. Logically, the lender should continue extending credit to the point where the losses from the most marginal bad payer taken on equals the profit from their good-paying counterparts – the point of break-even.

It has also been established that a scoring model predicts the proportion of bad payers (bad rate) at each score. It follows then that if an organization knows how many good payers it needs to balance the losses from each bad payer, it can set a cut-off at, and above which, customers will be accepted, because their risk is less than the break-even point.

Figure 4.12: Break-even model

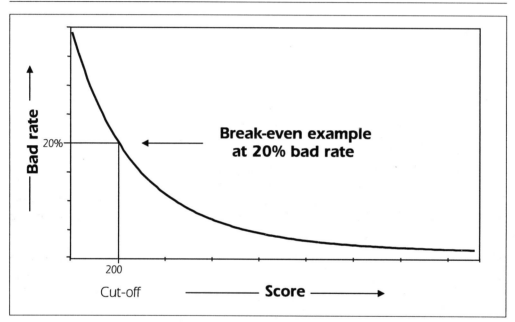

For example in Figure 4.12, if four good payers are needed to cover the cost of one bad payer, then the cut-off should be set at the score which predicts a 20% bad rate (i.e. where one out of every five applicants is expected to be 'bad'). In this case the cut-off would be 200.

In reality no organization can claim to fully understand break-even, even with a mature portfolio. Too many factors can influence the view of break-even, including volatility in lending rates, and difficulties in determining the time required to allow an account to come into profit.

As a practical alternative, organizations consider the trade-off between the acceptance rates at any given cut-off score and the subsequent overall bad rate expected from those accepted. The figures for this type of analysis come from the score distributions and are summarized in Figure 4.13.

Figure 4.13: Trade-off table

Cut-off score	Accept rate	Bad rate
0	100.0%	7.25%
170	99.2%	7.0%
195	93.9%	6.0%
202	90.6%	5.5%
212	84.2%	4.7%
222	75.5%	3.9%
240	56.8%	2.7%
265	29.5%	1.5%
280	16.3%	1.0%
Previous policy	**90.4%**	**6.25%**

Figure 4.13 demonstrates the range of opportunities available for the scorecard analysed in Section 4.2. The higher the cut-off the lower the acceptance rate and the lower the resulting bad rate from those accepted, and vice versa. (The statistics in Figure 4.13 are computed from those in Figure 4.5.)

The most common approach is to compare the results of the previous policy versus the opportunities presented by the scorecard. In this example the organization might consider setting its cut-off between 195 and 202. At 202, acceptance rates would be maintained at just over 90% and provide a drop in overall bad rate (from 6.3 to 5.5%), whereas 195 would allow for increased volumes (from 90.4% to 93.9%) at a similar past bad rate.

Super-pass and super-fail cut-offs

Where a scorecard contains a combination of credit bureau and application form and/or existing customer record characteristics, lenders have the opportunity to set additional cut-offs.

A 'super-fail' cut-off can be set at the point of the normal acceptance cut-off minus the maximum points that can be achieved from the bureau characteristics. Applications are scored based on their application form/existing customer record characteristics and declined without a bureau check if this score is so low that they would still fail to reach the acceptance cut-off even if they achieved maximum points from their bureau characteristics.

'Super-pass' is the converse. It is the normal acceptance cut-off plus the minimum points that can be achieved from the bureau characteristics. Applications can be accepted without a bureau check if their score from the application/customer characteristics is so high that they would still pass the acceptance cut-off even if they achieved minimum points from their bureau characteristics.

The rationale for this type of super-pass/super-fail policy is to reduce credit bureau search fees. Many companies operate a super-fail policy; fewer use a super-pass cut-off. Most organizations check for default and delinquent account information at the credit bureau even where there is a high pre-bureau score, particularly where the scorecard is assessing customers new to the organization. For repeat-business applications, from existing customers, super-pass policies are more likely to be used where existing account history shows the customer to be an acceptable risk.

(Note, most card organizations make a bureau search to fulfil money laundering identity checking requirements. In these circumstances a super-pass policy based on application form data is not worthwhile.)

An alternative approach is to set super-pass/super-fail cut-offs based on the scorecard bureau characteristics. This is most effective where the scorecard model has introduced the bureau characteristics before the application form characteristics (see page 39-40). The rationale for this approach is to increase operational efficiency and customer service, by minimizing data entry (initially only name and address is required) and being able to provide an acceptance decision for a proportion of applicants in the shortest possible time.

Declared and shadow limits

In general terms a limit is the maximum amount the lender wishes to extend to the applicant. For card products this is the declared or credit limit; for personal loans this is the principal loan amount. Setting limits must balance company exposure with customer requirements and expectations. Setting high initial limits may result in an unnecessary level of credit exposure that is subsequently hard to control. Initial limits should therefore reflect risk and be sufficiently high to make the product attractive to the applicant.

Most lenders set initial limits based on score as a measure of risk. Ideally this should be combined with some indicator of likely usage. In general, the lower the risk and the higher the predicted usage, the higher the initial limit offered.

Setting of initial limits/loan values also takes into account the amount of credit requested by the applicant. For some card limits, and for most for personal loan amounts, the decision is supported with a debt burden analysis. This aims to determine whether a customer has the funds to re-pay the credit facility applied for. It compares existing financial commitments (declared outgoings from the application form and information on other debt commitments found at the credit bureau) with applicant income. Where there is sufficient disposable income to meet the repayments of the new facility (and score criteria have been met), the requested amount is granted. Where there is insufficient disposable income, revised terms are proposed (see page 58).

Some companies facilitate this process by providing a budget planner and repayment table for customers to complete before their application is submitted. This allows customers to calculate the monthly repayments they can afford and therefore the credit limit or loan amount/period they might apply for.

Some lenders also set a second limit, known as a shadow limit. This is generally higher than the declared limit; it tends to be set primarily based on risk (score) and it tends towards the absolute maximum amount the lender might wish to extend. The purpose of this initial shadow limit is to manage requests from the customer for additional credit in the period immediately after acceptance, i.e. before customer performance is established. Amounts within the shadow limit are granted without further credit checking; amounts in excess of the shadow limit are declined, or possibly subjected to further credit checks.

Setting product facilities

Score can also be used in setting product facilities. In general, there is a relationship between product usage and risk. Some organizations refine their understanding of usage by building specific usage scorecards. In general, the higher the score the lower the risk and the lower the likely usage of the product. The opposite applies for low-scoring high-risk customers.

In response to this phenomenon, organizations offer more incentives to their low-risk customers to improve usage and take-up of their product. Tactics include:

● differential pricing – lower interest rates for high-scoring applicants;

● 'priority status' product offerings – e.g. a platinum or gold card;

● greater range of product facilities – the higher the score the greater the range of facilities offered; and

● additional product offerings with guaranteed acceptance, e.g. with a limit equal to the shadow less the declared limit set on the product applied for.

The lower the score and the higher the risk, the fewer are the incentives offered to applicants.

Organizations also use score to manage downgraded acceptance conditions for high-risk applications. The aim is to increase acceptance rates but maintain tight control over potential bad debt. Typical mechanisms include higher interest rates (set to reflect the additional bad debt expected from this group), low limits, no cash advance facilities, and obligatory payment by direct debit.

4.4 Strategy and Scorecard Monitoring

Role of monitoring

Like all management processes, evaluation of credit strategies depends on a feedback loop (see Figure 4.14). For score-based lenders, decisions are determined by a small group of policy managers who do not see individual cases. Here, management information is crucial for effective control.

Figure 4.14: Feedback loop

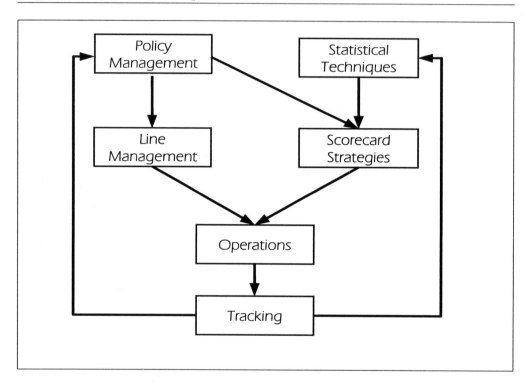

The tracking information derived from scoring is needed in order to understand:

● the overall state of risk on the portfolio;

● the effect of current policies; and

● how well the scorecard is working.

Effective management information must be timely and address the key elements in the lending policy, such as scorecard cut-offs and limit setting. Most risk management departments produce monthly or quarterly management reports, containing analyses of acceptance rates, override rates, application profiles and default trends.

For senior management, the most useful of these reports link scorecard performance measures with portfolio profit and loss, balance sheet and provision figures. They compare actual and previously expected default performance and relate key decision and action points to results. Where appropriate, they also refer to other information sources, for example, from an appropriate benchmarking consortium.

Monitoring the new applications decision process

In Figure 4.14 the monitoring of new applications seeks to evaluate policy results (the route into 'policy management') and validate scorecard effectiveness (the route into 'statistical techniques'). Industry-standard analyses divide the monitoring of new applications into 'front-end' and performance reports.

Front-end or early warning reports

The purposes of the front-end reports are to:

● determine the degree to which scorecard policies are being adhered to; and

● give an early indication of how well the scorecard is likely to work for the applications being assessed by that scorecard.

Scorecard adherence can be measured through an analysis of acceptance rates by score. Figure 4.15 demonstrates a portfolio where there is poor adherence to the cut-off policy, with 50% of cases in the scoreband above the cut-off being declined when they should have been accepted.

Figure 4.15: Accept rate by score

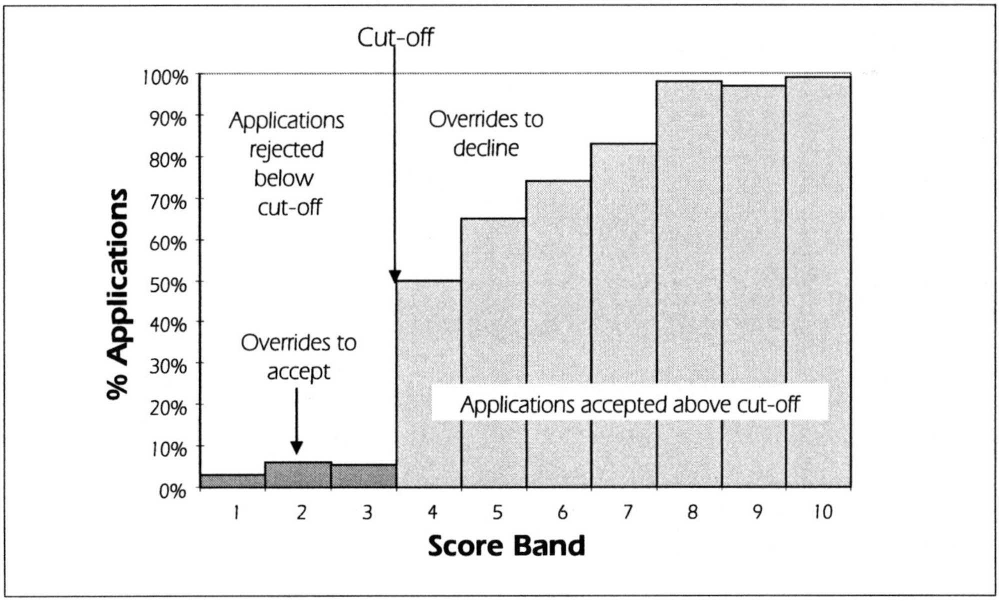

This type of situation should be followed up by override analyses to determine why cases have been accepted below the cut-off and declined at or above the cut-off. (See also Section 4.5).

It is important in this type of scorecard adherence analysis to identify cases that are accepted or declined regardless of score. These generally equate to the exclusion types identified in the scorecard development. A separate memo note of these cases is required, to monitor trends over time. They should not be included in any acceptance by score analysis.

Front-end reports also show how compatible the current applicant profile is with the scorecard. The profiles are measured by comparing the score distributions of the current group with a benchmark group – generally the scorecard development sample. Comparisons of the underlying scorecard characteristics are also made to pinpoint any significant areas of change.

The idea is that if the two profiles are similar, then the risk-to-score relationship predicted by the scorecard will apply to the current group. In Figure 4.16, the current applicants have a higher score profile than the benchmark. If the cut-off was set at 220, the benchmark expected acceptance rate would be 77%, whereas the current applicant group would have an acceptance rate of 88%. Over time the two profiles will gradually diverge and the risk-to-score relationship will deteriorate. These outcomes become clues for the renewal of the scorecard.

Figure 4.16: Applicant profiles comparison

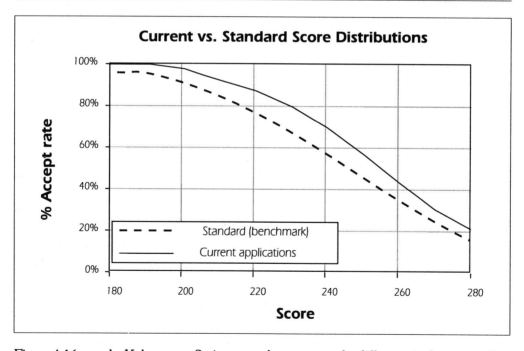

Figure 4.16 uses the Kolmogorov-Smirnov graph to compare the difference in the two profiles. The K-S statistic is used to measure the distance between the two curves and quantifies the statistical significance of any profile shift.

Performance reports

As performance experience begins to accumulate, the risk-to-score relationship must be validated. Industry-standard reports showing delinquency by score are used to demonstrate this relationship. Again, comparisons with expected benchmarks are the key to determining how well the scorecard is working.

In Figure 4.17, risk is measured by dividing the number of good accounts at each score by the number of bads (odds). The scorecard is working almost as effectively for the recent accept group after 12 months as for the benchmark group (the slope of the odds-to-score line is at the same angle for each group). However, the risk is higher at every score for the recent accept group compared with the benchmark.

Figure 4.17: Odds:score comparison

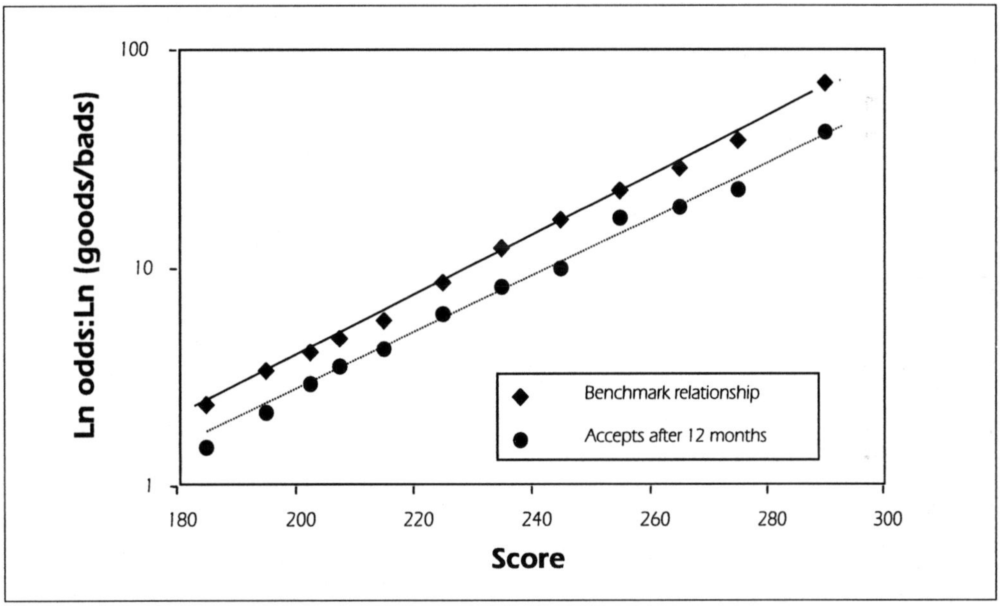

For new scorecards it is essential to monitor this risk-to-score relationship regularly after implementation – probably after 3, 6, 9 and 12 months for each month's worth of accounts taken on. This will give an early warning of how well the scorecard is working and whether the target risk-to-score relationship is likely to be achieved. This is then fed back into a review of the key policy controls.

All the scoring reports shown so far are based on numbers of accounts. Increasingly, organizations are attempting to better understand the relationship between score and their key profit drivers. This is enhancing their ability to determine cut-offs, and assess the impact of limits and differential pricing.

The Figure 4.18 example shows, for a credit card product, the typical relationship between the provision requirement and the net interest revenue, combined into a value of contribution. This clearly quantifies the counterbalancing sources of revenue and credit losses over the score continuum. It also demonstrates the negative relationship between risk and activity referred to in Section 4.3 on page 51. This is a major challenge for all lenders in managing card accounts.

Figure 4.18: Contribution by score analysis

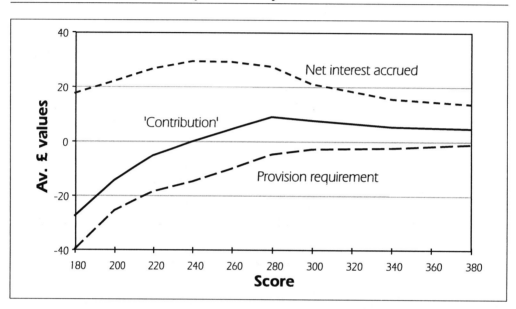

Identifying scorecard adjustment/redevelopment requirements

Beyond looking at the overall risk-to-score relationship, scorecards should be examined for misalignment.

Assume that a scorecard includes the characteristic 'type of accommodation'. At any given score, the risk should be the same whether the applicant is an owner or a tenant. In Figure 4.19 this characteristic is misaligned because the risk is lower for owners than for renters across all scores. In this case the attribute score for renters needs to be reduced by eight points to bring it into line with the owners attribute. Alternatively the attribute score for owners needs to be increased by eight points to bring it into line with the tenants attribute.

Figure 4.19: Misalignment analysis

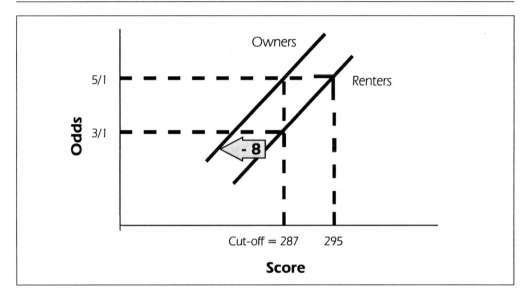

Lenders can gain significant short-term benefits from realigning one or two characteristics in their scorecards. However, it is unwise to take this analysis too far because of the correlation between the characteristics. Where there is critical misalignment across a range of characteristics, a full scorecard redevelopment is required.

4.5   Referral Management and Overrides

Every scorecard is used within a policy framework. This framework allows for rules to be incorporated into the underwriting process in addition to the scorecard assessment. Applicants accepted when their score is below the cut-off are known as overrides to accept, or low-side overrides. Those rejected where their score is equal to or above the cut-off are known as overrides to reject, or high-side overrides.

In some instances, applicants will be declined regardless of score, e.g. under-age or bankrupt applicants. In other cases applicants are accepted regardless of score e.g. staff applicants where the product is linked to their employment contract. In these cases the override decision does not require an operator review and can be handled automatically by the application processing system.

Other areas of the policy framework require operator input. These cases are known as referrals.

Types of referrals

There are three main categories of referrals, namely identity validation, manual reviews and changing the account conditions (see also Chapter 10).

Identity validation

The recruitment process encompasses more than just assessing creditworthiness. It also needs rules to check applicant identity and address – both for fraud detection and to fulfil money-laundering regulations.

For these reasons, some applications are referred for verification. Rules are generally based on:

- inconsistencies found on the application form;
- identity documents;
- address confirmation documents;
- checking for duplicate applications;
- recent bureau searches;
- suspect address matching; and
- suspect fraud matching.

Credit bureaux can play an important role in alerting lenders to suspect fraudulent applications. In the UK, the bureaux hold an industry-shared database of fraudulent names and addresses available to member organizations (CIFAS). In addition, other score-based/expert system products are available for fraud detection at the application stages.

Manual review

In theory, a score summarizes all the information known about an applicant to predict future risk. However, situations do arise where information exists that is outside the scope of the scorecard. In defined cases the lender manually reviews applications to compensate for any known weaknesses in the scorecard model.

Typically these situations arise where:

- there is information that applies to a only tiny proportion of applicants – this cannot be analysed statistically for inclusion in the scorecard;
- information becomes available that was not available when the scorecard was built;
- information is not accurately reflected in the score because of reject inference problems during the scorecard build; or
- information is not accurately reflected in the score because of data capture problems or incomplete recording within the scorecard build sample.

In the last three cases the referral rules are a temporary 'fix' until the information can be incorporated accurately into the scorecard.

Changing the account conditions

Sometimes, applicants pass the acceptance cut-off, but do not fully meet the criteria for the product or limit applied for. Frequently this occurs where the limit or loan amount requested exceeds the limit the lender is willing to grant. This occurs where the applicant's score is too low for the amount applied for, and/or where there appears to be insufficient disposable income to meet the monthly repayments. In these cases the application is referred while revised (downgraded) conditions are negotiated with the customer. Often the customer does not take up the revised offer and the application is rejected.

Policy rule formulation

To maintain management control, rules for handling referrals should be automated where possible. Ideally, the application processing system should guide the operator's investigations and decision making.

For 'identity validation' referrals, the objective is to determine whether the application is genuine, not to re-assess creditworthiness – scoring has already assessed repayment risk. Those that have passed the cut-off and are proved to be genuine are subsequently accepted. Those that are not considered genuine are declined and coded with the reason for decline, both for operational and reporting purposes.

The key is to capture all the data used to make the decision, plus the reason for the decision. The policy rules, decision reasons and decision outcomes can be evaluated to enhance future policy and scorecards.

Scoring or manual decision making

Scoring gives management control over the acquisition-to-bad debt relationship. If an improvement in quality is required, the cut-off is increased. If additional volumes are required, the cut-off is lowered, with an accompanying forecast of bad debt deterioration. In addition, scores are quick to compute, allowing speedy decisions.

Manual underwriting by comparison is less consistent than scoring because different individuals place a different emphasis on different elements of an application. It is also more labour intensive, harder to monitor and more difficult to effect improvements in the decision process.

It should be noted that some lenders use score only as a guide. As an example, a lender could amplify the application form information by contacting the customer and confirming critical data by astute questioning. This telephone contact demonstrates to the customer the interest the lender takes in attracting new customers and the service levels that it can provide.

The lender then uses the additional/confirmed information to more aggressively assign loan amounts or credit limits. For card products, higher limits are given to ensure that customers put the card at the front of their wallets, and to maximize balance transfers at an attractive teaser rate of interest. The rationale is to give more flexibility to the customer and to ensure the card is actively used with higher rolling balances.

In order to subsidize this process both delinquency and bad debt losses must be lower than normal industry levels.

Scoring in these circumstances is used as a guide to ensure that lower-scoring applications are scrutinized more closely. The philosophy is to look for ways to accept an application, rather than take on only mid- to high-scoring applications which may not turn out to be profitable (because higher-scoring applicants tend to be less credit active).

Impact of overrides

The impact of overrides includes:

- lost potentially good business (declines at and above cut-off);

- acceptance of some below-breakeven-quality business (accepts below cut-off);

- lower operational efficiency as a result of reviewing applications; and

- reduced management control over the acceptance policy.

The impact of overrides is measured initially in terms of business volumes. Figure 4.20 demonstrates a simple report showing decision by scores above and below cut-off.

Figure 4.20: Overrides table

Score	Accepts		Rejects		Total		Accept
	No.	%	No.	%	No.	%	rate
Up to cut off	130	0.5%	2,356	42.7%	2,486	7.3%	5.2%
Cut of and up	28,409	99.5%	3,165	57.3%	31,574	92.7%	90.0%
Total	**28,539**	**100.0%**	**5,521**	**100.0%**	**34,060**	**100.0%**	**83.8%**

In this example 92.7% of applicants scored at and above cut-off, but only 90% of those were accepted. Of the 7% scoring below the cut-off, 5% were accepted. Without overrides 93% of applicants would have been accepted; with overrides the acceptance rate was 84% – a net loss of 9% of the potential customers.

Subsequently, the impact of overrides is measured by observing the performance of those accepted below cut-off. This should be compared with the performance predicted by the scorecard and the performance of accepted accounts at the cut-off (to determine whether acceptance of cases below cut-off is worthwhile).

The performance of overrides above the cut-off cannot be observed because they have been declined. Estimates of their performance can be made, although structured tests are needed to validate estimation assumptions, before refining the referral rules, or other elements of the lending policy.

4.6 Decision Delivery Systems

In the past, most organizations with automated application processing systems (see Chapter 10) had all the scorecard, cut-off and referral parameters set up and managed by systems programmers. Any enhancements to scorecards and associated policies required these same programmers to make system changes.

Leading credit organizations now have control over the implementation and change of credit policy through the use of parameterized decision delivery systems. Typically called 'strategy manager' tools, they allow the user to set up and change scorecards and policy rules. This method frees the user from the bottleneck of the systems enhancement process, because parameters can be changed at any time.

Most strategy manager tools are PC-based and interface with the applications processing system. Changes can be made immediately, although most are made overnight. Many organizations make changes at a month end, where possible, to ensure clear reporting of the consequences of the change.

The systems themselves are made up of a set of components. One leading system offers the following components:

● strategy definition – allows strategies to be designed;

● strategy execution – implements the strategies;

● data manager – organizes access to internal and external data sources;

● reporting – evaluates the strategies;

● scoring – implements the scoring elements, e.g. scorecard, cut-offs; and

● bureau connection – determines when to search the credit bureau.

The flexibility offered by a strategy manager system is vital in a fast-moving, competitive market, where the lender continually seeks to enhance strategies. It is particularly important when a new scorecard is implemented, or a new product is launched, to allow initial strategies to be refined.

5

FRAUD SCORING

This is a specialist subject in its own right that will be covered only in outline here. The emphasis will be on the practical problems of introducing and using fraud scoring systems.

Firstly, scoring for application fraud is a very different undertaking from transaction fraud scoring. The first is a one-off assessment where the objective is to identify the most suspicious applications before the credit facility is granted, i.e. before there are any financial losses. It is as equally applicable to personal loans as it is to credit cards. Transaction fraud scoring seeks to identify unusual or inconsistent changes in transaction behaviour patterns in order to limit potential losses.

In both cases, the type of model that is used is relatively unimportant. It may be a neural network, an expert system, a statistical model or a combination of these. The features of a successful system include:

- flexibility (of the system and the scorecard) to adapt as new fraud trends emerge;

- champion/challenger testing and monitoring to introduce new strategies to overcome new trends; and

- the use of workflow and queuing systems to react very quickly to identified cases.

5.1   Application Fraud Scoring[1]

The process for developing these scorecards is largely the same as application scoring (except there is no reject inference phase) – see Chapter 4. A sample of fraudulent and non-fraudulent accounts is extracted from a sample window (typically 12 months to avoid any seasonal influences). As many characteristics as possible are extracted and/or generated from the sample, which may include bureau or other external data, application data, source of the application and early transaction data. Each fraud account needs to contain a marker indicating the type of fraud that it had been subjected to. The data is then analysed for patterns, and a model(s) is constructed using the most appropriate method.

Each type of scorecard development has its own unique considerations, and fraud scoring is no exception. Fraudsters learn and adjust their methods very quickly, so there is a need for the characteristics in the scorecard to be balanced. If the scorecard is dominated by, say, two very strong characteristics, it is likely that this will become common knowledge enabling the

---

[1] Mout, M.I. (1998) *Stemming Application Fraud*, InterAct98 Forum, Fair, Isaac & Co Inc, San Francisco

fraudster to 'fix' his application details in respect of these characteristics to enhance his chances of being accepted.

The scorecard is used alongside an application risk scorecard as part of the applications processing function. It may be an integral part of this system or it may be a separate system. The model will rank-order the risk of the applications being fraudulent. Once the highest risk applications have been identified, then additional checks are undertaken. The potential difficulty here is that some genuine applicants will be caught in this net, with the consequent additional cost of unnecessarily checking these and the potential loss of goodwill.

5.2   Transaction Fraud Scoring[2]

The objective of transaction fraud scoring is to reduce losses and increase recoveries, and at the same time maintain the goodwill of genuine customers. It is unrealistic to expect to be able to eliminate all fraud – this is not cost effective when having to work within limited resources (both budgetary and people). The optimal solution is achieved by using a combination of scorecards within a flexible scoring system together with workflow systems for individual case management.

Scoring system and process

An effective system has five main components:

- Scorecards or other predictive models together with pattern recognition capabilities;

- Strategy design and testing facilities that should be capable of being modified rapidly in response to new fraud patterns;

- Post-authorization (or transaction) scoring capability which scores recent transactions to identify potentially fraudulent ones, flags the higher-risk accounts for real-time scoring for their next transaction and posts them to a workflow system for case management. This review may be an on-line or batch process;

- Authorizations scoring in real time for the most suspicious cases. This happens while the cardholder is still in the store waiting for authorizations approval; and

- Workflow or queuing systems for investigators to review and work the accounts posted from the post-authorization scoring process. This system, which interfaces with the authorizations and main accounts systems, should also have queuing facilities that enable accounts to be prioritized and those with the greatest exposure worked first.

A fraud scenario might entail a series of transactions that occur in rapid succession, i.e. within an hour:

- Transaction no. 1 is approved routinely and its post-authorization score does not indicate anything suspicious;

[2] Jennings, A (1997) *Smart Ways to Fight Transaction Fraud*, Fair Isaac International Conference, Birmingham, UK

- Transaction no. 2 occurs 15 minutes later. This is also approved routinely but this time the post-authorization score indicates a suspicious situation. The system flags the account for real-time authorization scoring if and when the next transaction occurs and moves it to the workflow system for manual review if no further activity occurs;

- Transaction no. 3 occurs, say, 20 minutes later. This time the real-time authorizations score is calculated. It indicates a very high likelihood of fraud such that the transaction is referred for voice authorizations. The post-authorizations score confirms the degree of risk and the new details are posted to the workflow system, where the account is moved up into a higher priority queue; and

- Transaction no. 4 also incurs a real-time authorization score which now indicates a clear fraud. The call is referred, the purchase declined and the retailer is requested to pick up the card.

For accounts posted to the workflow system, either as a result of the above scenario or because they have been identified after the event, the score (with or without other criteria) is likely to be used to rank order the accounts into different priority queues.

Transaction-fraud strategies

In the days before fraud-scoring systems were commonplace, a typical fraud identification strategy might have looked like the example in Figure 5.1 where very few criteria were used to differentiate accounts, and the consequent actions were straightforward. In this example the only criteria are the transaction value and the number of recent purchases.

Figure 5.1: Simple fraud strategy

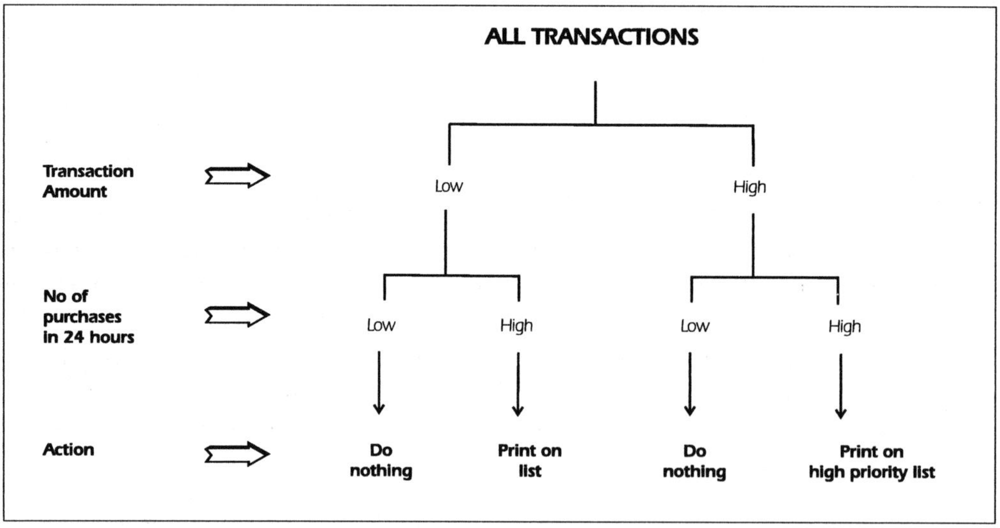

The introduction of the infrastructure described above enables much more refined strategies to be used that take into account many more factors, some of which are shown on the left hand side in Figure 5.2. The fraud scores in this example have been grouped into low, medium and high bands, and the different actions, which may be anything appropriate, are labelled as A, B, C, etc. for the sake of simplicity. Other characteristics that have been shown to be significant can also be tested.

Figure 5.2: Score-based fraud strategy

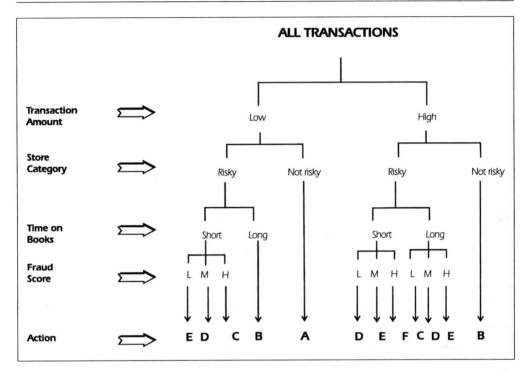

Using these criteria explicitly in a strategy rather than incorporating them into a scorecard means that they can be evaluated individually and modified rapidly should the need arise.

Transaction-fraud scorecard development issues

The development process is, in principle, the same as any other type of scorecard project (see Chapter 4). With transaction fraud scoring, the goods are genuine transactions and the bads are the fraudulent ones. Given that 99.9% of all transactions are genuine, extracting a sufficiently large sample of accounts with fraudulent transactions can be particularly difficult. This is one reason why pooled scorecards can be more realistic and more robust than individual ones. (Pooled scorecards are developed from data contributed by multiple lenders, all of which have the use of the end product. Because of the sheer volume of data as well as the variety within it, pooled scorecards can be very powerful.)

It is also likely that behaviour patterns on authorized transactions will vary from those on unauthorized ones. This then brings a further subdivision into an already-small sample.

There may also be a question mark over the quality of the fraudulent data, depending on how accurate or consistent the lender has been in applying fraud markers to the accounts.

6

BEHAVIOURAL SCORING

Behavioural scoring is a statistically-based tool for predicting different types of future behaviour on a credit account. Lenders use it for making on-going decisions on open accounts.

Behavioural scorecards are more powerful than application scorecards, particularly for revolving or open-ended credit products that generate a lot of account activity. This is because behavioural scores are based primarily on dynamic account performance information and they are computed regularly. Behavioural scores provide a regular, up-to-date assessment of an account's likely future status.

The use of application scorecards within the new applications process is relatively straightforward. They are used to make a one-time decision. By comparison, decision making on live accounts is more complex, because:

● each customer already has an open credit facility – and therefore some level of financial risk already exists;

● many decisions may be taken on an account by different business areas – requiring co-ordination across these areas to avoid conflicts; and

● customer behaviour is multi-dimensional – risk is only one dimension to be considered.

6.1   Types of Behavioural Scorecards

The first behavioural scorecards were built to predict future risk. Typically these types of scorecard influence risk decisions in the account management, collections and recoveries areas of the credit cycle. They can also be incorporated into marketing selection programmes.

Behavioural scorecards can be built to predict other dimensions of future behaviour, including revenue, propensity, usage, attrition, contactability and fraudulent activity. Behavioural scores therefore can be built to influence decisions across the whole credit cycle.

Some scorecards are used on their own to direct decision-making, whereas others are used in combination with each other.

Risk-based behavioural scorecards

Account management scorecards

Account management scorecards are built to predict future risk on accounts that are currently up to date.

They are generally used to manage limits during the life of an account. The overall aim is to increase the average balances of good, interest-bearing accounts, while reducing or containing the average balances of the bad, loss-making accounts.

Scores are used to set limits on an account to reflect the amount the lender wishes to extend at a given point in time. Often these limits are set in conjunction with usage information or usage scores. For credit card products, limits are used to control authorization decisions on retail purchases and cash advances; for loans, limits help with top-up loan decisions.

These risk-based scorecards, and their associated limits, also provide the marketing function with useful information for prospect selection and pre-approval opportunities, for selling additional products and offering incentives to increase account usage.

Collections and recoveries scorecards

Collections and recoveries scorecards predict the future performance of customers who are already delinquent. They are used to set risk-based collections and recoveries strategies. The overall aim is to either reduce collections/recovery costs for the same level of repayment, or increase repayments for the same level of collections/recoveries expense. The aim is also to retain future profitable customers, i.e. to avoid strategies that may increase repayments but which may also lead to the unnecessary closure of lower risk/future profitable accounts.

Scorecards for other dimensions of behaviour

Usage scorecards (card products)

Based on account usage patterns, these scorecards predict future levels of activity and are used in retention and incentive programmes. Often usage scores are combined with account management scores to set on-going limits.

Attrition scorecards

Similar to usage models, attrition scorecards attempt to predict accounts that are likely to close, become inactive or settle early. Again, they are used in retention and incentive programmes.

Churn/early attrition scorecards

Churn or early attrition scorecards help to identify short-life accounts, i.e. those likely to move regularly between lenders to get the best deal. This applies particularly to recently opened accounts, which were given an incentive to apply and are nearing the end of their incentive period (e.g. lower APR for the first six months). These accounts are also known as flippers.

(Note, these types of scorecards can also be built on data available at application time and can therefore be incorporated into the account-opening decision.)

Response scorecards

These are based on previous take-up of marketing offers. They predict future response and help to improve the cost effectiveness of marketing campaigns through the better targeting of offers (see Chapter 3).

Pre-screening/pre-approval scorecards

These predict credit risk for direct mail prospects and are often used in conjunction with response and account management scorecards. The aim is to be able to market guaranteed additional product offers.

(These types of scorecards can also be built for pre-screening mailing lists of new customers – see Chapter 3.) Using pre-screening/pre-approval and churn/early attrition scorecards helps lenders to gain market share and/or long term profitable accounts, while managing or reducing their acquisition costs.

Contactability scorecards

Contactability scores predict the likelihood of reaching the correct customer on the telephone. They are based on previous collections history and are used in a collections environment where they can optimize call lists for power diallers . They can also be used to optimize tele-marketing operations. The aim in each case is to improve productivity.

Collections promise scorecards

These supplement collections and contactability scores by predicting the likelihood of collections promises being kept. The aim is to increase payments for each telephone contact that is made.

Fraudulent activity scorecards

Fraudulent activity can be predicted from unusual spending patterns on open-ended products. The scores rank order the probability that the spending has come from the real accountholder. Accounts with suspect spending can be suspended and/or the customer contacted to verify usage. Neural networks and expert systems are more usual for predicting potential fraudulent activity than are score-based models (see Chapter 5).

(Fraud models can also be built on data available at application time and can therefore be incorporated into the account-opening decision to identify and prevent application fraud.)

Customer scoring

Multiple-product organizations use customer scoring to provide a customer-level basis for cohesive strategies across their product range and credit cycle stages. These models are discussed further in Chapter 7.

6.2   Advantages and Disadvantages of Behavioural Scoring

Advantages

The advantage of using behavioural scores is that they distil complex patterns of performance into a single easily usable value (the score). The score relates directly to a particular dimension of behaviour – risk, usage, propensity, etc. By structuring information about these different dimensions behavioural scores help to simplify and coordinate decision making across the credit cycle.

Without behavioural scoring, management of accounts is governed by judgmental rules, some of which are automated. Often they are very complex and require some manual intervention for decision making. The parallel with this is manual underwriting for new applications. Behavioural score-based strategies replace judgmental decision making, just as application scorecards take the place of manual underwriting for new applications.

Simplification of the decision-making process enables lenders to better understand the cause-and-effect of their lending actions and therefore continually improve their strategies. In addition, the use of score-based strategies across the credit cycle helps organizations to achieve a better balance between customer acquisition and retention strategies.

Companies with behavioural scoring therefore have the potential to realize:

● improved sales-to-bad debt ratios;

● improved operational efficiencies;

● improved customer satisfaction and therefore retention; and

● greater portfolio control.

Disadvantages

It is hard to find specific disadvantages for using behavioural scoring. However, some organizations do not realize its full potential because of poor formulation or execution of score-based strategies.

Behavioural scoring demands heavy investment in the management, analytical and systems infrastructure of the organization. It often results in some magnitude of organizational change. Where there is effective use of scores these costs are more than compensated for by the benefits listed above.

6.3   Developing Behavioural Scorecards

General principles

The basic principles for building any behavioural scorecard are the same as for an application scorecard (see Chapter 4).

The differences from application scorecard building are:

● composition of the sample;

● performance definitions;

● data sources;

● generation of characteristics; and

● generally, no reject inference phase.

The behavioural time line model in Figure 6.1 illustrates all the required definitions and potential data sources. These all depend on the type of scorecard, product and company experience.

Figure 6.1: Time line model for behavioural scorecard development

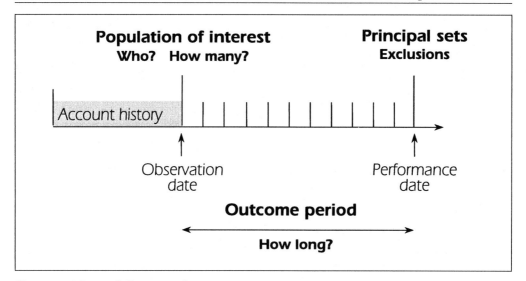

Composition of the sample

The sample is the set of accounts used to build the scorecard. It needs to reflect the group of accounts for which the scorecard will be used in the future (population of interest), e.g. accounts entering collections may be the population of interest for a collections scorecard.

Performance definitions

The performance definitions reflect the purpose of the scorecard. A scorecard predicting risk needs to have good and bad accounts defined at the performance date. An attrition scorecard may use active and inactive account definitions.

Data sources

Internal databases are the most important sources of data for building a behavioural scorecard. Characteristics for analysis and inclusion in a scorecard are derived from transactional and account performance data, e.g. number of times in arrears in the last six months. Other account histories may be included where appropriate, e.g. response to past marketing programmes for a response scorecard, or collections history for a collections scorecard. Some behavioural scorecards include application data, although the value of this information reduces as the account matures.

Data from external data sources such as credit bureaux may also be included (see Chapter 2). In the UK, reciprocity rules state that only default or negative information from shared account information databases held at the bureaux may be incorporated into marketing or account management type scorecards (see Chapter 17). Any shared account information can be included in risk-based collections or recovery type scorecards.

The importance of the bureau data depends on the product. It is less important for open-ended products where there is a lot of internally available, transactional data. It is more important for fixed-term products where transactional data is limited to payments or missed/partial payments. The decision to include bureau data in a scorecard should balance its contribution to the power of the scorecard against the cost of acquiring the data, for both the development and for its on-going use.

Creating characteristics and attributes

Data acquired for the scorecard development has to be structured into characteristics and attributes ready for analysis. There are numerous combinations that can be derived for this purpose. For example, arrears history data can be used to create many different characteristics based on frequency, arrears level and time period:

- number of times delinquent in the last 3, 6, 9, 12 months or lifetime (since opened);
- worst level of delinquency in the last 3, 6, 9, 12 months or lifetime; and
- number of times with two or more payments missed in the last 3, 6, 9, 12 months or lifetime.

Typical characteristics (see Figure 6.2) are derived from:

- delinquency history;
- usage history;
- static information;
- payment/purchase history;
- collections activity;
- revolving credit transactions;
- customer service contacts;
- promotions history; and
- bureau data.

Figure 6.2: List of example behavioural characteristics

1. **Delinquency history:**
   - ever in arrears or in arrears in the last x, y, z months
   - maximum arrears levels
   - number of times at arrears level x, y, z
   - number of months since last delinquent

2. **Usage history:**
   - balance-to-limit ratios
   - balance trends
   - retail purchases-to-cash advances ratios
   - open to buy (limit minus balance)
   - current balance-to-maximum balance ratios

3. **Static information:**
   - time on books
   - account type
   - customer age
   - application score

4. **Payment/purchase history:**
   - payment-to-balance ratios
   - purchases-to-payment ratios
   - purchase frequency
   - type of retail goods purchased

5. **Collection activity:**
   - outcomes/contact frequency/method

6. **Revolving credit transactions:**
   - number and type (retail/cash)

7. **Customer service contacts:**
   - in-bound/out-bound contacts

8. **Promotions history:**
   - Number of offers by type and outcomes

9. **Bureau data types** (reflecting restrictions on the use of positive data):
   - generic scores
   - shared account information
   - ratio of open accounts now compared with three months ago

For each characteristic, valid attributes are defined, which are subsequently grouped together based on the predictive nature of each attribute. As with application scoring, the most powerful characteristics are included in the scorecard build. This process takes into account any overlaps of information across the characteristics.

Developing a collections scorecard

This section gives a detailed example of sampling and data issues relating to the development of a collections behavioural scorecard. Parameters for other scorecard types are listed in Section 6.4.

Sample definitions

The population of interest for a collections scorecard is frequently based on accounts that are one payment down (arrears 1) at a given point in time, or accounts as they enter collections. As a risk-based scorecard, definitions of goods and bads after a specific outcome period are required.

The outcome period, or performance date, is determined in part by analysis of the rate at which accounts return to current, or in order. Figure 6.3 illustrates the type of analysis that might be used.

Figure 6.3: Analysis of recovery over time

Delinquency status	Observation date: month						
	0	1	2	3	**4**	5	6
Current		68.9%	78.2%	83.4%	**85.8%**	86.8%	87.2%
1 payment	100%	10.7%	8.7%	5.2%	**4.0%**	3.2%	2.9%
2 payments		20.5%	3.3%	2.9%	**2.5%**	2.4%	2.3%
3 payments			9.9%	2.6%	**1.6%**	1.5%	1.4%
4 payments				5.9%	**1.9%**	1.3%	1.0%
5 payments					**4.2%**	1.2%	1.1%
6 payments						3.6%	0.8%
7+ payments							3.4%
< 3 payments	100%	100%	90.1%	91.5%	**92.3%**	92.4%	92.4%
3+ payments			9.9%	8.5%	**7.8%**	7.6%	7.6%

In this case, the majority of accounts return to order after one month, and there are very few incremental accounts returning to order after month 4. To avoid the mis-classification of a good, but to ensure the development sample is as recent as possible, the outcome period in this example is likely to be set at four months.

The other factor to consider is the period over which the current collections process runs. In most organizations, accounts are passed to the recoveries section after four to six months. The life of the collections process should be used in conjunction with the analysis of recovery over time to set the outcome period.

For a collections scorecard, the definition of good and bad often equates to the collections department's view of success or failure. Frequently the definition is based on the number of payments in arrears, e.g.:

- good = less than three payments in arrears at the performance date; and
- bad = three or more payments in arrears at the performance date.

Sometimes these definitions are enhanced with information about paying arrangements or broken promises.

An alternative to the collections entry scorecard is to build a set of sequential collections scorecards. The idea is to score accounts each month, using a scorecard relating to the time they have been in collections. The outcome period for each scorecard is one month and generally a bad is defined as an account that has moved to the next stage of delinquency during the month. This approach is more difficult to implement operationally and to monitor, but has value where there is still transactional activity on the account during the early stages of delinquency.

Data sources

For a collections scorecard, data sources generally include the operating systems, e.g. account opening, billing and collections, and internal databases, e.g. credit scoring monitoring database.

Sometimes credit bureau data is included, depending on product (see page 71).

Figure 6.4 summarizes typical parameters for a collections entry scorecard in the form of a time line model.

Figure 6.4: Collections entry scorecard parameters

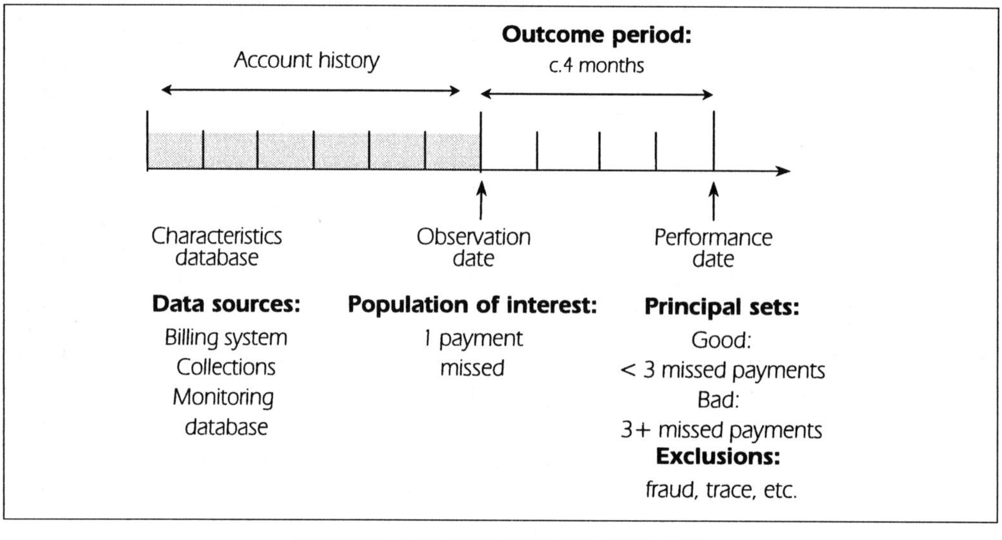

Figure 6.5: Mature account management scorecard

Account history

Outcome period:
9 (to 18) months

Observation
date

Performance
date

Data:
Characteristics
database
Performance
Arrears/payment ratios
Bureau
Generic score and/or
negative information
Promotions
Insurance/subsequent loan offers
Transactions
Revolving credit activity

Population:
Current and
active and
> 3 months on book

Principal sets:
Good: < 2 payments
Bad: 3+ payments

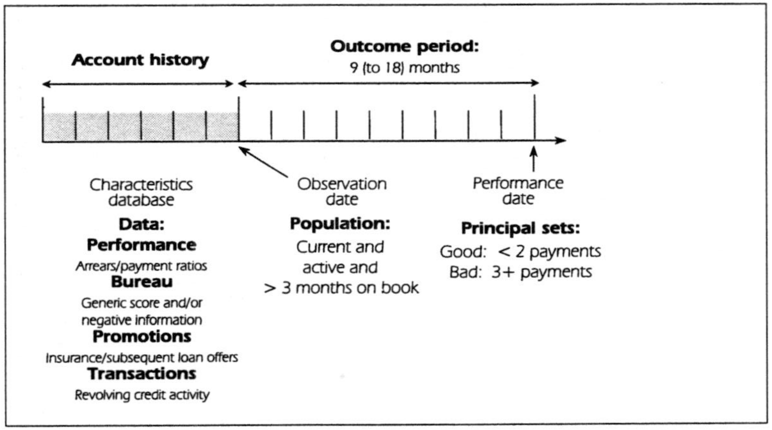

Figure 6.6: Early account management scorecard

Account
history

Outcome period: c.3 months

Observation
date

Performance
date

Data:
Characteristics
database
1st. period usage
Transactions

Population:
Current and
active and
<3 months on book

Principal sets:
Good: current
Bad: 2+ payments
or excess > 20%

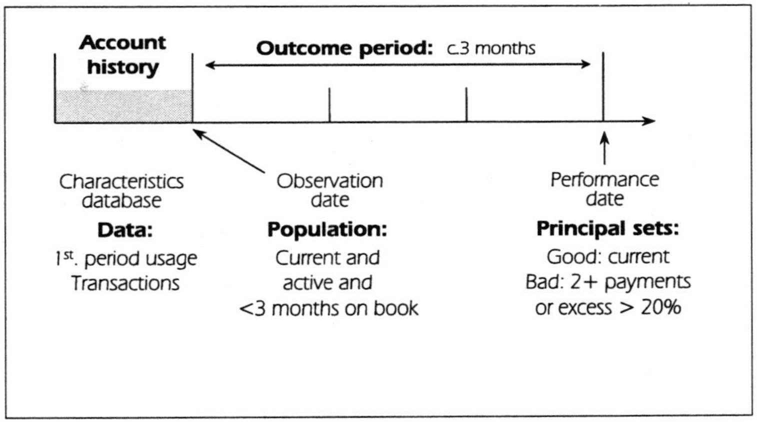

Figure 6.7: Attrition scorecard

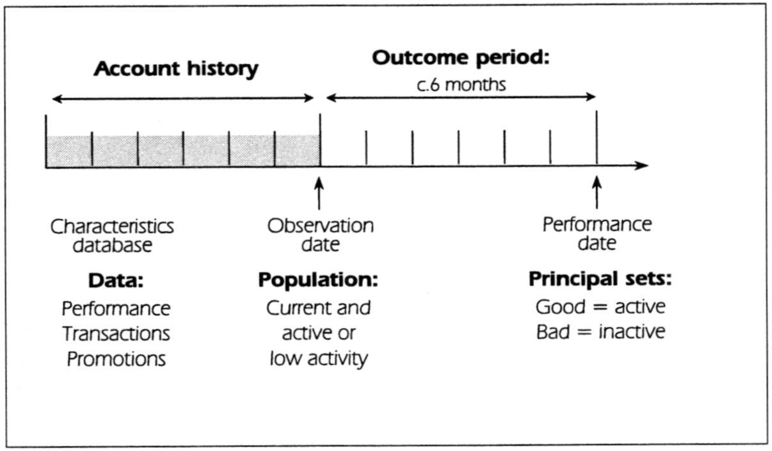

Account history

Outcome period:
c.6 months

Observation
date

Performance
date

Data:
Characteristics
database
Performance
Transactions
Promotions

Population:
Current and
active or
low activity

Principal sets:
Good = active
Bad = inactive

Figure 6.8: Revenue scorecard

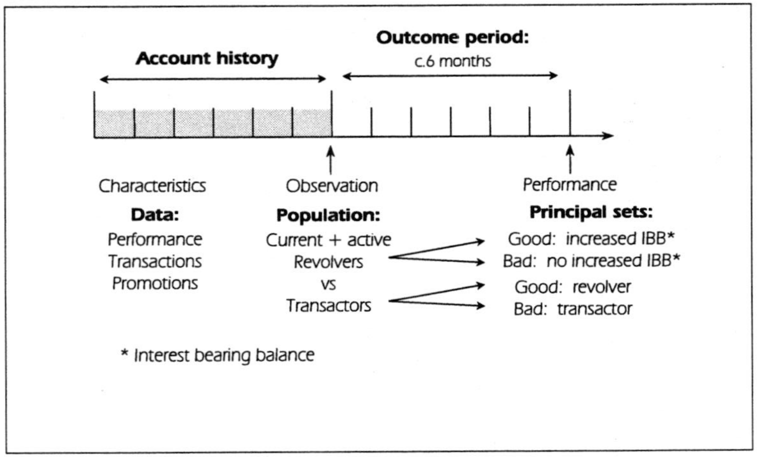

Account history

Outcome period:
c.6 months

Observation
date

Performance
date

Data:
Characteristics
Performance
Transactions
Promotions

Population:
Current + active
Revolvers
vs
Transactors

Principal sets:
Good: increased IBB*
Bad: no increased IBB*

Good: revolver
Bad: transactor

* Interest bearing balance

Developing other behavioural scorecards

Figures 6.5-6.8 (overleaf) give a summary of each of the key decision points for a range of other scorecards.

6.4   Strategy Setting

Once applicants are accepted, there are a multiplicity of decisions that need to be taken, as a result of the way customers manage their accounts. This section looks at example strategies and the issues surrounding these strategies, for each stage in the credit cycle.

In examining these strategy opportunities, it is important to understand:

- behavioural scores themselves do not set the strategies;

- given that the aim is to influence customer behaviour (e.g. grow the balance of good, interest-bearing accounts), the results of a new score-based strategy cannot necessarily be predicted accurately through analysis;

- formulation of good strategies is based on empirical evidence; and

- controlled experimentation with strategies is required to provide the evidence and direction for strategy setting and subsequent enhancements (see Section 6.5).

Limit strategies

The objectives of limits

Limits are a key mechanism for managing open-ended credit accounts. Declared limits are used to communicate to the customer the amount of credit he or she has available. They also set the maximum level of exposure for the lender, assuming customers are not allowed to go into excess (above their limit).

As discussed in Section 4.3, all new accounts are given a declared limit. For an open-ended product, such as a credit card, the declared limit can be adjusted over time, according to the demands and performance of the customer.

Poor management of declared limits leads to the average balance on the bad, loss-making accounts being significantly higher than the balances on the good, interest-earning accounts. Organizations with poor limit management tend to react to the demands of their customers rather than anticipate their needs and ability to handle higher credit limits. These companies need greater numbers of good accounts to pay for the higher losses from each bad account.

An effective limit management strategy redresses the ratio of good-to-bad balances. It takes into account both risk and customer demand for additional credit. Not only will these accounts become more profitable, but also there should be a positive knock-on effect on application acceptance rates as the view of break-even changes (refer to Section 4.3).

Shadow limits

Some organizations manage their limits through shadow limits. These are undeclared limits, primarily designed to allow a tolerance of spend above the declared limit.

Shadow limits are often set based on a combination of the existing declared limit, and a risk predictor, such as an account management behavioural score. They are revised regularly, generally monthly, following the computation of the account management score.

As an example, a high-scoring, low-risk customer, might be given a shadow limit that is 10% higher than the declared limit. If the declared limit was £500 the shadow limit would be £550. If the declared limit was £1000 the shadow limit would be £1100. Figure 6.9 illustrates how shadow limits might be calculated. As the risk rises (as the score falls), the difference between the declared and the shadow limits should fall.

Figure 6.9: Calculating shadow limits in relation to the declared limit

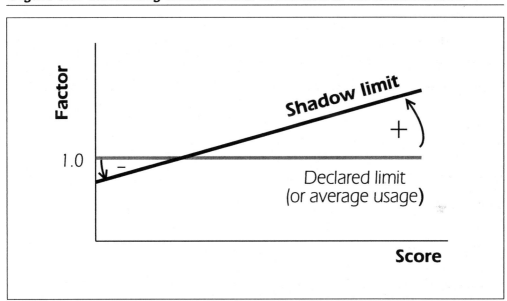

An alternative method is to add on a given amount to the declared limit, such as £50 for a low-risk customer, regardless of the declared limit. If the declared limit was £500 then the shadow limit would be £550. If the declared limit was £1,000 then the shadow limit would be £1,050.

Generally, the shadow limit exceeds the declared limit for medium- and low-risk accounts. Where the shadow exceeds the declared limit, it can be used to allow leeway for temporary spend, and may also be used to adjust the existing declared limit. This gives good customer service while safeguarding company exposure.

In some circumstances, an organization may view the declared limit on an account as too high (very high-risk cases). The shadow can be set below the declared limit, to reflect the desired limit. In practice, lenders are obliged to lend up to the declared limit where the customer is up to date, and the shadow has to be overridden. However, the reduced limit can be invoked if, or when, the customer misses a payment because at that point he or she has broken the terms of the agreement.

Target limits

Some organizations also set a target limit, which determines the absolute maximum limit the organization is prepared to lend the customer (not just a tolerance level). The limit allows for borrowings across multiple products. Setting these limits follows the same principles as for shadow limits.

For medium- and low-risk accounts, the target limit is generally set above the declared and shadow limits. For marketing activity the differential between the declared and target limits provides a guide for limit increase promotions, spending incentives and additional product offerings, such as personal loans to existing card customers.

For very high-risk accounts, where the shadow limit is below the declared limit, the target may be set equal to the declared limit. This allows the customer to spend up to the declared limit while up to date. Such accounts are excluded from promotional activity.

Although limit management is key for open-ended products, target limits also have a role in fixed-term products. The idea here is to regularly compute a maximum limit for the account holder, based on repayment performance (risk score). This can be used to offer further loans, either in response to an enquiry from the customer for a top-up, or as part of a marketing programme. Loan amounts below the target can be automatically approved, whereas those above the target are either negotiated down to the target or refused.

Target limits help organizations to be proactive. Over time this leads to positive changes in the relationship between good and bad balances.

Appetite for credit

Appetite for credit is the customer's need or desire for additional credit. Ideally, the setting of shadow and target limits should also take this into account. This can be achieved by including a further dimension of behaviour, such as an average balance-to-limit ratio or a usage-related score, when setting these limits. This then achieves a balance between customer need for, and ability to repay, further credit.

For example, a low-risk high-usage customer may be given a target limit that is 30% above their declared limit whereas a customer with the same risk but medium-usage may be given a target limit 20% above the declared limit. The lower the expected usage, the lower is the increment between the declared and shadow/target limit for any given level of risk.

Including the usage dimension is particularly important in setting target limits for use in limit increase promotions. Limit increases to low-usage customers may generate some additional spending and balance growth, but it is often not sustained. Credit exposure to the company is increased unnecessarily. When any of these customers do default they are likely to use all the credit available, leading to a mismatch between the level of good and bad balances. The usage element allows this type of incentive to be targeted more effectively.

Alternative methods

Not all organizations use shadow and target limits. An alternative method is to the review the declared limit each month, as an appropriate risk score is computed (e.g. an account management-type score). The declared limit may then be adjusted to reflect customer need, risk and the recency of their last increase. Any change is then communicated to the customer.

Limits for retail and cash advance transactions

The terms and conditions of some card accounts allow for different limits to be set for retail and cash advance transactions. In practice the customer is given a declared limit of which only a defined percentage can be used for cash advances. In these cases, organizations may set separate shadow limits for each of the two transaction types. Having a separate cash advance limit helps to manage risk for customers who use their card primarily for this purpose. As a group these customers are higher risk than those who predominantly use their card for retail purchases.

Authorizations

Card authorizations

Authorizations is the real-time process by which a card issuer decides to accept or refuse transactions that are above the floor limit (see Chapter 12).

In the past, judgmental rules were used (sometimes automated) to determine authorizations. These rules allowed not just for acceptance or refusal, but also led to limit increases. A proportion of cases was decided manually, where an account condition was outside the mainstream rules.

Using shadow and target limits dramatically simplifies the authorizations process. In principle, transactions are authorized up to the target limit without review. Lenders allow the declared limit to be increased to cover the transaction, up to either the shadow or target limit, depending on their individual policies. Any transaction that takes the balance above the target limit is refused.

When used with modern point-of-sale technologies, shadow and target limits make the authorizations process more efficient and easier to monitor. This has resulted in operational cost savings and improved control. In many cases, no manual credit decisions are required and the focus of the authorization operation has become fraud prevention rather than credit sanctioning (see Chapter 12).

Lenders that revise their declared limits regularly to reflect need and risk (rather than using shadow limits) authorize all transactions up to the declared limit without review. Where a transaction takes the balance above the declared limit, a tolerance is applied, for example as a percentage or amount above the declared limit. Within this tolerance, the transaction is authorized and the account is assessed for a limit increase once the transaction has been posted to the account. Outside the tolerance, the transaction is declined. In effect, the tolerance acts as a shadow limit.

These methods apply only for transactions with a value above the floor limit because all those below this limit are automatically approved.

Personal loan 'authorizations'

Where target limits are set for loan accounts, strategies may be put in place whereby any subsequent top-up loan request can be authorized up to that limit. This reduces the need for the customer to submit a revised application form, although proofs of income may still be required. Speedy loan decisions (binding or in principle) increase the chance that a customer will take up that offer. These strategies aim to improve the volume of loan business, while ensuring the risk on any specific loan is within acceptable limits for the company.

The differential between the outstanding loan amount and the target limit can also be used for cross-product selling, for example, offering a credit card with a limit up to the difference between the two. Giving customer services access to this information allows them to cross-sell where appropriate, whenever a customer contacts the organization. Again, these strategies aim to improve the volume of lending while ensuring the risk on any product/amount offered is within acceptable limits.

Similar cross-selling principles can be applied where a credit card is the primary product held by the customer. The aim may be to offer a personal loan up to the difference between the declared and target limits. In these circumstances, strategies should take into account the maximum repayment amount that would result from any loan offered. For example, the differential between the declared and target limits might be £3,000. The amount offered might be reduced for a short loan period, or increased for an extended repayment term.

Supporting marketing programmes

In the past, in-house direct marketing programmes tended to be applied without much differentiation to all eligible customers, as defined by judgmental rules. Most of these rules sought to exclude customers based on delinquency, rather than pro-actively select them for a particular offer.

Today, marketing selections are much more sophisticated, taking into consideration likely response/usage/attrition and likely future acceptance/maximum credit available (i.e. combining marketing and risk criteria).

Chapter 3 introduced the idea of targeting customers using a matrix based on risk and response. Similar principles can also be used for targeting promotions to the existing customer base by combining dimensions of risk and usage. Different tactics or offers are then applied to accounts in the different segments, e.g.:

- very high-risk accounts – exclude from promotions regardless of activity – reduce limits if they enter collections;

- low-risk, high-usage – prime targets for credit products – offer limit increases in stages (to observe increase spending and performance in relation to these higher limits); or

- low-risk, low-usage – target incentives to increase utilization of the credit facility, e.g. lower interest rates/alternative products.

Collections strategies

The collections function aims to maximize the amount collected in relation to the operational cost of running the function. However, collections effectiveness must also consider the longer-term relationship with the customer and potential future income. It is not just a case of collecting the overdue amount, but bringing the account into order for future business, in as cost effective manner as possible. In many organizations, the early stages of collections are viewed as, or projected as, a customer service function.

Behavioural scorecards are powerful predictors of risk which can help both the economic and strategic objectives of collections.

Figure 6.10 illustrates the performance of a typical collections scorecard. It shows the proportion of accounts charged off six months after entering collections, by the percentile of cases from highest to lowest risk (ranked by increasing score). Collections scores allow organizations to tailor their strategies according to risk.

Figure 6.10: Typical collections scorecard risk-to-score graph

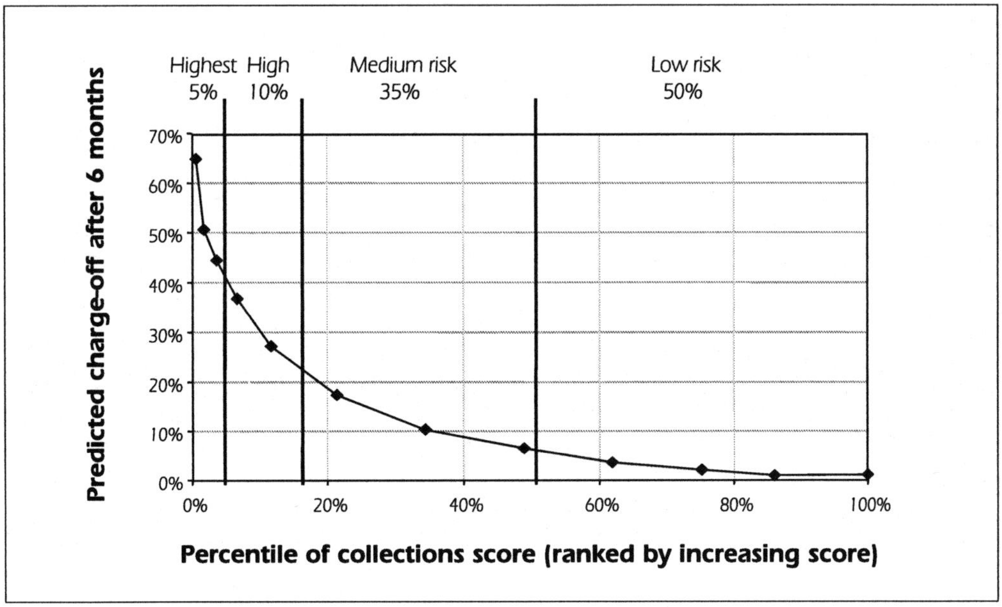

Developing strategies

The principles for developing a collections strategy are to:

- define an overall goal, e.g. improved cash flow for the same operational resource, or maintain performance with less resource;

- devise a strategy to meet this goal, e.g. concentrate resources on the highest-risk accounts;

- segment accounts into risk bands as they enter collections, e.g. into four risk bands as illustrated in Figure 6.10; and

- develop tactical plans for each segment to reflect risk and to meet the defined strategy, i.e. decide on the sequence of actions for each segment, in line with the strategy.

If the goal is 'improved results for the same resource', one strategy might be to take more immediate, severe action on the highest-risk accounts. This seeks to maximize immediate recoveries on this segment, where a future relationship with the customer is not sought. Medium- to low-risk accounts may be treated with a more conciliatory approach; the long-term potential of these accounts is of greater importance than immediate returns.

To achieve these objectives the availability and cost of resources must be considered. In this case, resources are concentrated on the highest-risk group. Progressively lower levels of resource are assigned to lower-risk groups.

An alternative strategy for the same goal may be to minimize effort on the highest-risk accounts. The aim here would be to identify can't-pays and won't-pays (highest-risk cases) as quickly as possible and send them to an external debt collection agency. Collector resources can then be focused on accounts with longer-term potential for the organization. More resource is given to the medium-risk and less to the lower-risk accounts. This avoids wasting collections resource on accounts (especially low-risk) that come back into order by themselves, i.e. self cure.

The overall distribution of resources for these two alternative strategies is illustrated in Figure 6.11. Here, level 1 represents the most intensive deployment of resources whereas level 4 represents the least intensive use of resources.

Figure 6.11: Distribution of collections resources

	Risk level			
	Very high	High	Medium	Low
Strategy 1 resource level:		2	3	4
Strategy 1 resource level:	4	1	2	3

Once the goal is defined, there are numerous choices to be made in designing strategies, segmentations and tactics. To determine the most effective approach requires test and control collections strategies/tactics to be run in parallel. These measure the success of different solutions, both in terms of immediate recoveries, and longer-term revenue/bad debt generated by accounts which have been subjected to different strategies/tactics.

Collections action plans

Collections action plans are a sequence of actions that are followed while an account is delinquent. They comprise three elements:

- message – e.g. customer service through to warning of legal action;
- method – e.g. letter, telephone, electronic mail, postcards, tele-message, house visit; and
- moment – i.e. timing of actions.

Traditionally collections plans have been determined by the number of days delinquent – the higher the number of days delinquent, the harsher the treatment. With a collections score, organizations tend to accelerate or extend their action plans to reflect risk. This has the effect of re-distributing resources across the collections portfolio, in order to meet their overall goals.

Figures 6.12-6.14 give three simple examples of collections tactics by risk. The examples assume that the relative rank ordering of risk (high, medium and low) persists throughout the 75-day collections action plan.

Figure 6.12: No differentiation by risk

Delinquency	Low Risk	Medium Risk	High Risk
30 Days	Statement Message	Statement Message	Statement Message
45 Days	Reminder 1	Reminder 1	Reminder 1
60 Days	Reminder 2	Reminder 2	Reminder 2
75 Days	Reminder 3	Reminder 3	Reminder 3

Figure 6.13: Prudent use of score

Delinquency	Low Risk	Medium Risk	High Risk
30 Days	Statement Message 1	Statement Message 2	Reminder 1
45 Days	–	Reminder 1	Reminder 2
60 Days	Statement Message 2	Reminder 2	Reminder 3
75 Days	Reminder 2	Reminder 3	Phone Call

Figure 6.14: Greater distinction by risk

Delinquency	Low Risk	Medium Risk	High Risk
30 Days	Statement Message 1	Statement Message 2	Reminder 1
45 Days	–	Reminder 1	Phone Call
60 Days	Statement Message 2	Reminder 2	Default Notice
75 Days	Reminder 1	Phone Call	Legal Action

The example in Figure 6.12 demonstrates a typical collections plan before a collections score was available. Figure 6.13 makes prudent use of score and Figure 6.14 makes more distinction across the risk categories.

Levels of payments should improve from groups subjected to the more intensive actions. Conversely, payment levels may decline from groups given less attention. The overall plan is successful if the increased payments from the groups receiving more intensive action exceed the reduction from the groups receiving less intensive action.

Another way of thinking about using score in collections plans is to ensure that a certain action is being taken on an account when it exhibits a specified level of risk.

An example is illustrated in Figures 6.15. Here, a high-risk account scoring 200 on entering collections has an expected bad rate of 20% when it reaches 30 days delinquent (arrears 1). A lower-risk account scoring 400 on entering collections has an expected bad rate of 5% at 30 days. By the time the 400 account reaches 90 days delinquent (arrears 3), the expected bad rate has risen to 20% (because the majority of 400s have already returned to normal, as expected). If, say, the default notice is sent to the 200 customer at 30 days then logically it should be sent to a 400 customer at 90 days, i.e. when the same level of predicted risk is reached. The same logic should follow through for all other actions.

Figure 6.15: Tailoring collections action according to risk

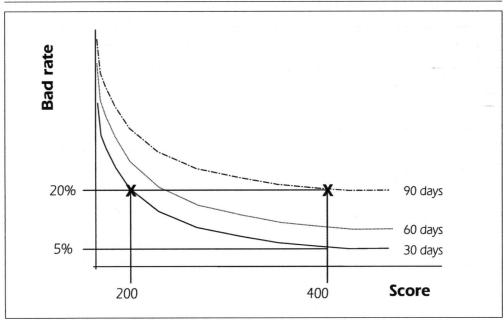

Uses of other scores in collections

Different scores can be calculated and applied across the spectrum of out-of-order accounts. Examples include:

- promise scores, estimating the probability that a customer will respect a promise to pay;

- contactability scores, to estimate the probability of successfully contacting the customer by telephone;

- application score for new account defaulters (until the behavioural score becomes more appropriate);

- trace scores for gone-aways/skip cases, to estimate probability of success in locating a customer – to direct the amount of in-house or external effort that should be applied – and what actions should be taken on located customers; and

- litigation/recoveries scores – calculated at the point where the account relationship is terminated – to determine whether to take legal action, use agents or write-off the account.

Scoring statistics can also support collections planning by predicting the volume of cases in each action plan (see Chapter 13). This helps resource budgeting. Some lenders also estimate provision and bad debt using monthly behavioural scores (see Chapter 9).

6.5 Experimentation

Leading organizations continually test new strategies and tactics to enhance their understanding of customer behaviour and to improve results.

Experiments are undertaken using a control and test methodology commonly known as champion/challenger. With its responsibility for risk-based strategy setting across the credit cycle, risk management is often the focal point for the instigation, testing and assessment of many experiments.

Example tests include assessment of:

- the impact of using different shadow and target limits on credit take-up and subsequent delinquency – evaluated by limit increases granted as a result of transactional activity (where the customer balance exceeds the declared limit but is within the shadow or target limit) and by limit increase offers sent to the customer as a marketing initiative;

- appetite for credit for the product held or alternative products;

- price sensitivity in relation to risk-based pricing strategies; and

- response to different collections tactics – good collections plans cannot be derived from first principles – it is essential to try different ideas, gauging customer reactions through experimentation and feedback monitoring.

Experiments are needed because it is not always possible to predict a customer's response to a change in policy. The goal of experiments is therefore to buy information about customer behaviour.

The principles of conducting experiments are similar to the ideas demonstrated in washing powder advertisements where a proportion of the washing is treated with a new brand and the results are contrasted with clothes washed with the existing brand. The two sets are then compared to prove how much whiter the new brand washes the clothes, in order to convert the user to this brand.

For credit experiments, a representative set of customers is subjected to a different policy. The effect on customer behaviour is measured and compared with the results of the normal strategy. Where the new strategy produces better results than the normal policy, the new strategy is rolled out to all accounts.

Sometimes, a new policy works for some customers but not for others. The best elements from each of the competing strategies are picked for the different groups of customers, and rolled out accordingly.

Characteristics of good experiments include:

- definition of very precise, measurable objectives – to systematically vary treatment gives clearer results than trying several variations within the one experiment;

- running over a limited duration – to limit the cost of experiments that produce poor or unexpected loss-generating results – and to hold management interest and ensure policies are reviewed as results become available;

- using a limited sample – again, to limit the cost of experiments that produce poor or unexpected loss-generating results – the sample needs to be big enough to allow for statistical conclusions, but no bigger;

- adequate operational planning – ensuring that any changes in policy for test groups can be handled effectively by the operational areas, that they are aware of these changes, and that they have a mechanism for giving feedback to those conducting the test; and

- definition of benchmark expectations and management reports for evaluating the tests.

Experimentation should be a continuous process – aiming to identify ideas that improve strategies and hence profitability, while eliminating those that do not give improvements. Companies experiencing success with champion/challenger have coherent test programmes, the supporting framework to analyse test outcomes and, above all, senior management commitment.

6.6　Strategy and Scorecard Monitoring

Focus

Effective management information is as critical for monitoring behavioural score-based decisions as it is for monitoring application score decisions.

Most organizations with behavioural scoring seek to continually improve their strategies and decision making on all accounts. Monitoring of behavioural score-based decisions tends therefore to focus on the comparison of champion and challenger groups.

Monitoring of scorecard effectiveness is also required. Scorecard statistics are helpful in monitoring portfolio profiles over time. These indicate whether overall portfolio quality is rising or falling, as an early indicator of future quality. Scorecard statistics associated with collections scorecards are valuable for operational planning. However, given that the aim of behavioural score-based strategies is to change customer behaviour, the observed performance-to-score relationship may not be in line with the relationship predicted by the scorecard development statistics. Care needs to be taken in interpreting variations between expectations and actual results. The more the organization is successful in influencing customer behaviour, the greater is variation that should be seen in actual results when compared with scorecard expectations.

Monitoring champion/challenger strategies

There are no universally accepted industry-standard reports for monitoring competing strategies. The specification of all reports should reflect the goals of the control strategy and should specifically measure the elements of policy that differ for the test group.

At a high level, a key measure of success is the relationship between the average good and the average bad balances. Where this relationship improves, then the overall profitability of the portfolio will also improve.

At a detailed level, the types of measures that should be tracked are:

● sales/credit take-up;

● balances;

● interest income;

● fee income (where appropriate);

● delinquency (numbers and balances by arrears levels and/or specific provision categories);

● write-offs; and

● operational costs.

Bringing these elements together allows a measure of contribution to be computed as an indictor of likely change in profitability. To do this also requires information on interest-funding costs (to calculate net interest revenue) and provisioning policy (to calculate provision from the balances outstanding). The calculation is:

Contribution = net interest + fees – provision – write off – operations costs

Information on attrition should be included with estimates of lost revenue and/or bad debt savings as appropriate.

One of the most effective ways of analysing different sets of accounts, which have been subjected to different policies, is to make comparisons on a per-account basis. Frequently the challenger or test group is much smaller than the champion or regular strategy group. Results need to be adjusted for this. Using a per-account measure simplifies the calculation and presentation of the results. Results of both the champion and challenger can then be factored up, to estimate what the financial impact would have been if either policy had been applied to all accounts.

In addition, comparisons should always be made against some benchmark or expected result. Actual results can then be used to adjust strategies, in order to achieve the desired results.

As indicated in Section 6.5, when comparing strategies, individual elements should be considered rather than the results of the champion or the challenger as a whole. Taking the collections example in Figure 6.11, the overall goal was to increase recoveries for the same collections resource. The two strategies deployed resources in different ways across four risk segments. The results for strategies 1 and 2 need to be compared for each risk segment. If the best results were strategy 1 for the very high-risk group, and strategy 2 for the high-, medium- and low-risk groups, more overall resource would be required to implement the best strategy for each segment. In this case the overall goal would be challenged, with a proven business case for increasing the collections operating budget (because all elements had benefited from more resource).

The time over which the results are measured is important. Strategy 1 may appear to be the best, in the collections example, for the very high-risk group after three months. However, strategy 2 aimed to identify the can't-pay, won't-pays in this group quickly and send them to a collections agency. It takes time for this process to take effect. Door-to-door collections may prove better over the longer period because these harder debts have been recognized earlier. Strategy 2 may therefore be the best over a longer period.

Whatever the tests, one approach to understanding the influence of any policy change is to undergo a three-stage analysis, as outlined below.

Immediate feedback measures

The objective of the first evaluation stage is to verify the operational consequences of any test:

- are policies properly implemented?
- are there any unexpected outcomes?

This evaluation should be based on informal feedback from operations and quantified where possible on operational performance reports.

Apart from looking for potential operational problems, the evaluation should measure early variations in activity and delinquency – notably turnover, take-up of facilities and recovery rates. Although a full picture is not available at this point, it should be possible to detect initial trends.

For collections experiments, roll rates can be studied. For experiments whose focus is increasing activity, the level of activity by scoreband should be reported.

Interim evaluation

The purpose of an interim evaluation is to focus on the goals of the experiment and on any notable 'side effects'.

The principal measures of portfolio performance at this stage might be:

- for collections experiments:

    - the rate with which accounts return to normal; or

    - the level of utilization on accounts in collections; and

- for credit experiments, such as incentives or limit increases:

    - an assessment of the effect on risk, by monitoring changes in the behavioural score distribution.

The conclusions of the interim evaluation can be strong enough in some circumstances to result in changes in the champion policies.

Final evaluation

The timing of the final evaluation depends on the nature of the policy test. A policy to modify limits is likely to take up to two years to show its full effects. A collections policy change may require only six months.

The evaluation should assess changes in the key profit drivers (revenue, credit losses and customer retention), plus operational and marketing costs, in relation to policies and actions taken.

The effect on delinquency is frequently the longest component to measure. This can be anticipated through the calculation of expected bad rates, determined by the behavioural scores. By doing this, policy interpretation can be made before the complete results of the tests are available. However, the risk-to-score relationship should be verified when actual performance data is available, before the evaluation is completed.

Scorecard monitoring

The techniques for monitoring behavioural scorecards are the same as for applications scorecards (see Chapter 4, Section 4.4). The key measures are:

- population profiles, as defined by score, which can be measured monthly following the computation of the behavioural scores; and

- the risk-to-score relationship, which can be measured after a period of time equating to the scorecard outcome period.

As already stated, the whole aim of using scores is to improve account strategies. If successful, population profiles and risk-to-score relationships should change.

For example, if a collections scorecard was built based on accounts that were treated the same regardless of risk, then the predicted risk-to-score relationship might look like the solid line in Figure 6.16.

Figure 6.16: Impact due to changes in strategy

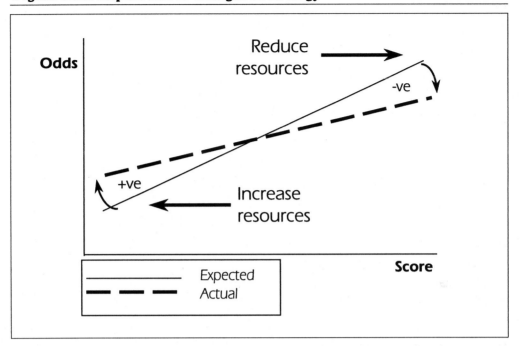

If strategy 1 from the collections example in Figure 6.11 was employed (the higher the risk, the more collections resource deployed), the risk-to-score relationship for the accounts subject to strategy 1 should flatten by comparison – the dotted line. This is because the more intensive action for the high-risk group should bring more accounts into order compared with past policies applied to this group. The performance of the low-risk group may deteriorate – at least in the short term – until the delayed/less intensive collections activity takes place. Success of the strategy depends on a financial evaluation of the additional gains from the high-risk group compared with the additional losses from the low-risk group. For scorecard monitoring, this change should be anticipated and communicated as part of the strategy planning process.

Thus, in the collections context, actions can influence the good/bad outcome of an account, i.e. an account may continue to miss payments under one strategy but come to order under a different strategy, and vice versa.

Limit-setting strategies tend to have less influence on the good/bad outcome of an account. Profiles and risk-to-score relationships are more likely to fit predictions for account management-type scorecards. However, monitoring reports should be able to identify where additional credit extended to a particular set of accounts results in higher delinquency than expected. Similarly, reports are needed to identify circumstances where additional credit is refused and where their performance turns out to be better than predicted.

Leading organizations also use behavioural scoring statistics in a wider management context, including:

● incorporating the monthly profiles of accounts by risk score into provision calculations; and

● using volumes by risk categories to help operational planning, e.g. collections workloads.

In these organizations scoring is a fully integrated part of the management process. Decisions are supported by empirical evidence. When the monitoring of strategies and use of scorecard statistics is poor, the benefits of using behavioural scoring are not realized.

6.7   Systems Infrastructure Requirements

Effective implementation of behavioural scoring systems requires extensive systems investment. Even where specialized software is bought from a third-party vendor, or used on a bureau basis, an extensive development and implementation programme is still required.

The principles are straightforward. The left-hand side of Figure 6.17 demonstrates a typical systems set-up for a credit product. At the centre is the accounts system. This cycles accounts monthly for the production of statements and other management information. From this, actions or parameters for handling accounts are generated (policy rules), including rules for authorizations and collections. These actions influence the customer who in turn generates transactions that are posted to the accounts system. The idea with behavioural scoring is to take account summaries from the accounts systems – generally monthly – either at the month end or at cycle time. The information is fed into a behavioural sub-system that then generates score-based action codes for posting back to the accounts system. These codes then drive the actions and communications with the customer.

Figure 6.17: Operating systems and behavioural sub-system

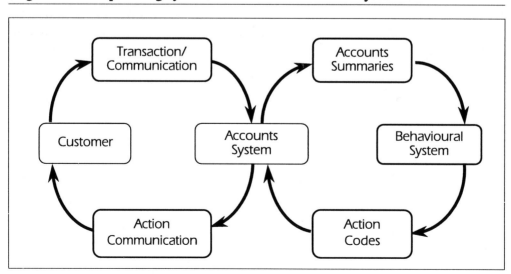

Within the behavioural scoring sub-system, (Figure 6.18), the account summaries are used to update a behavioural history file. This contains all the characteristics required for calculating scores and holds information for tracking purposes. Scores are then calculated and strategy codes set which direct, for example, cross-sell, authorization and collections policies. These codes allow champion and challenger groups to be identified and for different strategies to be defined.

Figure 6.18: Behavioural scoring sub-system components

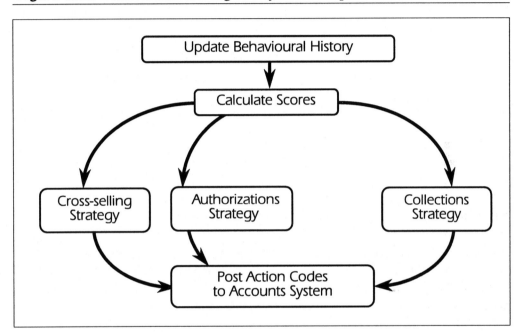

Limit setting may also take place in the behavioural system (declared/shadow/target limits) which may, in turn, influence parameters set for other policy areas (Figure 6.19). Strategy codes and limits are then posted back to the accounts system for actions by the operational and/or marketing areas.

Figure 6.19: Behavioural scoring sub-system with limit setting module

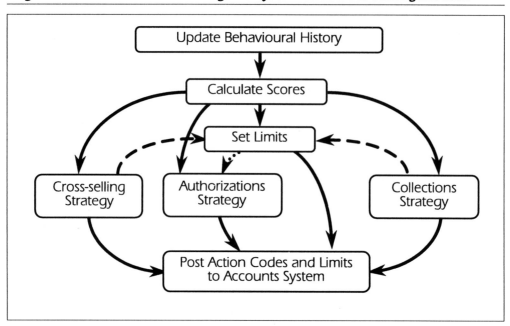

The first behavioural systems were limited in their ability to translate scores into effective strategies. They were programmed into the system which meant that any changes were cumbersome and expensive to implement. Today, strategy manager systems allow user control over the setting of scorecard and policy parameters, and the mechanisms for defining test and control groups are more flexible. Organizations with these flexible systems are able to learn from, and adapt to, changing customer circumstances more easily than those relying on more traditional methods of managing customer behaviour.

7

CUSTOMER SCORING

All the discussions about scoring so far have focused on a single product or process. Application scorecards are developed to assess applicants for a specific population, e.g. Visa card or personal loan, and behaviour scorecards are designed for specific purposes, e.g. collections for a personal loan portfolio.

7.1   What is Customer Scoring?

Every lender's ultimate ambition is to predict future profit from the outset of a new customer relationship. This has always been problematic (and is still particularly complex to achieve) and as a result, risk evolved as the surrogate for profit in terms of scorecards. In recent times, more financial products have become available, and there is more variation within products, as well as more competition between more lenders. When this is coupled with less long-term customer loyalty, lenders need greater skills for differentiating between potential good and bad customers and skills that can focus on retaining the good customers. One solution to this is customer scoring, i.e. looking at the customer's total exposure across all the products he or she holds with any one lender.

The paths shown in Figure 7.1 illustrate how the performance on each account held by a single customer contributes towards both account-level scores and the overall customer score.

Figure 7.1: Account scores and customer scores

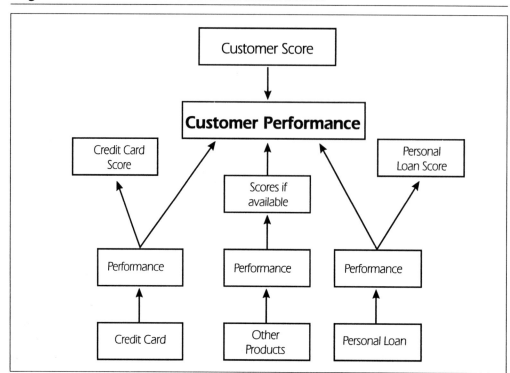

A customer score is defined as:

A single number that summarizes all relevant customer data and indicates the likelihood of a specific customer event occurring in a predefined time period.[1]

Customer *scoring* is the process whereby this single number is regularly calculated and stored for future use. The components of this definition are:

- 'All relevant customer data' – only products, and data from those products, that are affected or relevant are included in the scorecard development;

- 'A specific customer event' – like behaviour scorecards, customer models can be developed to predict different outcomes. Risk is most common, but attrition is another customer-level activity; and

- 'A predefined time period' – all scorecards are constrained to be valid only within a specified future time frame. This varies with the outcome, i.e. risk may be predicted over the next 12 months, whereas attrition may look at only the next three months.

The customer score is a broader and less sensitive measure than account scores that are, by definition, more focused. For best effect, the two should be used together in a complementary manner.

[1] Groome, G. and Gill, L. (1998) *'Customer Scoring – Practical Issues for Development Success'*, InterAct98 Conference, Fair, Isaac and Company Inc., San Francisco

7.2   Areas of Application

Organizations

The organizations that benefit most from customer scoring are the large, multi-product lenders, mainly banks and building societies. They often have subsidiary specialist companies with a particular lending focus, e.g. mortgage or insurance companies. Many of their customers have two or more products from across the group, e.g. some lenders do not sanction a personal loan or credit card unless the current account is also held by the same group of companies. Lenders that offer only a single product do not benefit from introducing customer scoring.

Once a lender does decide to invest in customer scoring, it needs to decide on the outcome it wishes to model. There are two main possibilities, although others are not precluded.

Risk

This is the most common measure or outcome. The total risk across a customer's total product holdings is assessed and summarized into a single score. This is then used to determine a customer-level credit limit, i.e. the total amount that the lender is prepared to advance to this customer, irrespective of product mix. In practice this might translate into a customer limit of £10,000 that can then be split into, say a £1,000 overdraft, a £5,000 personal loan and £4,000 on a credit card. Lending products that are secured on an asset are usually excluded.

An alternative approach is to calculate the total amount that the customer is capable of repaying and apportion that across the various products.

Attrition

Initial recruitment is one of the most expensive processes in a lender-customer relationship. Therefore, having successfully acquired new customers, the lender needs to maximize this cost and opportunity. A customer who holds but seldom uses a card may be a good customer but is not profitable and good customers might be tempted away by competitive offers. Attrition scores alert the lender to the likelihood of customers either becoming dormant or closing their accounts and appropriate actions can be taken to modify the customer's behaviour. This may mean either trying to prevent the closure happening (i.e. the good customers), or being satisfied when the bad ones do leave.

Functional Applications
Marketing

Having an overall view of a customer's risk together with his or her credit limit, and possibly with an attrition assessment, provides the basis for very focused and customer-specific marketing. Cross-selling other products at any opportunity (point of sale, telephone, etc.) is straightforward and comparatively risk-free, and mailshots can become more targeted and cost-effective. Specific anti-attrition campaigns can be designed and aimed at only those customers most likely to close. Customer scoring is also one means of bridging the marketing-credit divide (see Chapter 3).

Application processing

If customer scoring is in place and an existing customer applies for a new product, the customer score is likely to be used as part of the assessment process. It may be used as well as, or instead of, application scoring or it may be an integral part of the application scorecard.

Collections

If collections activities are undertaken on a group basis rather than a product basis, the customer score can be used as a measure for prioritizing collector queues and workloads.

7.3   Advantages and Disadvantages

The main consideration is the serious investment and long-term commitment that is required.

Advantages

The main benefits arise in the areas of cross-selling, up-selling, utilization of products and customer retention. Utilization of products is likely to include encouragement for credit cardholders to spend more and/or take extended credit, or to offer top-ups to good personal loan customers. Cross-selling entails offering other, appropriate, products to good customers, preferably at the time when they most need them.

At an organizational level, customer scoring for risk provides a new, high level of financial control. If lending is operated through a branch system, there were previous problems of lending being done without any knowledge of other products that the customer may hold. With customer scoring for risk, an overall and integrated picture is available regardless of geography or time, i.e. consistency in decision making is improved.

Overall customer service and revenue can be increased while operating costs and bad debts can be reduced.

Disadvantages

There are no direct disadvantages in the sense that some other activity is precluded if customer scoring is in place. However, there are huge costs associated with its introduction. Direct costs include, systems, scorecards, specialist staff and retraining existing staff, and there are organizational and structural implications. A customer-scoring project for a major lender can take several years to fully implement.

Customer scoring is not the ultimate and only tool for large lenders. Its contribution to overall customer management strategies may be marginal, assuming that product-based scoring (i.e. at account level) is in use.

7.4   Organizational Impact[2]

Customer scoring can be the catalyst for changes to the way that lenders are structured. Traditionally this has been along product lines, with all responsibilities for a customer's account (from marketing to closure) being held within a product-based operation. With customer scoring the focus shifts from the product to the customer, and ownership of (i.e. responsibility for) the customer becomes more difficult to define.

The lender may have to move to a functionally-based structure or a combination of both product and function. Some functions may already operate at a non-product level, including risk management and IT. These would encompass customer scoring in the normal course of their work. Other impacts at functional level include:

- Marketing campaigns should be instigated at customer or cross-product level. Branch staff can be given clear guidelines about up-selling or cross-selling at the point of sale so that opportunities are not missed;

- Application processing could be done at a customer level, with multiple scorecards being stored in a common application processing system which would include access to the customer score for existing customers; and

- It might allow customer-level collections where all the customer's debts are aggregated up and pursued as a single debt, although there maybe legal reasons that do not make this practical.

Each organization will need to assess it own situation in this regard. Whatever the outcome, it is clear that every lender that introduces customer scoring needs uncompromising commitment from all levels of management from the managing director downwards.

---

[2] Jennings, A.N. (1996) *'Strategic Approaches to Relationship Management'*, InterAct96 Conference, Fair, Isaac and Company Inc., San Francisco

8

PORTFOLIO MANAGEMENT

Every credit company needs to understand the repayment behaviour of its customers. In particular, each company needs to know whether levels of delinquency are rising or falling compared with their expectations, and the causes of changes in delinquency.

To do this they need to be able to understand repayment behaviour in relation to their internal credit and marketing policies, and in relation to outside economic and market influences – i.e. to link 'cause and effect'.

The rationale for understanding repayment behaviour is to respond to changes and to project forward bad debt expectations (see Chapter 9).

8.1   Terminology

For credit card products, the term delinquency covers both 'arrears' (missed payments) and 'excess', where the cardholder's balance exceeds the credit limit. For personal loans, only arrears/missed payment delinquency is possible.

Most lenders categorize delinquency by arrears level. Some lenders also categorize delinquent accounts where:

● there is special action taking place, e.g. accounts which are being sued or are with an external debt collection agent; and

● there is excess greater than a defined parameter but no arrears (where there is excess and arrears, arrears tend to take priority).

8.2   Key Management Reports

Debt analysis

Most organizations report on the delinquency of accounts by number and balance value at each month end. Most often this is a finance department function and the output is used to calculate the month-end provision (see Chapter 9).

Figure 8.1 gives a typical example of a debt analysis report, showing both the numbers and values of accounts in each category.

Figure 8.1: Debt analysis report

Debt category	Numbers of accounts		Outstanding debt	
	No.	%	£'000	%
Current	740,000	82%	400,000	80%
Arrears 1	83,000	9%	40,000	8%
Arrears 2	20,000	2%	12,000	2%
Arrears 3	8,000	1%	6,000	1%
Arrears 4+	13,000	1%	10,000	2%
Litigation	14,000	2%	12,000	2%
Agents	22,000	2%	20,000	4%
Total	**900,000**	**100%**	**500,000**	**100%**

This report gives an overall picture of the state of the total portfolio. It is used to determine changes in portfolio trends when the values are monitored over time. As such, the data from this report are often the main components of any bad debt projection (see Chapter 9).

However, although the debt analysis gives overall trends, it is at too high a level to give management a full understanding of the underlying dynamics of the portfolio.

The dynamic performance cohort matrix

The key management tool for understanding these dynamics is the performance cohort matrix. This is a triangular matrix that tracks the delinquency of accounts opened in a given time period (cohort) by time on book (since opened) – see example in Figure 8.2. This matrix is also known as a dynamic cohort matrix, or delinquency pyramid.

Figure 8.2: Dynamic performance cohort matrix

Open date (cohort)	Time on Books (months since opened)						
	3	6	9	12	15	18	21
Period 1	2.3%	4.0%	6.0%	7.2%	7.8%	8.0%	8.1%
Period 2	2.6%	4.8%	6.6%	7.8%	8.5%	8.8%	
Period 3	2.4%	4.1%	5.9%	7.3%	8.0%		
Period 4	2.3%	3.9%	6.1%	7.2%			
Period 5	2.4%	4.1%	5.9%				
Period 6	2.2%	4.0%	Performance Measure:				
Period 7	2.3%	Arrears 2+					

Typical reporting dimensions are:

● monthly or quarterly cohorts, defined by account opening date (shown as 'periods' in the left-hand column);

● reporting of performance at each month end after opening, or quarterly; and

● reporting a performance measure of, for example, 'currently two or more payments in arrears'.

Each month or quarter a new cohort is added to the report and performance is updated for all the other existing cohorts. Monthly reporting is generally preferable to quarterly reporting in order to have the first opportunity to identify significant changes in performance.

Life cycle effect

In a dynamic cohort matrix, the dominant pattern is the life cycle effect – the evolution of delinquency based on time on books. This provides a benchmark pattern of delinquency, as it emerges, from the beginning of the credit cycle.

If the portfolio were stable, the values in each column of the matrix would be the same, allowing for some degree of random fluctuation. This is because each column represents performance of accounts at the same age and each set should have the same level of delinquency at each point in time after account opening. In reality, many internal and external factors of change may influence the performance different cohorts.

Figure 8.3 illustrates the 'life cycle curve' graphically, based on the figures taken from period 1 in Figure 8.2. A life cycle curve corresponds to a single row of a dynamic performance matrix report.

Figure 8.3: Life cycle effect

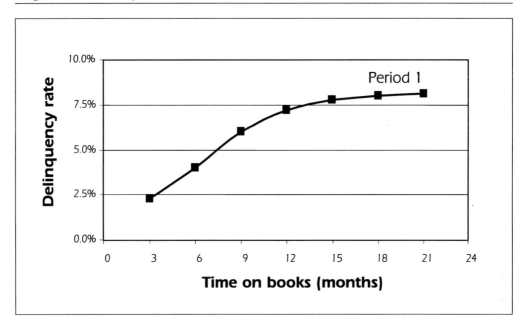

In this example, the rate of delinquency rises rapidly during the first 12 months after recruitment, and continues at a slightly slower pace for the next 6 months. After 18 months the rate of increased delinquency is significantly slower, reaching a plateau (maturity) by 21 months. This life cycle curve is typical for a consumer lending portfolio, although the level of delinquency and point of maturity will vary by portfolio. This life cycle benchmark is important in detecting sources of portfolio change, which can be related to both internal and external influences.

It should be noted also that even if the life cycle were always consistent, total portfolio delinquency would still vary over time , depending on the volumes of business in each cohort. For example, a sudden increase in new account volumes would initially suppress total portfolio delinquency. This is because all of these high-volume new accounts would be in the early stages of their life cycle where delinquency levels are low. In these circumstances the average age of accounts on book would fall.

New account effects

In practice, accounts opened in different periods will be of different quality. This is due to variations in marketing and/or underwriting policy, or to changes in the market. For instance, a drop in cut-off score normally leads to an increased level of delinquency at each level of exposure. This effect is known as a new account effect. It results in different life cycle curves for business originated in different periods.

As an example, in Figure 8.2 the delinquency for business written in period 2 is worse, at each level of exposure, than the accounts opened in period 1. Figure 8.4 shows life cycle curves for these two cohorts. The two curves have essentially the same shape, but are at different levels.

Figure 8.4: New account effect

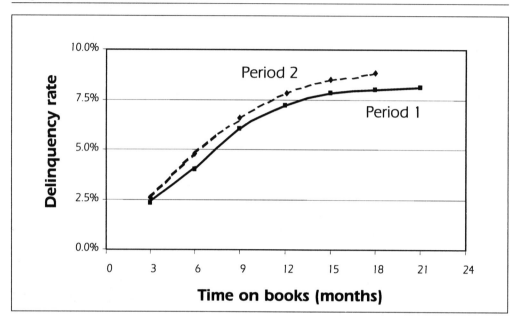

In general, a sudden or marked shift in the life cycle pattern for a new set of accounts, while the existing accounts follow the established trend, can be related back to internal company policy changes (e.g., marketing or underwriting strategies). A gradual shift would be more indicative of economic or market changes.

Portfolio effects

New account effects are related to differences in the quality of business written. Sometimes, two cohorts that display the same patterns in the early months (up to a random fluctuation) later perform in significantly different ways. For example, a new collections policy may shift the performance of the whole portfolio. It will affect different cohorts at different points in their life cycles. This is known as a 'portfolio effect'.

Generally, portfolio effects are caused by changes in internal account management or in the external credit or economic environment. As with new account effects, internal causes tend to lead to more distinct changes whereas change related to external factors tends to emerge more gradually.

Portfolio effects are found by comparing the diagonals of the cohort matrix, each of which corresponds to a fixed observation date. Figure 8.5 is the same as Figure 8.2 updated by one period, i.e. with performance as at the end of period 8.

Figure 8.5: Cohort matrix demonstrating portfolio effects

Open date (cohort)	Time on Books (months since opened)							
	3	**6**	**9**	**12**	**15**	**18**	**21**	**24**
Period 1	2.3%	4.0%	6.0%	7.2%	**7.8%**	8.0%	8.1%	**8.3%**
Period 2	2.6%	4.8%	6.6%	**7.8%**	8.5%	8.8%	**9.2%**	
Period 3	2.4%	4.1%	**5.9%**	7.3%	8.0%	**8.6%**		
Period 4	2.3%	**3.9%**	6.1%	7.2%	**8.3%**			
Period 5	**2.4%**	4.1%	5.9%	**7.7%**				
Period 6	2.2%	4.0%	**6.6%**					
Period 7	2.3%	**4.4%**			Performance measure:			
Period 8	**2.8%**				Arrears 2+			

In the Figure 8.5 example, the most recent set of observations (on the lowest diagonal in bold) shows a significant difference from what might have been expected on the basis of prior experience across all cohorts of debt. For example, at the end of period 5, delinquency was 2.4%, 3.9%, 5.9% and 7.8% after 3, 6, 9 and 15 months on book, respectively. As at the end of period 8, delinquency was significantly higher at 2.8%, 4.4%, 6.6% and 8.3% after 3, 6, 9 and 15 months respectively.

In addition, period 1 delinquency, which appeared to have reached a plateau of 8.1% after 21 months, had risen to 8.3% at the end of period 8 (24 months exposure). Unexpected change in delinquency across mature cohorts is a good indicator of a portfolio effect because this cannot be due to factors influencing recruitment.

Note that period 2 performance was ignored in the comparison of period-ends 5 and 8 because a significant new account effect had already been detected for that cohort. In practice, both new account and portfolio effects can be taking place on a portfolio at the same time, requiring careful interpretation of results. Figure 8.6 demonstrates graphically the two effects for the Figure 8.5 portfolio example.

Figure 8.6: Portfolio and new account effects

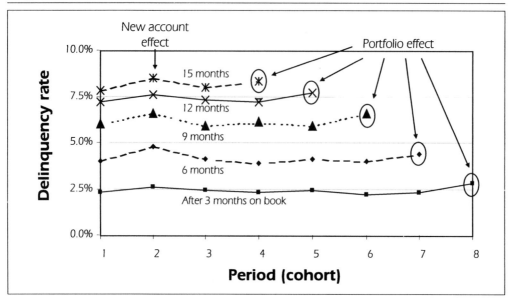

In Figure 8.6 each line represents a different time on book. The distance between the lines shows the life cycle effect. They are wider apart for short time on book and closer together for long time on book. If all cohorts were performing in exactly the same way, the lines would be straight and parallel with each other.

However, in this example there is a peak in the line for every level of exposure for the period 2 cohort. This demonstrates the new account effect where delinquency was higher for this cohort compared with all others in the matrix.

With the exception of the period 2 data points, each of the lines is relatively straight (allowing for a random fluctuation), until the last data point on each line. Each of these represents performance as at the end of period 8 (the lowest diagonal of the matrix). This is a portfolio effect. In each case the line rises to reflect deterioration in delinquency across all cohorts even though all (excluding period 2) were following the same early pattern of delinquency.

Performance measures

The performance measure used in the cohort matrix depends on the purpose of the report. A 'current-arrears' measure is generally used to monitor the current state of the portfolio. It shows both improvements and deterioration in performance for mature cohorts.

A 'currently 2+' measure is recommended because it avoids fluctuations caused by operational problems, which influence the incidence of cases one payment in arrears, and it is more sensitive to early changes in delinquency patterns than using an arrears 3+ measure.

When using a current-arrears measure, consideration must be given to the treatment of charged-off and written-off accounts. If these are excluded from the report as the charge-off or write-off happens, performance of cohorts from which these accounts have been removed will appear to improve. If the report is being used to monitor volumes of delinquent cases for collections purposes this is valid. If the report is being used to monitor portfolio trends this will give a misleading picture.

A 'maximum-arrears performance' measure may also be used for the report. Maximum arrears is the highest level of arrears recorded on an account and is sometimes known as 'historic' or 'worst' arrears. In this case the pattern of arrears observed in the report can only ever rise. This form of reporting tends to be used for scorecard development purposes when determining the rate at which bad accounts emerge after account opening (see Chapter 4, Section 4.2).

Other uses of the report

Portfolio management is not just about managing delinquency. It involves understanding all dimensions of behaviour that influence the key profit drivers. Credit portfolio profit drivers and related behavioural patterns include:

- bad debt losses – delinquency – dictated by recruitment and collections policies;

- revenue – spend, revolving balances, interest, fees – directed by recruitment, limit and pricing policies; and

- persistence – activity and retention – influenced by pricing and marketing offers.

The performance cohort matrix can be used to measure any of these dimensions. Examples include reporting on:

- credit sales – retail purchases versus cash advances;

- credit usage, e.g. balance-to-limit ratios;

- balance growth, e.g. average interest-bearing balance;

- net income revenue;

- activity, e.g. used in last six months; and

- time to closure.

Matrix reporting also has applications in collections and recoveries. Here, collections, litigation, and external agents recovery rates can all be monitored, based on cohorts of debt entering the different parts of the collections and recoveries process. In the context of collections and recoveries, these matrices are more commonly referred to as tranche reports and are discussed in Chapters 13 and 14.

9

THE THEORY OF PROVISION

9.1   Definition of Provision

Provision is an accounting term defined in the Companies Act 1948 as:

> *any amount written off or retained by way of providing for depreciation, renewals or diminution in the value of assets, or retained by way of providing for any known liability of which the amount cannot be determined with substantial accuracy.*

For lending organizations, provision is a fund set aside to cover the cost of bad debt, whether this arises from non-payment due to financial hardship or from outright fraud. The provision recognizes that the actual value of outstandings reported on the company's balance sheet is less than the stated value, because some borrowers will default on some or all of their repayments.

9.2   Reporting Provisions

In each accounting period (generally at each month end), a new provision is calculated based on the outstanding balances in defined delinquent or 'impaired' debt categories. The new provision is entered on the balance sheet.

The change in provision between the current and previous accounting period, plus the value of write-offs made during the current accounting period, is known as the current period's bad debt charge. This is entered on the profit and loss statement and is generally reported as a percentage of outstanding balances. An example is illustrated in Figure 9.1. Here, the £25,000,000 bad debt charge is the sum of the increase in provision during the year plus the bad debt write-off during the year.

Figure 9.1: Bad debt charge reporting *vs.* outstanding balances

Bad Debt Charge	£'000	Calculations	
Balances at end of year	500,000	A	
Bad debt provision at end of year	30,000	B	
Bad debt provision at end of previous year	20,000	C	
Increase in bad debt provision during year	10,000	D	B-C
Bad debt write off during year	15,000	E	
Bad debt charge at end of year	25,000	F	D+E
Bad debt charge as % balances	5%	G	F/A%

Reporting of fraud debt varies by organization. Some express losses due to fraud as a percentage of outstandings, others as a percentage of credit sales, and some use both measures. Figure 9.2 gives an example in which the fraud charge (the change in provision and write-off due to fraud) is reported as a percentage of credit sales.

Figure 9.2: Fraud charge reporting *vs.* credit sales

Fraud Charge	£'000
Credit sales during year	300,000
Fraud charge at end of year	6,000
Fraud charge as % sales	2%

Debt categories

Lenders generally distinguish between two types of provision:

Specific provision takes account of cases that already show significant problems ('impaired'); for example, fraud, suspect-fraud, litigation or with-debt-collection-agent cases. Sometimes specific provision is made on trace/gone-away, customer query or insurance claim-pending cases.

General provision allows for payment problems that are not yet manifest in particular cases. It covers payment problems from cases outside the specific provision categories. Generally this includes accounts that are in the first stages of delinquency. Sometimes a general provision is made for in-order accounts (see Section 9.4).

Organizations vary in the way provisions are made. Some use only specific provisions, others only general provisions. Most use some combination of the two.

Calculating provision

Provision is calculated as a percentage of outstanding balances in each of the defined debt categories. This percentage reflects the likelihood that a debt in a particular category will be written-off. In general, the more significant the problem, the higher the provision percentage will be.

For example, it is prudent to have a higher provision for accounts that are with an external debt collection agent than for accounts which are one payment in arrears, because less monies are likely to be repaid by agency cases.

If a given debt category has a provision level of 40%, this means that the lender expects 60% of balances in that category to be repaid. A category with a provision of 5% means that the lender expects 95% of balances to be repaid.

When a balance is written off, there is a release in provision and a corresponding increase in the bad debt charge. For example, if a case with a 40% provision and a balance of £1,000 is written-off, the provision will reduce by £400 and the bad debt charge will increase by the net £600.

Reports

Reports for calculating provision should show the distribution of debt by provision categories. A simplified typical report, which includes both specific and general provision categories, is given in Figure 9.3.

Figure 9.3: Distribution of debt report

Debt category		Outstanding debt		Provisions	
		Col. 1	Col. 2	Col. 3	Col. 4
		£'000	Col. %	Actuary %	£'000
General	Current	400,000	80.0%	0.5%	2,000
	Arrears 1	40,000	8.0%	1%	400
	Arrears 2	12,000	2.4%	5%	600
	Arrears 3	6,000	1.2%	15%	900
	Arrears 4+	10,000	2.0%	40%	4,000
Specific	Litigation	12,000	2.4%	60%	7,200
	Agents	20,000	4.0%	70%	14,000
Total		**500,000**	**100%**	**6%**	**29,100**

The report should give the provision percentage (the proportion of the balance to be provided against – column 3 in Figure 9.3) for each category of debt, along with the calculated amount of provision required (column 4). The provision percentage is also known as the actuary percentage.

In reality, a greater number of debt categories would appear on this report, in line with the provision categories defined by the lender. Some organizations report arrears levels as far as 12 or more payments missed. Others split the current and early arrears categories according to risk, defined initially by application score and subsequently by behavioural score.

The example in Figure 9.3 demonstrates that the higher the arrears level, and the more impaired the balances, the higher the actuarial provision percentage applied. The provision rates for the specific categories are higher than for any of the general categories.

The total provision percentage is found by taking the sum of the provision amounts across each of the debt categories, as a percentage of total outstanding balances. In Figure 9.3 this is £29,100 as a percentage of £500,000, i.e. 6%.

This report is required at each accounting period end to calculate the provision requirement, to determine portfolio trends and to identify provision adjustments.

9.3 Forecasting Bad Debt for Existing Portfolios

Organizations need to forecast debt movement in order to determine their provision requirement. The starting point is to project future performance based on past experience. Forecasts should be based on these projections and modified to take into account factors that will/may influence the projections. Factors include both changes to internal policy and the external economic and business environment. Projections should also be modified using analyses of the performance cohort matrix. As discussed in Chapter 8, this is a vital tool for understanding portfolio dynamics, allowing managers to understand the cause and effect of internal and external agents of change.

Two methods for projecting bad debt are the net roll-rate model and the Markov Chain model.

Net roll-rate models

The most common method for projecting debt movement is based on net roll rates. Although this method is widely used in the industry, it has a number of weaknesses which are highlighted below.

Net roll rates give the proportion of balances in each delinquency level that will roll forward to the next delinquency level one month later. All improving accounts are assumed to move back to a current status. A simple example is given in Figure 9.4. It shows the movement of debt between two months, May and June:

Figure 9.4: Net roll-rate report

Status	Balances May £'000	Balances June £'000	Roll-rate calculation
Carried Fwd[1]	–	20,000	20,000/25,000 = 80%
New Spend[1]	–	5,200	–
Total Current	25,000	25,200	–
Arrears 1	1,500	1,250	1,250/25,000 = 5%
Arrears 2	400	300	300/1,500 = 20%
Arrears 3	240	240	240/400 = 60%
Arrears 4	200	180	180/240 = 75%
Write-off[1]	–	160	160/200 = 80%

[1]Figures for month 1 not required in the demonstration calculations.

In Figure 9.4, of the £25,000 total current balances in May:

- 80% is carried forward as current debt in June – shown as the £20,000 carried forward in June of the £25,000 total current debt in May; and

- 5% (£1,250 of the £25,000) rolls forward into arrears 1.

Similarly, of the May arrears 1 debt (£1,500), 20% (£300) rolls forward into arrears 2, and so on through the arrears levels.

For completeness, Figure 9.4 shows balances relating to new spend. Together new spend plus the carried forward current balances from the previous month give the total current balance.

Provision requirements can be calculated from these net roll rates.

Example method 1

The simplest method is to focus on the roll rates across the debt categories. The provision percentage for any category of debt is given by the product of the roll rates through the successive levels of delinquency.

Figure 9.5 demonstrates this method.

Figure 9.5: Simple calculation of provision percentages

From-to:	Roll rate	Debt category	Provision calculation %	Provision %
	Col. 1	Col. 2	Col. 3	Col. 4
Current– Arrears1	5%	Current	5 x 20 x 60 x 75 x 80%	0.36%
Arrears 1-2	20%	Arrears 1	20 x 60 x 75 x 80%	7.2%
Arrears 2-3	60%	Arrears 2	60 x 75 x 80%	36%
Arrears 3-4	75%	Arrears 3	75 x 80%	60%
Arrears 4-write-off	80%	Arrears 4	80%	80%

Here the roll rates are taken from Figure 9.4. The provision percentage calculations (column 3) start from the bottom of the table and work upwards. The provision percentage for arrears 4 relates directly to the roll into write-off, i.e. 80%. The percentage for arrears 3 is the product of the rolls from arrears 3 to 4 and from arrears 4 to write-off, i.e. 75% of 80% = 60%, and so on for each debt category.

In reality more debt categories would be included in this analysis, including a roll from the highest arrears category into recoveries, rather than straight into write-off. This is because write-off processing is not always carried out in a consistent manner and can affect the results. In addition, the roll to write-off from recoveries occurs over a long period that does not match the monthly roll rate pattern of debt across the early arrears stages.

To overcome these problems, the provision percentage for the recoveries categories (e.g. litigation or with debt collection agents) is calculated based on the recovery rate experienced for each recoveries category over the long term. For example, if the recovery rate was 20% then the provision percentage would be 80%. The percentages for the pre-recoveries debt categories would then be calculated as above.

Example method 2

A second method takes payback rate into account in order to calculate the future bad debt arising from the amount currently outstanding. For this, a current-to-current carried forward roll rate is calculated. This is the ratio of debt outstanding from the previous period that is still outstanding – and in order – one period later (80% in figure 9.4). The write-off provision then corresponds to what would arise if all spending were stopped on the portfolio and payments applied to existing debt.

The bad debt prediction is made by multiplying through the roll rates for a given initial distribution of debt. In Figure 9.6, the roll rates from Figure 9.4 are applied to the debt shown at end May. For example, the June arrears-1 value of £1,250 is 5% of the £25,000 current balance in May; the July arrears-1 value of £1,000 is 5% of the £20,000 current balance in June, and so. It is possible to calculate the write-off arising with an infinite horizon, by use of simple formulae. A provision level (percentage) corresponding to each arrears status can then be derived.

Figure 9.6: Application of roll rates

Status	Roll Rate	May £'000	June £'000	July £'000	Aug. £'000	Sep. £'000	Oct. £'000	Infinity £'000
Current	—	25,000	—	—	—	—	—	—
C/forward	80%	—	20,000	16,000	12,800	10,240	8,192	0
Arrears 1	5%	1,500	1,250	1,000	800	640	512	0
Arrears 2	20%	400	300	250	200	160	128	0
Arrears 3	60%	240	240	180	150	120	96	0
Arrears 4	75%	200	180	180	135	112	90	0
Write-off	80%	0	160	154	154	108	90	0
Cum. write-off		0	160	314	468	576	666	1,006
Tot. outstanding		27,340	21,970	17,610	14,085	13,360	9,018	0

Model applications

The net roll-rates model works tolerably well for products where:

● there is no spending except on accounts that are current;

● delinquency is defined as time since last payment;

● all the accounts in a particular status either move on to the next state or return to current status; and

● all accounts in a given arrears status have about the same chance of rolling on the next status in the coming period.

Model limitations

Implicitly, a roll-rate model assumes that debt that does not roll on to the next state is repaid in full. This assumption is not correct. Usually, barely enough is repaid to restore the balance to order and the remaining balance is still at risk. This faulty assumption leads to systematic biases in the estimated provision levels and is especially prone to error in estimating the timing of write-off.

Roll-rate models assume that there is a strict succession of states, corresponding to months delinquent. The model breaks down where:

● accounts can jump between arrears states, because of part-payments;

● spending occurs on accounts in arrears; or

● accounts can stay in the same state for several successive periods, leading to roll rates of more than 100% and causing severe anomalies in the results.

Where a behavioural scoring system is in use, or there is some other statistical method to classify the risk on individual accounts, roll rates are unsatisfactory because they do not take this extra information into account.

Roll-rate models do not allow for modelling of the effect of future spending patterns. Hence, they are of little help in the financial management of a portfolio.

Markov Chain models

An alternative method for forecasting provision is the Markov Chain model. This classifies accounts in states at successive observation points. The model uses a transition matrix that gives the probability of an account in a given state moving to any other state between the observation points. The matrix is then modified to take account of movements in balance and financial changes.

Figures 9.7 and 9.8 illustrate a transition matrix using simple arrears states:

Figure 9.7: Transition matrix – balances £'000s

Month 1 Status (May)	Total	Paid back	Current C/forward	Arrears 1	Arrears 2	Arrears 3	Arrears 4	Write-off
Current	25,000	4,995	**18,877**	**1,128**				
Arrears 1	1,500	175	970	100	**255**			
Arrears 2	400	25	120	15	25	**215**		
Arrears 3	240	12	18	5	15	15	**170**	5
Arrears 4	200	3	15	2	5	10	10	**155**
Total	27,340	5,210	20,000	1,250	300	240	180	160

Figure 9.8: Transition matrix percentages

Month 1 Status (May)	Total	Paid back	Current C/forward	Arrears 1	2	3	4	Write-off
Current	100%	20%	**76%**	5%				
Arrears 1	100%	12%	65%	7%	**17%**			
Arrears 2	100%	6%	30%	4%	6%	**54%**		
Arrears 3	100%	5%	8%	2%	6%	6%	**71%**	2%
Arrears 4	100%	2%	8%	1%	3%	5%	5%	**78%**

Figure 9.7 shows the distribution of balances between two months, May and June. The balance values are converted into probabilities or percentages by dividing the month-2 state value by the month 1 source-state value (shown in Figure 9.8).

For example, of the May current debt:

● 76% is carried forward as current debt in June – (18,877 of 25,000); and

● 5% rolls forward into arrears 1 (1,128 of 25,000).

Of the May arrears-1 debt:

● 65% rolls back to current (970 of 1,500);

● 6.67% (rounded to 7% in the table) remains at arrears 1 (100 of 1,500); and

● 17% rolls forward into arrears 2 (255 of 1,500).

The matrices show that the majority of delinquent balances do roll forward – the diagonal in these matrices shown in bold. For example, £215 of the £400 in arrears 2 in May rolls into arrears 3 in June, and so on. The only exception in this example is the arrears 1 debt, the majority of which returns to current after one month.

The advantage of the Markov Chain approach is that is takes into consideration balances that do not follow the majority trend. Also, although the states in the Figure 9.7 and 9.8 examples are defined only in terms of arrears, other important factors that influence future repayments can be used to define states – such as behavioural scores and time on book. Examples include:

● in-order (arrears state), new account (defined by time on book), and low risk (defined by score);

● in-order, new account, high risk;

● in-order, established account, low risk;

- in-order, established account, high risk;

- mild out-of-order, low risk;

- mild out-of-order, high risk, high balance;

- severe out-of-order, paying arrangement;

- CCJ issued last 12 months;

- paid back; and

- written off.

One disadvantage of the model is that it can give spurious results if the subdivision of states is too fine, resulting in too few data points in some states. Also, if the definition of any state is dependent on application or behavioural scores, when these scorecards are up-dated the model must also be adjusted.

However, this approach improves on the net roll-rates model because it:

- allows states to be defined in more general terms, not just current level of delinquency;

- takes account of spending patterns on out-of-order accounts;

- takes full account of the movement of debt between states;

- gives better projections on repeat-delinquents and accounts that do not move straight through the delinquency chain; and

- gives clearer input for budgeting future delinquency and final loss levels.

9.4 Forecasting Bad Debt for New or Rapidly Growing Portfolios

Bad debt forecasts are based on analysis of past experience. Good models provide projections and incorporate sensitivities, to reflect management's judgment of the impact of future business plans and on expectations about the national economy and the credit environment.

With a new portfolio there is no past experience. Initial provision forecasts should incorporate expectations from the set-up business plan, management's judgment, experience from similar products and expert industry experience. For example, provision for fraud is likely to be disproportionately high for a new portfolio, compared with a mature portfolio. This is because fraudsters are attracted to new products/schemes and fraud cases are identified and quantified faster than bad debts.

Forecasts for rapidly expanding and new portfolios should consider the difference between the overall and underlying delinquency patterns. For each cohort of debt accepted, the underlying delinquency pattern follows a life-cycle curve, as described in Chapter 8. In general, for a consumer credit product, the life-cycle curve shows that the majority of bad payers are found between six and eighteen months after acceptance (although the precise pattern varies by portfolio).

The life-cycle pattern shows that it is misleading to assume that all the up-to-date balances in a new or rapidly expanding portfolio will be paid back. Accounts that are newly opened and mildly delinquent will not repay at the same rate as more established accounts at the same level of delinquency. Logically, this means assigning higher provision rates for these milder delinquent categories than would be the case for a more mature portfolio, and assigning a provision against new account up-to-date balances.

One solution for managing rapidly expanding and new portfolio provisions is to apply provisions to newly acquired debt. This is often called inception-time provisioning. It takes into account the higher concentration of new and therefore up-to-date debt than exists in a mature, stable portfolio.

In practice, this is achieved by forecasting and reporting bad debt by age of account. Typically, two or three age-of-debt breakdowns are used, for example, accounts less than 12 months on book, 12-24 months and greater than 24 months on book. These breaks should reflect the observed life-cycle delinquency of the portfolio.

If provision rates from a mature portfolio are applied to a new or expanding portfolio, overall bad debt, when measured as a percentage of total outstandings, will be underestimated. This will produce an artificially good picture in the early stages of growth. As the portfolio matures, and more specifically when the pace of growth slows, the provision requirement will rise rapidly. The business will face a double difficulty – less dynamic growth compounded by an apparent deterioration in quality.

9.5 Managing Provisions

A number of business areas are involved in determining the formula and the level of provisions. These usually include:

- risk management;
- collections and recoveries;
- finance;
- internal audit; and
- external audit.

The first three are instrumental in the forecasting process, bringing together specialist modelling skills and practical business knowledge. In addition, one of these usually carries the prime responsibility for the level of bad debt, i.e. it holds the bad debt budget and is responsible for any variations from that budget.

The auditors have responsibility for ensuring the validity of the actuarial percentages and in some cases are responsible for the calculation of these values.

External auditors must be satisfied with the formula for arriving at the provision level and have the responsibility for ensuring provisions represent a fair and true picture of the book in the company accounts. Where they are not satisfied with the formula, they can appoint external professional actuaries to determine the state of the book. As such they carry out their role on behalf of the non-executive directors and shareholders of the company.

Together, this group is responsible for

- understanding the state of the portfolio;
- determining whether provision is adequate;
- determining whether provisions need to be increased; and
- determining whether some part of the provision can be released.

Changes in provision have a direct impact on profits. Any increase reduces profits by the value of the increase, whereas any release in provision increases profits by the value of the release.

It is essential, for prudent and legal reasons, for a lender to maintain an adequate level of cover for bad debt. During a period of economic growth, where the portfolio is performing well, there is likely to be an opportunity to release provision. However, any release must allow for economic downturns. Therefore, most organizations look to manage their provision, to smooth the cost of bad debt over the economic cycles and avoid unexpected or unnecessary fluctuations in company profits.

Thus, for most organizations the bad debt forecast is the cornerstone for predicting provision requirements. These forecasts tend to be reliable over relative short periods and most forecast for the forthcoming 12 months. Because economic cycles occur over the longer period, the actual provision entered into the company accounts may vary from the forecast requirement, to take into account the need to manage provisions over the longer term.

10

APPLICATION PROCESSING

10.1   Application Processing Department

Objective of Application Processing

Every lender aims to maximize the returns on the monies spent on recruiting new customers, while at the same time taking on only those applicants who will be both an acceptable level of risk and generate profitable business in the future. The application processing department aims to fulfil these latter two criteria while making the accept/decline decision in as short a time as possible to generate initial customer goodwill.

Overview of the department

Typically the work flows through the department as illustrated in Figure 10.1 opposite. This is a simplified outline intended to place the process in context and give an overall picture.

Many other functions occur in parallel with these, the main ones being fraud checks and money laundering verification checks. The manual review process is applied to applications that fall outside the mainstream decision process. The criteria for determining this vary with each lender.

10.2   Pre-scoring Processes

Application form

The type of information that is requested from an applicant is given in Chapter 2, where Figure 2.1 illustrates a typical application form. Each lender has its own variation that reflects its own policies, scorecards and marketing requirements.

Telephone applications

Increasingly much new business is being written via the telephone. Applicants are encouraged to have a copy of the application form in front of them (although this is not mandatory) and the telephonist asks the questions, guiding them through the form and the process. Each answer is keyed directly into the application processing system so that none of the manual pre-processing associated with paper applications is required.

Figure 10.1: Flow through application processing department

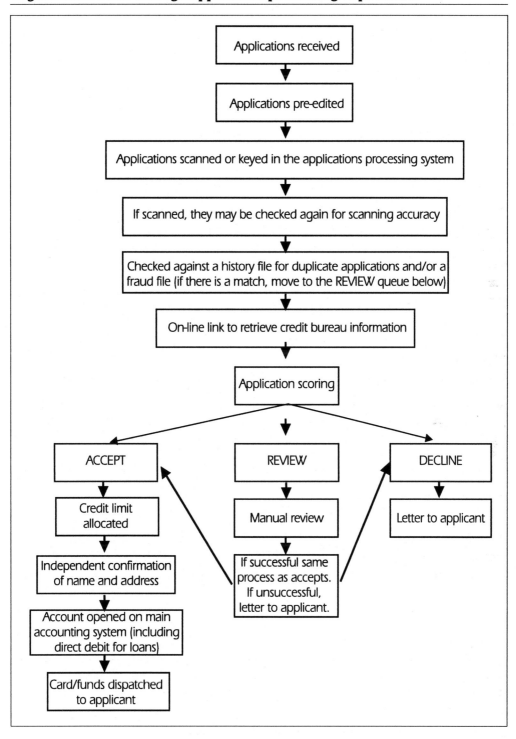

The applicant usually receives a decision in principle immediately. Sometimes an outright decline is given, but in all other cases proof of identity is required before the decision can be confirmed. From this point on, the processing is identical to paper-based applications.

Manual pre-editing

Applications arrive by a number of means:

- post but from a variety of sources, and in a variety of styles;
- fax – likewise in a variety of styles;
- telephone; and
- the Internet.

The variety of styles and sources usually depends on what marketing activity has been undertaken in the recent past. Leaflets picked up from branches may be more elaborate than single sheet inserts placed in magazines, or there may have been a campaign of pre-approvals where much of the detail is cleanly pre-printed.

Once the postal applications are opened they go to the editing section. Applications received by fax are treated in the same way. Internet-based applications are discussed in Section 10.8.

Hand-written documents vary enormously in clarity, legibility and completeness of detail. It is imperative that they are 'cleaned up' to ensure accuracy before they are assessed. This might entail tidying up the handwriting, inserting missing postcodes or phoning the applicant because there are too many missing details. Although this is a relatively straightforward process, it is nevertheless essential and time-consuming.

Data capture

This can be achieved in a number of ways. It may be done in-house or on a bureau basis by a computer bureau, another card issuer or a credit reference agency.

Traditionally clerks would be employed to key all the data into predefined screens and fields on an application processing system, and in many organizations this is still the case. The order of the screens, and the fields within each screen, are designed to reflect the layout of the application, making it easier and speedier for the operator. There are rules behind most of the fields to ensure accuracy and compliance with both the lender's policies and any legal requirements.

Alternatively a scanner can be used for data capture. It employs software called OCR (Optical Character Recognition) to convert the scanned image into a format suitable for creating a digital file which then becomes the basis for application scoring and all subsequent computer-based actions.

At the time of writing, however, scanners are not sufficiently sensitive to reliably interpret every character it reads, particularly with elaborate handwriting. Therefore to ensure accurate data entry, a second editing function is required. This entails comparing the screen image of the document (which highlights characters that are unclear) with the paper original, and where necessary making corrections to the screen image.

Data validation

Every application processing system has in-built rules to ensure that the data that is entered into each field is appropriate, of the right length, and in the correct range of values. Typical examples are:

- names contain only alpha characters, no numbers;

- postcodes are in the format of aann naa (where a is an alpha character and n is numeric), although there are occasional exceptions, e.g. W4;

- age or date of birth is only numeric and is the appropriate length. The year must include the century, i.e. 19xx or 20xx; and

- fields like years in job, or years at address or time with bank are all numeric and are either one or two digits long and are in the range 1-50 (for example), or are captured as four numerics for months and years in the format mmyy.

If any data entered breaches these rules, a warning message appears on the screen at the time of input. If the message is caused by a keying error, the operator can correct it and continue. If however, the original data is incorrect, then the system may put the application data into a pending file, while the physical application is outsorted for resolution. This may be by telephone or by returning the application by post.

Data verification

Each issuer has its own policies that are reflected throughout the whole process, but some rules are likely to be common to most systems. These may derive from items that are mandatory for scoring or account opening, legal requirements or anti-fraud, common-sense checks. These typically include:

- name and address (including postcode) and date of birth are the minimum number of mandatory fields covering the whole application;

- there will be a minimum total number of mandatory fields for the whole application form, reflecting scorecard and account opening criteria;

- if the applicant is under age, then decline – a legal requirement;

- if the applicant is over x, then decline or review. This might be a lender's policy, where x might be 70 or 75;

- cross-check that time at address, time in job, and age all make sense in relation to each other. For instance if an applicant says he or she is 27 years of age, but also says he or she has been 15 years in the job, then something is clearly adrift. It may be a genuine error or it could be first-party fraud;

- similar checks can be used for any other common-sense combinations;

- if the application is for a personal loan, then bank details and the direct debit mandate are likely to be mandatory;

- some lenders may explicitly ask the applicant to agree to retrieving and using personal data from a credit reference agency. They may chose not to process the application if this permission is not granted; and

- if the application is not signed and dated, it is not a legally binding contract and it must be returned to the applicant before any further work is done on it.

Duplicate and fraudulent applications

Fraudsters frequently submit multiple applications, often with slight variations of the details on each. This is more likely to be a problem for the large-volume lenders where the perception is that they will receive far too many applications to notice a few duplicates.

People who have recently been declined may also reapply fairly quickly thereafter, in the hope that something will have changed to their benefit and they will be accepted (i.e. not with fraudulent intent).

Modern application processing systems contain a history file against which all new incoming applications are automatically checked. This file contains enough details from each application to enable a comprehensive matching process to be undertaken quickly and efficiently. Each lender decides the criteria for an entry remaining on this file. Some may delete entries after six months; others may retain them for several years. Alternatively there may be a link between the application processing system and specialist system for detecting fraudulent applications which will be more sophisticated than the process just described (see Chapters 5 and 11).

If there is a match against the history file then the details of both the current and the previous applications are written to a match file. This file is generally printed at the end of the day's work, ready for a reviewer to assess the next day.

10.3   Credit References

There are four reasons for taking a credit reference as part of the application reviewing process:

- to verify the applicant's name and address from independent sources (a requirement of the Money Laundering Regulations for credit cards);

- to assess the applicant's current level of financial commitment;

- to see whether the applicant has, or has had, a good or bad financial track record – this may vary from missing the occasional payment through to having several CCJs; and

- as a fraud prevention measure.

Taking the credit reference

In application scoring terms, credit reference information is almost always significant. However there is a direct cost attached to each enquiry or search made. The question that arises for every lender is 'in which order do I process – the applicant-provided information first or the bureau data?' The trade-off is this:

- Applying the scoring process to the applicant data first enables the best cases to be accepted automatically and the worst cases to be identified and declined immediately. A bureau search need only be done on the rest, thereby saving the cost of the bureau search and increasing speed of decision making on this group. However, this potentially slows the operational efficiency for the remaining applications because this part of the process now becomes two sequential functions, i.e. scoring, followed by the reference.

- Conversely, take a bureau search on all applicant details by automatically sending the enquiry on-line from the application processing systems to the bureau. The reference data is returned immediately and is included in the application scoring process. The costs are increased and it may also increase the efficiency of the process overall. This approach also ensures that the maximum amount of data is captured, which is important for future scorecard developments.

Both approaches are equally valid and are wholly the choice of the lender. Some of the criteria that will have an impact on this decision are:

- cost of a search: large-volume lenders are usually able to negotiate rates that are significantly lower than the standard, published price;

- the target time for getting the plastic card/personal loan cheque to the customer: if this is a tight limit then increased efficiency may be seen as being more important; and

- the volumes of applications that are likely to be declined regardless of the bureau information: the fewer the case, the lower the savings, alternatively, if thousands are being declined, then the savings could be significant.

In practice, lenders vary their search policy over time as circumstances change, for example, where the credit bureaux pricing structure changes. If their application processing system includes automatically searching a bureau, then switching this off may require reprogramming that part of the system – or at least resetting some parameters.

Using the data

Chapter 2 provides full details of the various types of data that are routinely retrieved from a bureau and it is assumed that the reader is familiar with this material.

Money laundering

All applications for running-credit accounts are legally required to have two independent sources of verification for both the name and address of the applicant. A credit reference provides one of these (see Chapter 16).

Over-committed and adverse information

The details returned from the bureau's shared information files will give an indication of the potential for over-commitment. It will also give an objective picture of the applicant's track record with other lenders. The scorecard may contain criteria for assessing both these factors, and they will be added to the overall picture and the final score.

Fraud prevention

The independent nature of the information retrieved from the voters roll will usually confirm the veracity of the applicant's identity. Additionally, if there has been any fraud, or even suspected fraud, there will a record on CIFAS files. The processing system will highlight this for manual review and each issuer must assess the detail on its merits and act accordingly, although most cases will be declined. If it is appears that the current application is also fraud-related, then a new entry to CIFAS must be generated for the benefit of the whole industry.

10.4   Post-scoring Processes

As the workflow illustrated in Figure 10.1 shows, applications now undergo different processes, depending on the outcome of the scoring process.

Accepted applications

For accepted accounts the application processing system:

- allocates the credit limit for credit cards; or

- allocates the loan amount and compares it with the requested amount;

- generates an entry to trigger opening the new account on the main accounts system; and

- generates an entry for the creation of the plastic card (for credit cards); and

- produces a cheque or generates an entry for automatically allocating the funds to the applicant's bank account (for personal loans).

Subsequently, if a direct debit needs setting up, this is done manually through a different, bank-based, system. All the paper is then filed away, but under the Money Laundering Regulations must be retained for at least five years.

Declined applications

For declined applications, the computer automatically generates a decline letter advising of the decision and outlining the process whereby the applicant can appeal. It may also advise which credit bureau was used and that the applicant can obtain a copy of his or her personal details from that bureau if required.

In the UK, it is illegal to decline an applicant on the grounds of ethnic origin, geography, sex, nationality or disability.

Credit referrals

These are the applications that fall into one or more reasons for manual referral (see Chapter 4, Section 4.5). In these cases most lenders seek further information from the applicant, internal records or another independent source. When this is added to the existing detail, an accept or decline decision can be reached.

- *Information from the applicant* might include asking to see pay slips or recent bank statements. If a work telephone number has been given then the lender might telephone the applicant at work – providing verification of his or her employment.

- *Internal records* will probably be consulted if it is known that the applicant has other accounts or products with the lender or the wider organization. For example, if a personal loan has been applied for, and the applicant states that his or her current account is with the same lender, then cross-checking these bank records both verifies the information given and provides an means of independent identification for money laundering purposes.

- *Another independent source* usually means an alternative credit reference agency. Although in theory the quantity and quality of information held by both bureaux should be the same, in actual fact it can differ, sometimes significantly. Searching a second bureau may well provide information that was not available from the first search.

Large-volume lenders are likely to undertake an automated second bureau search for reasons of operational efficiency.

Reviews for other purposes

Money laundering

The regulations require that, for all running-credit accounts, two checks are made independently on the name and the address. If a credit bureau is used as one source of confirmation for, say, the name, then a second, different source must be used to confirm the address. CIFAS files are an acceptable alternative.

For face-to-face lending (e.g. in a branch) this is less of a problem because the lender can ask to see the applicant's driver's licence or other credit/debit card. However in distance or direct lending, this is not possible. If therefore the applicant already has an existing relationship with the lender, this makes the process easier because these records are deemed to provide adequate independent verification. If the applicant is new to the lender, then making a search on a second bureau is the most efficient way forward. If that fails for whatever reason, then contact must be made with the applicant to request sight of some paper-based identification (see Chapter 16).

Suspected fraud

There are two types of potential fraudulent application:

- The form has genuinely been completed by the applicant who has used his or her real name and address. However he or she has 'massaged' some of the answers on the form to enhance the chance of being accepted. If this massaging is significant (e.g. 'at this address for ten years', whereas the voters roll shows only four years) it warrants further investigation. This is an example of first-party fraud.

- If the name and address on the form are fictitious or are the real details of another person, i.e. not the signatory, then this is third-party fraud. This warrants fast action, an entry on the CIFAS system to alert other lenders and the application is declined.

Both of these areas are usually the domain of trained fraud identification staff. If a reviewer in the application processing department is at all suspicious, he or she should immediately pass the details to the fraud team. In a modern applications processing systems which employs workflow and queuing methods, then separate queues are likely to be established for fraud cases. The reviewer needs only to transfer the suspect case into this queue and a fraud reviewer will pick it up for assessment.

10.5   Giving Reasons for Declines and Appeals

There have been ongoing debates for many years regarding the need to give the applicant a specific reason for declining an application. Similarly, should a lender declare that application scoring is the main vehicle used for assessing an application?

In the USA it is a legal requirement that a reason(s) is given, and when application scoring is employed, this becomes more difficult. The application score is a composite of all the factors in the scorecard, and it is particularly problematic to identify a single cause. However, the revised *Guide to Credit Scoring* is recommending that this practice be adopted routinely.

Equally, the *Guide to Credit Scoring* also recommends that, where application scoring is in use, this fact should be openly published. (See Chapter 17, Section 17.3.)

Appeals

Best practice has always required that lenders have a procedure whereby applicants who have been declined, may appeal. This usually requires that the applicant provides additional information that will enable the lender to reassess the decision and that a different person from the original reviewer reconsiders the case. Whether or not the decision is reversed depends on the policies of each lender.

This requirement for an appeal procedure is embodied in the *Guide to Credit Scoring* (see Chapter 17), which has laid down best practice since its first publication in 1983.

If the applicant asks which credit bureau has been used, then the lender is obliged (under the Consumer Credit Act) to pass on this information, including an address where the applicant may purchase a copy of the file. (See Chapter 16, Section 16.1.)

10.6   Safe Card Dispatch

The methods and intricacies of embossing the plastic card and writing the details onto the magnetic stripe are outside the scope of this course. This function is often outsourced to plastic card manufacturers and, because an unsigned card is the plastic equivalent of an unsigned cheque, the process is steeped in security measures.

However, the lender has the discretion to choose its preferred method of despatching cards. There are a number of options, and lenders often vary methods over time to try and stay one jump ahead of fraudsters. (One of the main sources of the fraudulent use of cards are those that have been lost or stolen between despatch and receipt by the cardholder, and misused by the interceptor.)

- *Regular mail in a plain envelope:* The difficulty with this approach is that, because the plastic is rigid, it is fairly easy to feel its shape through the envelope. This is probably the cheapest method albeit it is also the highest-risk one.

- *Registered mail or recorded delivery:* This is safer than the standard postal service, but it costs significantly more.

- *Delivery by courier:* This may be undertaken in high-risk areas or as a short-term response to known fraud activity in a particular area.

- *Collect from a branch:* Occasionally a lender asks the cardholder to collect the card from the organization's nearest branch. Although this is a very safe approach, it is not always popular with cardholders.

- *High-risk addresses:* Certain types of addresses have always been particularly risky. These include university halls of residents (where mail is often left in public areas), mail box addresses and blocks of flats where the letterboxes are near the front door and are easily accessible. Wherever possible, lenders ask for an alternative, safer, delivery address. This is a particular problem each summer, when most new students apply for cards before going to college or university.

All cards are sent out encased in a 'card carrier', which is a folded paper holder with slots that hold the card in place. The Consumer Credit Act also requires that a copy of the regulated agreement is also sent out with the plastic – and this is also true for all replacement and reissued cards.

Similar safeguards may be employed for the dispatch of personal loan cheques.

10.7   Managing the Department

An application processing department almost always operates under conditions of varying workloads. These depend on marketing campaigns, both the number and success of campaigns running at any one time. Therefore there is a need for good communications with marketing (see Chapter 3) and detailed capacity planning. Some departments work on a fixed 9 - 5.30 basis and offer overtime to cope with peak loads; others operate shifts that can be switched on or off as required.

At an individual level, the volumes of day-to-day work that are expected from operators and reviewers are pre-defined, and are often the basis for performance-related pay schemes. These volumes, or rates of processing, are measured by the application processing system and reported to supervisors or managers on a daily or weekly basis. These throughput figures are also used in the capacity planning process.

10.8   Internet Applications

The ability to apply for loans or credit cards via the Internet is increasingly common, although this method appears to be more fraud-prone. Some of these web sites ask a limited number of questions and rely heavily on credit reference data. Others ask at least as many, if not more, questions than a paper-based application. One of the limitations of this service is that UK-based lending is available only to UK residents. All Internet applications are processed using application scoring and credit reference data. All accepted applications still require proof of identity in the same way as conventional applications.

As it currently stands, the law still requires a paper-based document containing a physical signature to ensure that a legally binding contract exists. Currently there is legislation under discussion that should pave the way for electronic signatures to be equally binding. (See Chapter 16, Section 16.4.)

11

FRAUD MANAGEMENT

This subject predominately affects the plastic card market, but it does also apply to a lesser extent to personal loan products. The key problems are application fraud for both cards and loans, and the multitude of ways in which actual cards, counterfeit cards, or just the card number can be used without the cardholder's consent.

11.1 Background and Trends

Plastic card fraud has been one of the fastest growing crimes in the UK ever since the first credit card company was established in the mid-1960s. Although figures are generally not available for the first ten years when there were only two main issuers (Access and Barclaycard) and virtually no store cards, it is estimated that in 1983 fraud loses were running at between 18p and 30p for every £100 of expenditure[1]. In 1988 the Access consortium devolved down to its constituent members, each of which became a card issuer in its own right. Subsequently, card issuers were able to offer both Visa and MasterCard products. This resulted in a massive increase in the number of UK-issued credit cards and a corresponding increase in the opportunity for, and potential 'benefit' of, fraudulent activity.

Through the late 1980s and early 1990s, fraud losses virtually doubled, reaching just over £165 million in 1991. The major banks and building societies agreed that collective action was necessary to stem the losses and in September 1990 they formed the Plastic Fraud Prevention Forum (PFPF). This group worked with the Home Office and Association for Payment and Clearing Services (APACS) members to set standards and introduce industry-wide fraud containment methods. As a result fraud losses fell to £83m in 1995. Since then it has continued to grow again in absolute terms. However if the fraud losses are considered as a percentage of the total value of transactions, then the figures halved over 12 months to reach 0.9% in 1998.[2] Despite this significant improvement, the largest single area of fraud loss is still from counterfeit cards, where 1998 losses were 48% of the total despite the reduction from 72% in 1995.

---

[1] Drury, A.C. & Ferrier, C.W. (1984) *Credit Cards*, Butterworths, London
[2] APACS (1999) *Fraud in Focus*, APACS, London

11.2   Types of Fraud

Fraudulent activity can occur at any stage of the credit life cycle and can take many forms. Often it is limited only by the audacity of the fraudsters, although the increasing use of sophisticated electronic technologies is helping to contain some of these approaches.

Application fraud

This covers any type of fraudulent activity that occurs before and during the applications processing stage. (See Chapter 10, Section 10.4.)

First-party fraud

This occurs when the named person is the genuine applicant, but some of the details given on the application form have been falsified. This may take the form of 'massaging' or, at the other extreme, blatant lying about some aspects of the applicant's situation.

Third-party fraud

This occurs when the applicant is a person other than the one whose details are given on the form. For example, the person filling in the form might be Mr A.B. Smith, but the name he used, and signed under, is Mr X.Y. Jones. This is done when the applicant knows that he will be declined in his own right, but knows enough about Mr Jones' circumstances to enable him to complete the form with a high chance of being accepted.

These situations apply as equally to personal loan applications as they do to plastic cards. Since the Money Laundering Regulations came into force (requiring all running-credit applicants to be independently verified) it is possible that this form of fraud may have been contained to some extent.

Card-based fraud

Losses from these types of fraud in the UK totalled £135m in 1998, and the main categories are shown in Figure 11.1.

Figure 11.1: 1998 Plastic card fraud losses[3]

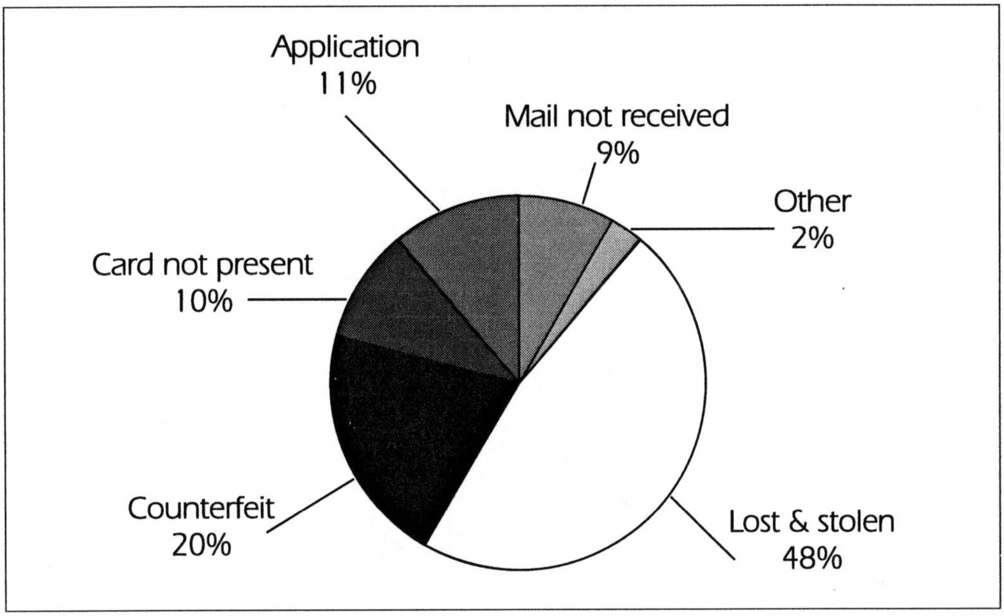

Lost and stolen

When the genuine cardholder either inadvertently loses his or her card or has it stolen, the potential exists for the recipient to either use it fraudulently or to sell it on. Transactions typically occur in the following 24-36 hours before the loss is notified and the account blocked.

Counterfeit cards

This usually occurs after the card details have been intercepted from a retail sales situation or from a phone/mail order situation – and now from the Internet. The genuine details are used to manufacture additional plastics. These may be used very quickly and then disposed of, or they may be stored away for quite some time before being used when the cardholder least expects it.

Non-receipt of cards

Reissued or new plastics are either intercepted in the post (or other delivery means) or from 'unsafe' addresses. These are often places where mail can be left in a communal or open area – halls of residence are a typical example. (See Chapter 10, Section 10.6.)

Skimming or cloning

This is a recent development in which a corrupt retailer (or an employee) swipes a genuine

[3] APACS (1999) *Fraud in Focus*, APACS, London

card through a small electronic device that captures (skims) and stores the details off the magnetic stripe. The details are then reused (in the form of counterfeit cards), sold on or used to make card-not-present transactions.

Transaction-based fraud

Card not present

This occurs when fraudulently obtained card details are used to make purchases over the telephone, by mail order or the Internet. Since the growth in the Internet as a source of remote shopping, this type of fraud has increased significantly (36% increase in the UK from 1997 to 1998)[4].

Overseas fraud on UK-issued cards

While this is not a specific form of fraud in itself, it is an area of growing concern and losses, particularly in Europe. Greater difficulties are associated with this area in respect of the cost of, and the reduced likelihood of, any preventative or recoveries actions across national borders.

Pre-empting authorizations

A newly opened account will have a large credit paid into it by cheque before any transactions have occurred or statement issued. Almost immediately there is significant spending on the card up to (if not exceeding) the value of the credit. Because there is a credit balance on the account every authorizations request is automatically approved. Several days later, the original cheque bounces, and the cardholder disappears. (It could be argued that this is a form of first-party fraud because the cardholder applied in the first place with the deliberate intent to defraud.)

11.3 Fraud Identification and Prevention

Many activities are designed with both identification and prevention objectives. The two concepts are interlinked and overlap in many ways, and the activities discussed in this section address both needs.

APACS initiatives

APACS has become the main instigator of industry-wide fraud prevention initiatives by directing and coordinating plastic card fraud prevention throughout the financial services industry. Working in close co-operation with national and international payment systems organizations, police and retailers, APACS, through the Plastic Fraud Prevention Group (PFPF), leads the research, development and implementation of anti-fraud initiatives.

---

[4] APACS (1999) *Fraud in Focus*, APACS, London

Fraud Intelligence Bureau (FIB)

In response to the growth in skimming, the FIB was set up as a central unit to confirm occurrences of skimming, alert participating banks and, at the same time, work with the police. The genuine cardholder is the first to notice transactions on the statement that he or she did not incur. When they are reported to the card issuer, they are passed onto the FIB for analysis. Three occurrences at a specific retailer constitute an alert; six hits are a confirmation, after which all members are notified. The FIB is a medium-term initiative that will run until chip cards become commonplace (see Section 11.4) and it is not concerned with application fraud.

International Hot Card File (IHCF)

This is an on-line, real-time system for participating members to notify other banks and retailers of suspect fraud cases. It is administered by APACS and operated by an independent computer bureau. It confines itself to possible fraud details only, i.e. it cannot be used for credit control purposes. It focuses on the two retail sectors that card issuers know to be among their worst problem areas, namely supermarkets and petrol stations.

Other APACS Initiatives

A number of committees exist to coordinate non-competitive activities such as setting international systems standards, point-of-sale terminal issues, and chip card roll-out.

CIFAS

Although details of CIFAS data were given in Chapter 2, CIFAS (the organization) is widening its membership to include non-credit grantors whose data is nevertheless beneficial in fraud prevention. As well as the original banks and building societies, members now include retailers, mail order companies, telecommunications companies, motor finance and insurance companies. It is also working with organizations such as the Benefits Agency, Customs and Excise and DVLA to share data for the common objective of fraud prevention.

The CIFAS system processes both application and transaction fraud and it recognizes seven categories:

- empty house fraud – false name with an existing address;
- impersonation – using the name and particulars of another person;
- massaging – using a genuine name and address with one or more material falsehoods in personal details with the intention of gaining acceptance, followed by a serious misuse of the credit facility;
- attempted fraud – the same as massaging but the application is intercepted before the credit facility is agreed and no misuse or loss occurs;
- selling on, or conversion, of goods to which the seller has no title, where the goods have been obtained under a regulated credit or hire agreement;

- first-party fraud – opening a credit facility for the deliberate purpose of fraud or fraudulent misuse of the facility, but using genuine name, address and personal details; and

- aiding and abetting.

A new category for fraudulent insurance claims is planned.

Payment Systems Organizations

Payment Systems Organizations (PSOs) are the umbrella organizations under whose brand name most internationally accepted credit cards are issued, e.g. Visa, MasterCard or Switch. These organizations operate international networks for authorization and transaction traffic, and their systems include fraud hot-list files for the benefit of all members. Unlike the IHCF, these hot-lists can also include credit control cases, e.g. over-limit accounts. (See Chapter 12.)

11.4 Fraud Prevention Strategies

There are other techniques and strategies in addition to those discussed above which are strictly fraud prevention approaches. These are operated as standard practice by all card issuers and merchant acquirers (discussed below as External Policies), and each lender also operates its own policies (discussed as Internal Policies). These are not mutually exclusive but work together to maximize fraud prevention possibilities for the potential benefit of the cardholder, the issuer and the retailer.

External policies

Retailer floor limits

Together with authorizations systems, this is one of the oldest fraud prevention techniques. Each retailer that accepts plastic cards, is assigned a financial limit (a floor limit) and in principle all transactions above this limit require permission (i.e. authorization) from the card issuer. The level of this limit is varied over time, and is lower for retailers of low-value transactions and vice-versa. If there is a sudden spate of fraudulent activity in a particular geographic area or a certain trade sector, floor limits may be reduced or set to zero as a short-term expediency measure.

Authorizations

This is the process whereby retailers are required to obtain the card issuer's permission to go ahead with particular transactions over a pre-determined floor limit. In the days before electronic card-swipe machines, all authorizations required a telephone call to the card centre. If the transaction was authorized, then a code was given to the retailer who hand-wrote it onto the paper voucher. This process could take several minutes – often to the irritation of the cardholder.

Since the advent of electronic terminals this has changed. Retailers with on-line terminals automatically have all transactions authorized, i.e. operating as though the floor limit were zero. If the terminal is off-line, it dials for authorizations only if the transaction value is greater than the floor limit. While this is transparent to the cardholder, an authorizations code is generated, transmitted back to the merchant and printed along with all the other details on the slip that the cardholder signs. This automation means that much more fraud prevention and identification can take place routinely and undetected by fraudsters. Telephone calls from the merchant to the authorizations centre are now permitted only under fraudulent or suspicious circumstances. (See Chapter 12 for full details about authorizations.)

Personal Identity Number (PIN)

These were first used in 1975 as an additional security measure for ATM transactions. PINs are either four- or six-digit codes and are successful only while the number is not committed to paper or passed onto another person. Some banks allow cardholders to chose their own PIN, whereas in other cases it is determined by the card-issuing system. PINs are frequently encrypted during transmission for authorizations as an additional security measure.

Holograms on cards

These were introduced as an industry standard in the early 1990s to inhibit counterfeiting. All Visa, MasterCard, Switch, Diners Club and American Express cards now contain holograms as a routine part of their design and manufacture.

CVV/CVC

Card verification value (CVV) or code (CVC) is an anti-counterfeiting measure. This is a number that is encoded on the magnetic stripe in such a way that any attempt to counterfeit the details on the magnetic stripe will fail because the CVV will be incorrect.

Chip cards[5]

Integrated circuit cards (ICCs) or chip cards are plastic cards that contain a built-in programmable microprocessor that can be coded with security, credit control, authorizations or other data. They will be used in conjunction with the merchant's terminal that will read the chip. They will identify genuine cards and make attempted fraud and counterfeiting both difficult and expensive. These cards are being hailed as the 'biggest fraud prevention milestone ever achieved in the card industry'. They have been developed to international standards after close co-operation between the international payment systems organizations and the UK is the first country to introduce them as standard.

Police, retailer and card issuer cooperation

Although the need for this sounds obvious, it was not until the mid-1980s that the industry

[5] APACS (1999) *Fraud in Focus*, APACS, London

acknowledged that fraud was a non-competitive, industry-wide issue that should be tackled by mutual co-operation. Many of the external, industry initiatives work as well as they do simply because of this mutual self-help approach.

Internal policies

Fraud systems

Systems for identifying application fraud are very different from those designed to track transaction fraud. There are several, commercially available, systems, which can be purchased for in-house operation alongside an application processing system, or used on a bureau basis. In either case, they work in tandem with the lender's accounts systems and they are based on scoring, other predictive techniques, or data matching methods. Identification of such cases enables pro-active responses to be undertaken on individual cases. They provide workflow and queuing capabilities, so that cases can be categorized and the most urgent worked as top priority (see Chapter 5).

PIN encryption

Encryption is a security technique in which electronic data is scrambled into a non-intelligible form for transmitting PINs from ATMs to the main computer. The process is designed to inhibit computer hacking (i.e. unauthorized access to a computer system). Encryption is increasingly being used in Internet transmissions of sensitive data including credit card details.

Security checks

Most banks and credit card companies (and many other organizations that hold personal data) ask for some data that is known only to the customer, e.g. mother's maiden name. If there is an occasion when the customer needs to telephone the bank or issuer, he or she will be asked these questions at the outset as confirmation of identity.

New card validation

Some issuers do not allow a new or reissued card to be used without first being 'validated'. This entails a telephone call to the issuer to confirm identity and security details before the account is activated. Some retail card schemes also use this approach; the cardholder may be asked for additional identification in the store before the card is activated.

New card receipt

Some issuers enclose a return slip with the card asking the cardholder to sign to the effect that he or she has physically received the card. Once this slip has been received, the issuer marks the account accordingly and the new card can be used.

Close accounts for lost/stolen cards

This is one of the oldest techniques for safeguarding the cardholder in the event that the card is lost or stolen. Once this fact is reported to the card issuer, the account is immediately closed and marked as a lost (or stolen) account. Any transactions subsequently posted to the account have to be confirmed as genuine by the cardholder. A new account is opened and a replacement card is sent to the cardholder (see Chapter 12, Section 12.4).

Card-not-present transactions

Because this is a higher risk sector, the rules for telephone and mail order authorizations are more stringent than face-to-face transactions. It is likely that all of these require authorizations regardless of the floor limit.

11.5 Fraud Recoveries

When deciding whether to attempt some recovery from losses through fraudulent activity, each lender has to decide between chasing the cardholder, charging the loss back to the merchant or carrying the loss. It is a question of balancing the costs against any likely returns.

Merchant charge-back

Under Visa and MasterCard rules, issuers have the right of charge-back against a merchant if a transaction goes ahead when the retailer has breached any of their card acceptance conditions, e.g. a fraudulent transaction is accepted but the merchant has not requested authorizations approval. The amount of the loss is invoiced to the merchant.

Card pick-up

The most usual method of achieving this is by asking the merchant to retain the card. This request can be made either by voice authorizations or automatically through the till or terminal. Outside agents may also be employed by the issuer to visit cardholders to recover the card, although this is more common for delinquency reasons.

Seizure of goods

Goods may be seized from the cardholder to the value of the loss if this is feasible. The goods are usually sent to auction and the proceeds often given to charities.

12
ACCOUNT MANAGEMENT

Almost without exception, the details in this chapter apply to credit and charge cards rather than to personal loans. It is important to understand the interrelated nature of the parties involved in a credit card operation in order to understand the workings of both authorizations and transactions (and the risks inherent in both).

12.1 Parties to a Credit Card Relationship

Cardholder – the account owner/the 'holder' of the plastic card, i.e. the debtor.

Card Issuer – the card company/the issuing bank/the organization that opens the account on behalf of the cardholder, issues the card, and manages the cardholder's account and to which the cardholder is liable. The card issuer may operate on behalf of third parties, e.g. charity credit cards are branded with the name of the charity, but the cardholder is liable to the organization that is managing the card on its behalf. Historically issuers were limited to banks, but non-finance organizations are now also issuers, e.g. one Internet service provider now offers a Visa or MasterCard and supermarket credit cards abound.

Merchant – the retailer who accepts the card as payment for goods or services. This may be a retail outlet, a mail order or telephone order company, or an Internet trader.

Acquirer – the bank/organization that recruits the merchant, manages the merchant's account and processes his or her transactions. The acquirer and the card issuer may be part of the same organization, e.g. Barclaycard is both an acquirer and an issuer, whereas a small building society or a supermarket may be an issuer only.

Payment Systems Organizations (PSOs) – the umbrella organizations (often, but not exclusively, Visa or MasterCard) are membership associations to which acquirers and issuers apply to join. They set the rules and regulations with which the issuers, acquirers and merchants must comply, and in return the acquirers and issuers can operate under the PSO's brand name, utilizing their money transmission systems which link merchants, ATMs and issuers across the world.

All five parties are bound by contractual agreements in different ways, and they are all interrelated in order to operate the worldwide credit card facilities.

Cardholder – Issuer

The cardholder applies to an issuer for a credit card, and once accepted, the card is issued and a regulated agreement exists between the two. This agreement imposes controls on both sides and ensures certain protection for the consumer. The cardholder's transactions are posted to his or her account, the issuer must send out regular statements, and the cardholder must regularly repay part or all of any outstanding balance. There are defined procedures for redress if the cardholder defaults on any payments.

Merchant – Acquirer

When a retailer decides that it wants to be able to accept credit card transactions, it applies to an acquiring institution/bank. The local branch of that bank becomes the retailer's primary point of contact regarding any aspect of his credit card business. For instance, the acquirer may supply the terminals, it determines the floor limit (in line with the PSO's regulations) and the level of merchant service charge. The acquirer also processes the merchant's transactions on a regular, usually daily, basis, applies them to his account, issues a monthly statement and undertakes settlement (i.e. reimburses the merchant for the value of the transactions it has deposited). The acquirer data captures the incoming transactions and forwards them to the relevant PSO for onward transmission to the card issuer.

An acquirer does not automatically accept every merchant that applies. Merchants whose business activities are illegal, borderline illegal, or disreputable, are likely to be declined, e.g. prostitutes or sex shops. Equally if the merchant appears to be financially unstable, it is also likely to be declined.

PSOs – Issuers – Acquirers

The PSO organizations are not banks in themselves, but associations of banks, whose members operate in more than 300 countries[1]. Their functions are to:

- promote the brand name(s) of the PSO, i.e. not that of the issuer;
- provide a means of authorizations and transmission of transactions;
- provide a means of clearing and settling transactions; and
- conduct collective development projects on behalf of their members.

They do not recruit merchants or issue cards.

The PSOs are largely competitive but co-operate on industry issues such as fraud prevention measures. They set the marketing, operating and administrative rules with which all members must comply. They also provide international communications networks for the transmission of authorization requests/responses, and transaction details back from the acquirer to the issuer. These networks also be used to distribute fraud hot-card files and warning bulletin files.

---

[1] www.visa.com

This is not to suggest that acquirers and issuers do not have any control over running their businesses. For instance, PSO rules dictate the format and the details of the information that is encoded onto the magnetic stripe on the back of the card, but the issuer is at liberty to set its own interest rates. Issuers can apply their own design or logo to the front of the card (provided they do not compromise the security features set in place by the PSOs). The PSO rules determine the size and shape of the card and dictate that the hologram is on the front in a specific position.

Issuers and acquirers can both be members of more than one card scheme; dual membership of both Visa and MasterCard is common.

12.2   Information Flows between the Parties

At a high level, the flow and exchange of information is conceptually straightforward:

●   cardholder pays for a purchase with a credit card;

●   an authorization request is automatically sent to be checked against the cardholder's account;

●   when it is approved, the authorization converts into a confirmed transaction;

●   the transaction details appear on the cardholder's next statement;

●   the cardholders pays (some or all of) the total balance so created by the due date;

●   the transaction amount is added to the merchant's account with the acquirer; and

●   the merchant is reimbursed for the cumulative value of that period's transactions.

It is important to realize that the authorizations data uses physically separate transmission systems from the transaction data. The detailed flow of information given below looks at the two independently, although they interlink at the point when the authorization is approved.

Authorizations flows

Figure 12.1: Information flows in credit card authorizations

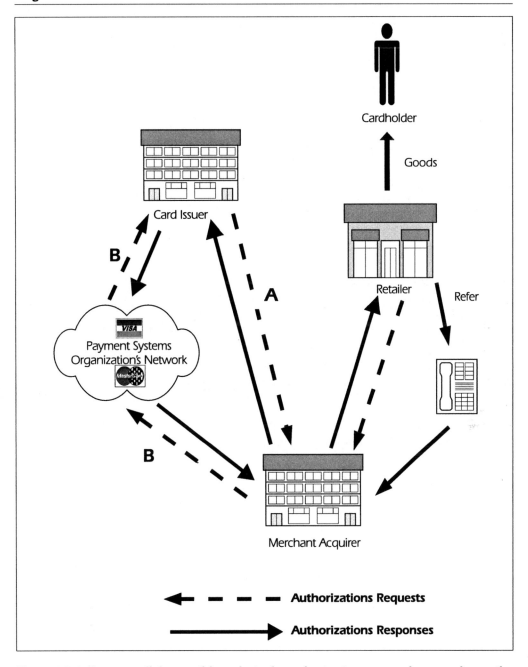

Figure 12.1 illustrates all the possible paths in the authorizations process between the retailer and authorizations request being granted, declined or referred, although there are some exceptions where only part of this path is taken.

Step 1: The cardholder makes a credit card purchase and the retailer swipes the card through a terminal or till. This generates an authorizations request which is sent automatically to the acquirer.

Step 2: This request takes either one of two paths:

● If the card which is being presented (e.g. NatWest) has been issued by the same bank that acquired the merchant (i.e. NatWest), the authorizations request is routed via path A, i.e. directly from the acquirer's system to the issuer's cardholder system.

● If the card presented (e.g. Nat West) is being used in a merchant signed up by a different acquirer (e.g. Barclays), path B is taken, i.e. via the PSO's systems and networks.

Step 3: If the amount of the transaction is within the cardholder's available credit and there are no adverse reasons on the account (e.g. fraud blocks), then a positive authorization response, together with an authorization number, is sent directly back to the terminal via its original route.

If the issuer chooses to decline the request for whatever reason, this response also follows the original route back to the merchant. The outright decline decisions are automated to the same extent and via the same route as the straightforward accepts, i.e. there is no manual intervention. Automatic accepts and declines probably account for 95% or more of all authorizations traffic.

Variations to the authorizations flow

● **Referrals**

If for some reason the system response is refer rather than accept or decline, it is sent back to the merchant by the same path as the incoming request, but now the retailer must pick up the telephone and speak directly to the card issuer. Depending on the nature of the problem, the card issuer either accepts or declines the transaction and this decision is sent back automatically via the same route as the incoming request. Refers probably account for less than 5% of the overall traffic, possibly even as low as 1%.

● **Transactions below the floor limit**

If the amount of the transaction is less than the merchant's floor limit, under PSO rules there is no requirement for an authorization. However, some larger retailers with on-line terminals automatically seek authorizations for all transactions regardless of value.

● **Card-not-present situations**

These occur with telephone or mail order purchases, and now also with Internet shopping, and more stringent merchant control and behaviour is required for these.

● **Paper-based transactions**

Occasionally paper-based sales vouchers are used instead of automated processing (e.g. if the authorization system is down). In this situation all transactions above the floor limit require manual authorizations.

● **Issuer does not operate an authorizations function**

Smaller and/or new card companies may choose initially not to establish an authorizations system nor a voice authorizations function. In these cases, the function is typically outsourced to the PSO. Incoming authorizations requests are checked against parameters supplied by the issuer to the PSOs, and a response returned from the PSOs.

Transaction details

Figure 12.2: Information flow of transaction details

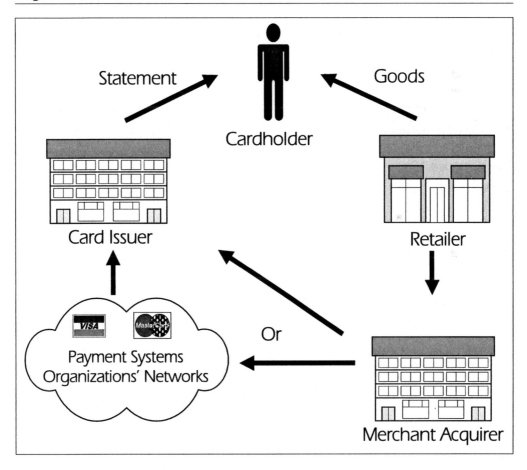

In the system illustrated in Figure 12.2 the financial data is transmitted on a one-way path from the retailer back to the cardholder's account.

In the store the cardholder signs the paper slip and leaves with the goods. The merchant's terminal either stores the transaction details for onward transmission at the end of the day or sends them in real time to the acquirer. (Off-line terminals operate on the basis of daily downloading all transactions in a single batch over the telephone line.) The details are forwarded via the PSO's systems to the card issuer, where the details are posted to the cardholder's account, usually in the following few days. At the billing point all transactions are printed onto a statement which is sent to the cardholder for payment.

In the same way as authorizations traffic, if the acquirer is part of the same organization as the issuer, the transaction is likely to bypass the PSOs and connect directly.

Variations

Although paper-based transactions are relatively uncommon in the UK, there are still many countries in which they are the norm. In this case, the merchant batches up his vouchers at the end of the day, and physically banks them at his local bank branch/acquirer. The paper vouchers are physically sent to the acquirer for data capture. This function may be undertaken by the acquirer itself or by an outside computer bureau. Once the details are captured electronically, they are posted to the cardholder's account.

Clearing and settlement

This aspect of the process is largely outside the scope of this book, but suffice it to say that the PSOs operate a clearing and settlement service between the issuers and the acquirers, and the acquirers do the same for the merchants. (This is the same process that banks operate when clearing cheques and paying out on them.) This service enables the merchants to be reimbursed within a few days for the cardholder transactions.

12.3   Authorizations Practicalities

Before the advent of electronic tills and terminals, the authorizations concept and process was:

● executed verbally via the telephone rather than digitally via computer networks;

● not an integrated part of the standard routine of using a credit card for either the cardholder or the merchant (i.e. was the exception, not the rule); and

● a credit control function as well as a fraud prevention/identification process.

Authorizations departments employed large numbers of people, often on a 24-hour rota basis. Decisions were made subjectively by the operator who viewed each cardholder account on the screen and made a decision based on predefined manual guidelines, possibly accompanied by some hard-coded rules. Behaviour scoring was in its infancy, as were the relevant PC and computer technologies.

Today the process is largely automated and around two-thirds of all transactions are routinely authorized. Decisions are made using complex predictive models, strategies and systems like those discussed in Chapter 6. These systems encompass all delinquency and over-limit possibilities and automatically make the accept/decline decision based on the applicable strategies. Because this is transparent to the operators still employed in an authorization capacity, the manual element of the function has become one of fraud prevention only.

However, in the intervening years, not only has the volume of cards issued escalated exponentially, but the degree of sophistication used by fraudsters has also increased. The need for, and the importance of, voice authorizations has not reduced in significance, merely changed in its nature. Visa and MasterCard rules indicate that a voice authorization should only be undertaken in situations where the merchant is suspicious about the person presenting the card. This includes anyone presenting an expired card.

Function and purpose of authorizations

This begs the question 'is authorizations a credit control or a fraud prevention function, or both'? The answer depends on who is being asked the question:

- in terms of the *concept* of authorizations and the systems that underpin it, it is both a credit control and fraud prevention/identification mechanism, albeit that all the credit control requirements are supplied automatically and unseen by any operator;

- in terms of the physical department that supplies the voice authorizations capability, it is strictly a fraud prevention/identification function because the PSO's rules dictate that this is the only circumstance under which a merchant should speak to an authorizations operator;

- in terms of credit risk management and behaviour scoring systems, it is primarily a credit control function, but if the issuer has the appropriate systems and scorecards then it may additionally be a fraud function; or

- the fraud prevention department would say that its primary objective is fraud prevention and/or identification.

Departmental structure

Authorizations departments are effectively call centres. Capacity planning and monitoring are essential features of the department where the volume of calls, the pattern of calls throughout the day/week/month and the length of calls are all used to establish operator volumes and rosters. The voice authorizations function is usually provided 24 hours per day, 365 days per year, but outside peak hours smaller issuers may chose to outsource this or combine it with an all-purpose call centre.

The department is likely to be structured in teams of 10-15 operators reporting to a supervisor. Operators are measured in terms of performance quality (e.g. amount of time idle, number of calls per hour, quality of the call) and these criteria are likely to be linked to performance-related pay schemes.

Co-operation between acquirers

Because acquirers are essentially competitive organizations, the Monopolies and Mergers Commission permits dialogue between them only for fraud prevention reasons. Visa and/or MasterCard may issue details of a sudden problem that acquirers are required to address, often by way of reducing floor limits in the affected area, but co-operation between them can result in a co-ordinated, and therefore more effective, approach to the issue.

12.4   Lost and Stolen Cards

The single biggest risk behind all plastic cards that have been either lost or stolen is the potential for fraudulent use. In the early days of credit cards in the UK, issuers would differentiate in their treatment of these two categories, but since fraud activity has escalated in both sophistication and frequency, all cards reported missing are treated as being stolen regardless of the circumstances.

There is an onus on cardholders to report the card immediately that they become aware that it is missing. If the delay in doing this is particularly prolonged and there is fraudulent use in the interim, then the issuer may chose to exercise his right (under the Consumer Credit Act) for the cardholder to fulfil a liability up to £50. In practice, card issuers seldom do this and they carry any losses themselves.

Card issuers, or their agents, offer a 24-hour service for being able to report cards missing. Once the call has been taken, the cardholder's account is closed immediately. A new one is opened and all existing and incoming transactions destined for the original account are automatically transferred to the new one. Any authorized user cards that are not lost/stolen have to be destroyed at the same time. Replacement plastics are issued within a few days.

12.5   Credit Limit Increases

These can occur because:

● the cardholder requests an increase;

● the account balance plus a new transaction will take the outstanding balance over the declared limit and a temporary increase is needed to cover this; or

● the lender is being proactive and offering an unsolicited increase.

Credit (or declared) limits apply to the whole account regardless of how many authorized users also have cards, so that the potential for increased risk may be greater if there are multiple users. Lenders generally impose (unseen to the cardholder) a minimum time gap between granting consecutive increases (see also Chapter 6, Section 6.4).

Solicited increases

Many cardholders typically request increases in the early summer (before holidays) in

December (for Christmas shopping) and to a lesser extent in January (to pay for excesses of Christmas). To what extent these requests are granted again depends on the behaviour or customer score or account history.

The customer service department responsible for this function is set clear rules about granting these requests. If shadow limits based on an account management scorecard are in use, the decision will be automated. Either way, the staff have target times in which to respond to the cardholder.

Temporary excess

This arises where the amount of the new transaction, together with the current balance on the account, makes the new balance exceed the declared limit. This situation may be detected at the point of sale provided the transaction is above the merchant's floor limit and the transaction is sent for authorization. If it is below the floor limit, then the excess is flagged up for review after the transaction is posted to the account. If shadow limits are in use, then either:

- a temporary excess is granted and the account reviewed for a permanent increase, or

- the shadow limit automatically becomes the new declared limit.

Unsolicited increases

This is a marketing activity that should be undertaken in cooperation with the risk management department. A high-level decision is taken about the maximum extra exposure the lender is willing to take on, and new strategies that support this can then be designed and tested. (Such strategies may have been established as part of ongoing behavioural scoring activities in anticipation of the next round of increases.) New individual declared limits are set in line with any shadow and/or target limits that have been established by the behavioural scoring strategies. Having selected the most effective set of parameters the individual accounts are identified and the necessary notification letters are produced. The new limit is updated on the accounts system at the same time and becomes effective immediately. If there is no behavioural or customer scoring in place, bulk unsolicited increases may be undertaken on the basis of bureau data and/or a set of judgmental exclusion rules, e.g. any delinquency in the last x months or any CCJs in the last y years.

If a cardholder telephones the issuer for any reason, then a proactive lender with either behavioural or customer scoring in place is able to maximize the telephone call by asking if the cardholder (in appropriate cases) would like an increase.

13

MANAGING DELINQUENT
ACCOUNTS

Every lender balances the trade-off between account volumes and subsequent risk when making account-opening decisions and when additional credit facilities are extended. As explained in Chapters 4 and 6, underwriting strategies aim to manage, not eliminate, risk. Lenders therefore expect a proportion of accounts to fall into arrears. They also expect some of their card customers to exceed their credit limit. Arrears and/or excess (over-limit) are called delinquent conditions. The purpose of the collections and recoveries functions is to manage delinquent cases.

13.1   Terminology

Different lenders use different terminology for activities associated with managing delinquent accounts. For clarity, the following phrases are used throughout this chapter:

Collections – the early stages of a delinquent account.

Recoveries – the later, harder stages of a delinquent account.

The dividing line between these two varies from lender to lender, depending on policies and practices.

Promises or arrangements – promises made by the customer to make a payment or series of payments by an agreed date(s).

Charge-off – a procedural and systems concept which occurs when the account is closed on the system and the outstanding debt moved into a financial category set up for potential bad debts. Any payments made by the customer can be allocated back to the original account.

Write-off – an accounting term indicating the debt is now considered unrecoverable and the amount goes into the bad debt category and will appear (cumulatively) in the company's annual accounts. Any payments made by the customer cannot be allocated back to the account.

13.2   The Operational Mission

The aim of collections and recoveries is to optimize collections effectiveness. In economic terms this means maximizing the amount collected in relation to the operational cost of running the function. However, collections effectiveness should also take into account the longer-term relationship with the customer and the potential for future income. If this potential is positive, then the objective should become customer rehabilitation with dignity. It is not just a case of collecting the overdue or excess amount, but bringing the account into order for future business, in as cost-effective a manner as possible.

13.3   Reasons for Delinquency

Non-payment

There are many reasons why a customer fails to make a payment. The majority are related to a customer's change in circumstances, and/or an inability to manage finances. Typical examples include:

- loss of job or marital breakdown – such changes cause disruption to the normal pattern of life, and in most cases a reduction in income, which results in temporary or longer-term payment problems;

- occasional missed payments, either because the customer forgot or was on holiday – these customers generally pay within the month and rarely require or experience any action from the collections department;

- incorrect set-up of a direct debit facility or set-up too close to the payment date – these are sometimes called 'technical arrears' cases and typically affect the first payment made on a new account; and

- disputes either with the lender, or more frequently with a retailer from whom they have purchased goods using the lender's credit facility – in these cases the customer may withhold payment until the dispute is resolved.

Regardless of the reason, at some point, soon after a customer has failed to make a scheduled payment, the account becomes a collections case. Timing of the transfer to the collections department and system is determined by company policy.

Excess

Excess occurs on card products when the outstanding balance is greater than the credit limit.

A lender endeavours to extend credit only up to the customer's declared limit, allowing for some tolerance above this limit e.g. up to the shadow limit. Given that most retailers operate a floor limit, below which all transactions are accepted, some customers may exceed their credit limit, either wittingly or unwittingly.

13.4   Organizational Structures

Collections and recoveries departments are organized around the flow of accounts as they progress though the stages of delinquency. Figure 13.1 demonstrates the relationships between the main functions, or units, within collections and recoveries.

Figure 13.1: Organizational structures

```
                              ┌──────────────────┐
                              │  Missed payment  │
                              └──────────────────┘
                                       │
                              ┌──────────────────┐
                    ┌─────────│ Enters Collections│
                    │         └──────────────────┘
                    │                  │
          ┌──────────────┐    ┌──────────────────┐
          │Special marker¹│    │ No special markers│
          └──────────────┘    └──────────────────┘
                  │                      │
        ┌──────────────┐  ┌──────────────┐  ┌────────────────────┐
        │Manual process│─▶│Special marker│─▶│Mainstream automated │
        └──────────────┘  │   removed    │  │collections process² │
                          └──────────────┘  └────────────────────┘
```

Payment brings account in order — Promise/arrangement — Identified as gone-away — Identified as suspect fraud — No contact/no promises/no payments/multiple broken promises after x days

Monitoring for payment(s) — Goes to Trace — Goes to Fraud — Identified as charge-off

Broken promise/arrangement — Problem resolved — Goes to Recoveries³

Leaves Collections — Cannot be found after x attempts — Confirmed — No payment for > x days — Paying arrangement

Balance paid

Identified as write-off — Leaves Recoveries

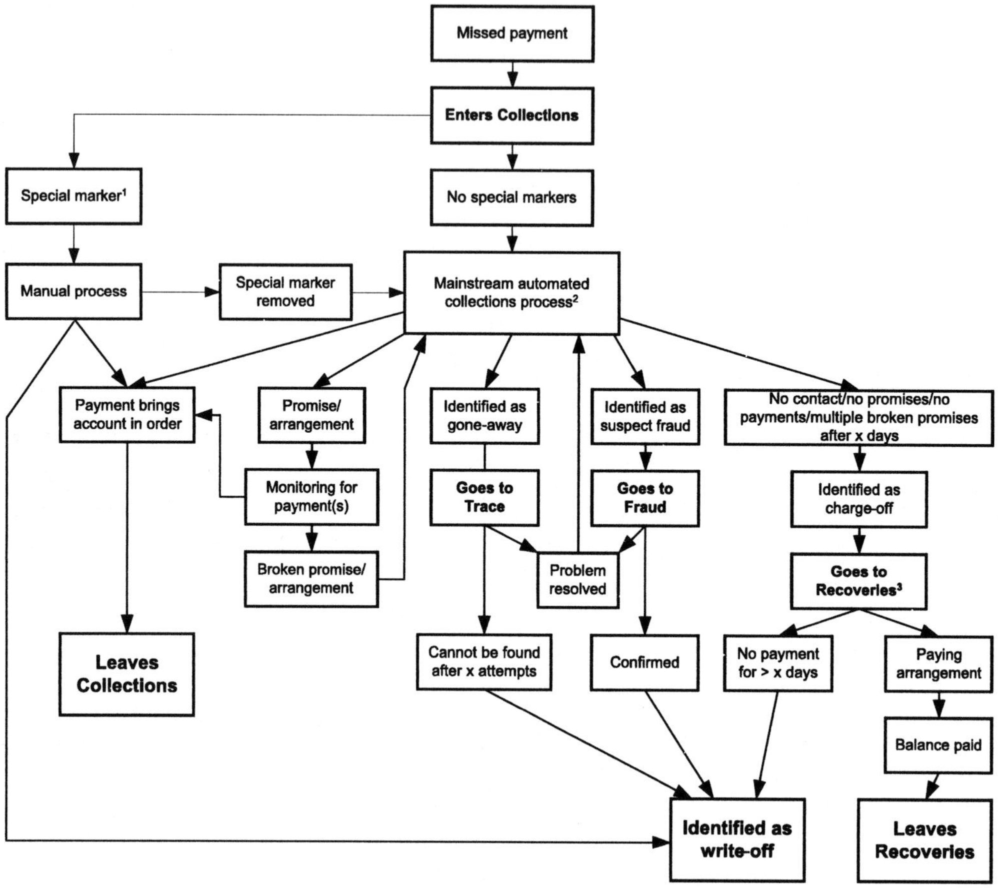

1   E.g. dispute, query, deceased, bankruptcy
2   Different action plans for different groups of accounts
3   Includes litigation and debt collection agents

Collections

Collections deals with early delinquent cases. Its aim is to bring delinquent accounts back into order while maintaining an on-going relationship with the customer (long-term retention approach). However the use of behavioural scoring allows companies to identify potential hard-core cases at an early stage of delinquency. For these a more economics-driven approach is likely to be taken.

Collections activity is generally conducted in-house and comprises teams of skilled collectors. It is sometimes part of, or viewed as an extension of, the customer services function.

Recoveries

Recoveries generally deals with hard-core delinquent accounts after collections have concluded their activities with the customer. Its aim is to recover all the outstanding debt while severing the relationship with the customer (economics approach). There is a statutory requirement for a default notice to be sent to a customer before payment of the full outstanding balance can be demanded. This default notice is the key action at the end of the collections and the start of the recoveries phases.

Recoveries actions generally involve third parties either through external debt collection agents (see Chapter 14) or through the courts (see Chapter 15). In each case recoveries tends to be predominantly an administrative function.

Other activities: trace and fraud

As a natural consequence of collection activity, some delinquent cases are deemed to be gone-aways, because the customer cannot be contacted at the address. These are called trace cases. Others may be identified as suspect-frauds. Many collection functions include separate sections to deal with these type of cases (see also Chapters 11 and 14). When/if the condition is resolved, the account is returned to the mainstream collections operation.

13.5   Customer Handling Policies

Types of collections cases

Collections cases are typically grouped into high-level categories, according to different conditions displayed by these accounts, e.g.:

- new account defaulters (first payment missed), subdivided into direct debit/non-direct debit payers;
- over-limit but no payments missed (card facilities only);
- missed payments but not over-limit;
- missed payments and over-limit (card facilitites only); and
- missed payments with/without over-limit with administrative markers that require special handling or negotiation, e.g. deceased, dispute, query, customer advised financial difficulties, or in negotiation with/represented by a Citizens Advice Bureau (CAB).

With new-account defaulters the objective is to identify and isolate any potentially high-risk or fraudulent accounts from other, genuine cases, where an error may have occurred when the account was opened. Subdivision based on payment method ensures problems with direct debit mandates are resolved quickly on behalf of the customer.

Sensitive cases, or those with specific circumstances, need to be removed from the mainstream collections process and handled individually. Generally, these accounts are characterized by a previous dialogue(s) with the customer or a representative.

Of the remaining delinquent accounts (missed payment and overlimit combinations), the rationale for differentiation is to allow letters and messages to be tailored to request appropriate action from the customer – e.g. to clear the arrears and/or bring the outstanding balance to within the credit limit.

Collections action plans

Collections action plans, as defined in Chapter 6, are a sequence of actions that are followed while an account is delinquent. They comprise three elements:

- message – e.g. customer service through to warning of legal action;
- method – e.g. letter, telephone, fax, postcard, electronic mail; and
- moment – i.e. timing of actions.

These plans generally follow a progressive path through the arrears stages, i.e.:

- one payment, or one month, or 30 days, down;
- two payments, or two months, or 60 days, down;
- three payments, or three months, or 90 days down;
- four payments, or four months, or 120 days down, etc.

The greater the degree of delinquency, the greater the risk of never getting fully repaid, and the more severe the action or approach taken. A collections action plan might therefore start with a customer service type letter or telephone call. For those who fail to make payments, requests for payments acquire a more persistent tone, followed eventually by the default notice and a 'letter before action' before transfer to recoveries.

Organizations without behavioural scoring frequently apply the same collection procedures to all cases in each high-level category. Sometimes these organizations also segment delinquent accounts into finer groups e.g.:

- with/without previous delinquency or collections history;
- high/low balance; and
- new/established account.

The idea is to either prioritize accounts for action based on a judgmental perception of risk, or take different actions according to risk.

Where judgmental or score-driven segmentation is in place, different collections action plans are employed to reflect segmentation rules and risk. Figure 13.2 illustrates a set of action plans that reflect arrears stages and risk as defined by a collections scorecard.

Figure 13.2: Action plans by risk

Delinquency	Low Risk	Medium Risk	High Risk
30 Days	Statement Message 1	Statement Message 2	Reminder 1
45 Days	–	Reminder 1	Phone Call
60 Days	Statement Message 2	Reminder 2	Default Notice
75 Days	Reminder 1	Phone Call	Legal Action

Where a promise or arrangement is made, the account is taken out of its action plan and monitored for payments. Where the promise or arrangement is broken, the customer should be placed back into an appropriate action plan.

Other conditions can arise which may result in a case being taken out of the plan, including:

● gone-aways, which are sent to the trace section;

● suspect-frauds, which are sent to the fraud section; or

● deceased, dispute, query, customer advised financial difficulties, or in negotiation with/ represented by a CAB, all of which are handled individually until the relevant condition is resolved.

Collector methods

Collectors use a range of different approaches to encourage the customer to pay. Their aim is to agree a repayment plan that the customer can meet and which is economically viable for the company. Ideally the payments exceed the rate at which interest is accruing on the account.

Where appropriate (and within company-set policies and procedures), the collector will (in negotiation with the customer):

● apply collections or late fees;

● increase the interest rate;

● reduce the credit limit;

● suppress interest (generally as a temporary measure);

- negotiate a product switch, e.g. from a revolving product to a structured loan;

- reschedule loan payments;

- offer a consolidation loan; or

- agree to a 'short settlement' – an amount agreed by both parties to close down the account which falls short of the true amount owed by the customer.

Lost contact or gone-aways

If at any stage it becomes clear that the customer cannot be contacted, these accounts are out-sorted and passed to the trace unit for different treatment. Gone-aways are commonly identified by:

- statements being returned as undelivered or not at this address;

- collectors telephoning the customer – where the person answering the telephone reports that the customer has moved; or

- collections letters being 'returned to sender'.

The amount of effort extended in locating a customer should balance the cost against the likelihood of finding the customer, and the likely success of getting a payment.

Trace units generally have a defined sequence of internal activities or action plans for confirming or finding a new address. For example, they may check:

- that the account has the details stored correctly using information from the application processing system and application form (mainly for new customers);

- any other account holdings within the company/group;

- with a bureau-based account information-sharing schemes for an up-to-date address from another lender;

- with GAIN files (subject to membership);

- with BT's directory enquiries for telephone numbers; and

- with the employer (details from the application form).

If any of these routes produces an address the case is passed back to collections. Sometimes a letter is sent asking the customer to get in touch, or make a payment, or saying that the lender will telephone them.

If internal trace activity fails the case is generally issued to a specialist external trace agent (see Chapter 14). Accounts may be issued to a second trace agent if the first agency cannot find the customer.

If both internal and external searches fail, a default notice should be sent out to the last known address. If the lender is a member of GAIN, an entry on the GAIN files should be generated.

Suspect and confirmed frauds

If at any stage an account is suspected as fraud, it is out-sorted and passed to the fraud unit for different treatment. However, there is often a fine dividing line between a suspect-fraud and a trace case. For this reason the two units need to work in close co-operation regardless of company structure or reporting lines.

It is prudent to write-off confirmed fraud accounts immediately or mark them in a way that allocates 100% provision (see Chapter 9) against the account, pending the write-off being actioned.

Recoveries

At some stage, the lender will decide that, despite all efforts to recover the situation and rehabilitate the customer, it is not economically viable to warrant further direct action. The defining point between collections and recoveries is the issuing of the default notice.

At this point the account is charged-off and it becomes a recoveries case.

These accounts are now potentially hard-core losses. The lender has to decide what the best course of action is, and this will vary for each case. The options are:

- send the account to a debt collections agent;

- keep pursuing it in-house using a specialist team;

- set up a repayment programme which the customer can afford, together with debt counselling;

- take legal action to recover the debt;

- write the debt off altogether; or

- sell the debt to a debt collections agency.

Money advice/debt counselling

Where appropriate, and possibly as early two or three payments down, the lender should suggest to the debtor that debt counselling may be helpful, and either offer internal advice, or supply details of debt counselling bodies (see also Chapter 17, Section 17.4). If the debtor follows this path through an external centre, the lender is likely to receive correspondence from the money advice centre. Negotiations about a repayment plan will take place between the debt counsellor (on behalf of the customer) and the lender. Once this has been agreed, the customer's account should be marked to indicate that a repayment plan is in place and mainstream collections activity suspended.

These accounts should be monitored in the same way as other collections or recoveries accounts. The customer's situation should be reviewed with the debt counsellor every three to six months to ascertain whether personal circumstances have changed, and if so whether more favourable repayments can be agreed.

There are two types of money advice centres available to the debtor, namely free ones (such as Citizens Advice Bureau) or independent commercial ones that charge a fee to the creditor. With the former, the full amount of all repayments is credited to the customer's account, whereas with the latter, the amount of the fee charged may be deducted from the repayment so that only the net amount is credited to the customer. This can result in a longer time period before the debt is fully repaid.

13.6   Organizing Departmental Activities

Collections

Collections departments are organized around small teams of clerical staff (or collectors) who report to a supervisor. Each collector is provided with access to the collections system and the accounts system, either of which may link into credit bureau files.

The teams work in one of the following ways:

- by account ownership;
- by days delinquent;
- by risk segmentation; or
- by defined account condition/special marker.

Being organized by account ownership means that, once an account goes delinquent, it is allocated to an individual or specific team to work. That individual or team retains responsibility for that account throughout its life in collections regardless of whether the account immediately rolls back into order or whether it goes on to recoveries.

The advantage of this cradle-to-grave approach is that an on-going relationship between individual customers and collectors can be achieved. This is thought to improve the chance of promises and arrangements being kept. The disadvantage is that an individual collector may not be available when a customer contacts the department, potentially negating the first benefit. Also, these individual relationships cannot be maintained where power dialling is used.

Being organized by days delinquent means that a team (or teams) works accounts only at a certain stage of delinquency. Those accounts that roll on are passed to the next team. The department might comprise any number of 5- and 30-day teams, several 60-day teams, a smaller number of 90-day teams, and so on.

The advantage of this approach is that collectors can be more focused on the type of account they are handling. New collectors become effective more quickly because there is less variety among the accounts handled, although lack of variety may require teams to be rotated frequently. For the approach to work effectively, collectors must be given incentives in a way that prevents them leaving the 'harder cases' to roll forward for their colleagues working in teams farther down the arrears chain. This approach is more adaptable to the use of power dialling.

Being organized by risk segmentation is a hybrid of the first two. Teams of collectors work accounts across the arrears stages but their focus is determined by the predicted risk of future non-payment.

Many organizations have a separate team that makes the 'recoveries decision'. Sometimes this team sits within collections and determines whether the account is ready for recovery action. If so, the most appropriate method is determined and the team ensures that all the necessary legal processes have been completed before sending the account to recoveries. Sometimes this team sits within recoveries. It fulfils the same role, except that it passes accounts back to collections if recovery action is deemed as not yet appropriate.

Outside the mainstream collections process a separate team may handle sensitive cases identified by an account marker, such a deceased, queries, insurance claims and disputes.

Other supporting administrative teams are also needed for activities such as post, training, systems support and capacity planning.

Trace and fraud

Trace is organized into administrative teams undertaking specialist investigation work and liaison with outside agencies. Fraud may be located in a separate department.

Recoveries

Recoveries is also a team-based operation with groups set up for handling accounts sent to external agents (see Chapter 14).

Where recoveries includes an in-house litigation process, a specialist team is required that understands the legal process for pursuing debts (see Chapter 15). The company should also employ a qualified solicitor to support this team.

13.7   Basic Systems Requirements

An effective collections system allows the organization to manage all elements of the collections and recoveries process. At a minimum, it includes the following functionality:

- customer contact management/diary facility;

- account segmentation facilities;

- account monitoring/administration; and

- liaison with outside agencies.

Workflow, telecommunication links, collector productivity and management information features are common to each area of activity. The ability of the chosen system to interface seamlessly with the existing accounts system is a primary consideration in the original purchase of the system.

Other common systems functionalities include:

- interaction with a power diallers; and
- litigation handling activities.

Collector screen facilities

Screen facilities should be designed to give sufficient information to the collector to pursue the customer in line with the collections actions plan. All screens should be straightforward. The initial screen should only display information that is needed at the point of contact with the customer. It must include:

- instant access to customer account details including payment history;
- brief notes made previously reflecting other customer contacts (last 1-3 notes);
- diary facilities to record promises/arrangements and review dates; and
- switches to other systems or databases including bureaux files.

This initial screen might also display any special or administrative markers and indicators of other account holdings.

Further screens should be available giving the full collections history and more detailed account information.

Dedicated screens are required for use in the trace and recoveries units. Separate functionality is required for litigation processing to reflect court procedures and timings.

Segmentation criteria

As accounts enter collections they are routed to a specified collections 'location'. This may be known as a classification, state, node or queue. Behavioural scores (or bands of scores), judgmental segmentation rules, type of delinquency (arrears/excess), or specific account markers are used as the basis for allocating accounts to their 'location'.

Each collections location has an associated collections action plan which determines when automatic letters are sent and when the account is presented to a collector for action.

Accounts may be re-assigned to different 'locations' as a result of, for example:

- markers being added to an account, e.g. a trace marker will re-assign the account to the trace location, a recoveries marker will move it to one of the recoveries' units;
- promise/arrangements which are held in another location pending payments or until their review date – to ensure automated actions do not take place and conflict with agreed arrangements;
- broken promises/arrangements which re-assign an account into a location with an appropriate action plan; or
- manual intervention.

Queues

In workflow systems, queues are groups of cases that are similar in some way, e.g. belonging to a specific 'location'. Collectors work through a queue and the system monitors the progress of the workload. If one queue is falling behind, a good system automatically moves cases into other collector's queue. Alternatively a supervisor re-allocates cases.

At the start of each day's work, the system automatically presents the collector with a list of accounts to be processed. Only those accounts requiring collector action are displayed. Where cases have a 'carry forward' date appended to them, e.g. for review in two weeks, the system diarizes them until that date then allocates them to the appropriate queue.

Queues are generally set up to reflect the underlying collections action plans (identified by 'location'). Within queues, accounts are prioritized for attention. This ensures the most urgent or highest balance cases are worked first. Queue prioritization can be interrupted in some systems by that day's scheduled appointments.

Queues can be set up for cases that need urgent or specialist attention, e.g. gone-aways. In these circumstances only those working within the trace unit have access to those queues.

Other functionalities

A good collections system includes power-dialling facilities. This is a mechanism for automatically dialling out and connecting customer with collector. It improves productivity by removing time wasted with busy, no answer or invalid numbers. Most collections systems download cases requiring telephone action into a dialler list for automatic actioning. The collections system needs to be able to interpret and record the outcome of the dialler activity. Some power-diallers can also be set up to manage in-bound telephone calls.

Collections systems should have the ability to identify cases without a telephone number where a telephone call is part of the action plan. Electronic or manual lists should be produced for searching for missing numbers and adding new numbers to the account record.

The collections system should record a collector identifier, and the date and time each time an account is actioned. This is used to audit collections actions and give feedback to individual collectors on their performance.

A range of management information is also required for strategic and operational purposes. This should be sufficient to determine the link between actions taken and customer response/outcomes. These include cure rates (accounts which have returned to order), promise rates, progression into recoveries/trace/fraud and write-off.

13.8   Managing the Collector Resource

Training

The availability of collections-focused training facilities is very important to the success of the function. Even for long-standing experienced collectors, it is important to ensure that their skills are maintained and their motivation and effectiveness is not diminished. This can be achieved by a number of aids as well as regular classroom sessions. Aids might include:

- aide memoirs, process maps or quick reference guides, which are incorporated into the collections system to answer any queries;

- system modules which ensure that standard procedures are followed precisely, i.e. the system drives the collectors actions in these situations rather than the other way round;

- supervisor call monitoring – listening in to collector telephone calls – to give direct feedback on approach and areas for improvement; and

- workstation assessments to ensure health and safety requirements are being met.

For all areas, regular training in the legislative framework which governs the credit industry, and collections/recovery methods in particular, is paramount.

Evaluation

Collections

Because they have first-hand contact with the customer, collectors have a direct influence over the success of the collections process. Evaluation of their performance should ideally focus on their financial success. However, this success is linked to the volume of customer contacts. Collectors and their supervisors are therefore assessed in terms of both the quality and productivity of their work. Individual and team measurements include:

- number of accounts worked, or telephoned, or written to, per hour;

- length and quality of telephone calls;

- number of accounts with a promise/arrangement made or coming back into order;

- number of accounts with a broken promise/arrangement or rolling into worse states of delinquency;

- average value of promises against average value of payments;

- cash collected (payments received) as a percentage of delinquent balances;

- case loads (number of cases per collector); and

- oldest case waiting to be actioned.

All these measures should be monitored over time and/or compared with a benchmark level of expectation.

Trace and recoveries

People working in these areas generally have contact with the customer only through third parties. They can influence the success of their operational units by the timeliness of their actions. Their evaluation should therefore be based primarily on turnround times and productivity. Examples of individual and team measurements include:

- volumes of cases issued for action, per hour;
- time taken to issue cases, e.g. to external agents;
- time taken to locate a gone-away;
- case loads (number of cases per operator); and
- oldest case waiting to be actioned.

Financial measures of success are governed more by high-level policies, e.g. agency selected for trace or collections work, or recoveries decision criteria, which dictate the type of recovery action to be taken. Measures of financial success are therefore more appropriate for monitoring policy rather than the individuals carrying out those policies.

Motivation

Motivation is key for maintaining collections success.

Ideally, collectors should be employed on a performance-related pay basis. A standard basic salary is topped up with further payments once targets have been met, with bonus payments for exceeding targets. The harder the collector works the greater the reward for both company and collector.

However, this ideal brings many practical problems. Workstations need internal systems to measure and report individual activities so that monetary rewards are allocated on a fair and visible basis. With collections it is not always clear which precise action generates a payment response and therefore it is difficult to assign success to a specific collector.

Financial rewards are easier to manage on a group basis. Again though, arguments arise over the quality of debt handled by different groups and therefore the relative ease of collections.

In one successful scheme, an organization set a target of x% reduction in bad debt by the financial year-end. Any additional improvement was split equally between the company and the collectors. Success was achieved through the whole collections area working as one team, with realistic targets and regular feedback on progress.

It is difficult to include operators in associated collections activities – trace and recoveries – in a performance-related pay scheme because their success relies primarily on third parties.

A more practical solution is for non-monetary incentives where departments run internal competitions (weekly, monthly or even annually) and have event days, all with themes that are aimed at increasing motivation, enthusiasm and therefore productivity.

13.9   Management Information

Management information is required to assist the collections units manage their cases on a day-to-day basis, and to give feedback to teams and individuals. Management information is also required for longer-term planning and measuring the success of strategies and tactics.

Good collections units provide senior managers with a regular information pack or analysis of collections results, which is reviewed by the company's credit policy management group.

The role of the policy group is to interpret changes in results as a consequence of the collections effort, other internal policy changes (e.g. changes in cut-offs for new applications) and external competitive or economic change. Typical questions addressed by the group include:

- 'What are the most cost-effective collections methods?'

- 'How much does collections through external agents cost compared with the agents' performance?'

- (where a deterioration in performance is detected) 'How bad is the collections problem, when will the problem peak and how will the peak be identified?'

To answer these questions a range of operational, debt performance and operation planning reports are required.

Ideally all reports are system driven. However, the very nature of many collections questions requires data to be brought together from a number of sources and may require some level of manual collation.

Operational performance and audit reports

Daily, weekly and monthly operational reports are required to determine the effectiveness of the collectors and operators in relation to the strategies and tactics set by the organization. Typical reports include:

- collector/operator performance (see Section 13.8);

- volumes of accounts worked/not worked on the power dialler;

- audits of high balance and 'long time in system without positive action' cases to highlight 'black holes' in the operation or cases representing unusual high risk;

- volumes of write-offs, by collections unit, level of delinquency and write-off reason (linked to write-off criteria – see Section 13.10); and

- high level reconciliation of accounts sent to external agents (full reconciliation is very time consuming and tends to take place only when a policy-set level of variance between agent and internals records is exceeded).

Policy performance reports

Regular reports are required to reconcile the 'cause and effect' of collections activities. The focus is on identifying the actions or tactics that make a material difference in performance.

Typical reports include:

- collections outcomes, e.g. cure rates over time since entering collections, which can be linked back to specific actions taken as a result of the defined actions plans;

- measuring the results of competing collections plans;

- measuring litigation recoveries by enforcement method;

- comparisons of external debt collections agents (see Chapter 14); and

- comparisons of different recovery methods (for comparable cases).

Capacity and budget planning reports

Actual and predicted volumes of cases (by case type) are required, to ensure there are sufficient collectors and other operators to carry out the collections activities on a day-to-day basis.

Longer-term predicted volumes are important in setting the operational budget. From these the required number of collectors/operators (the highest cost element of the collections budget) can be calculated. These volumes also drive cost estimates for third-party activities.

Examples of immediate and longer-term planning reports include:

- predicting day-to-day and near-future workloads;

- estimating case volume changes when collections strategies or tactics are changed; and

- making use of bad debt forecasts for longer-term workload projections and budgeting.

Portfolio reports – debt movement

All companies have a bad debt forecast, generally developed in the form of a provision model (see Chapter 9). The purpose is to determine the likely future cost of bad debt to the business. The model aims to predict changes in provision and write-off over time, generally up to 12 months into the future, taking into account past trends and anticipated changes in business opportunities.

In many organizations, collections has responsibility for the level of bad debt (i.e. the bad debt budget). Collections should therefore have input into the bad debt forecast. They require reports that monitor trends and performance against the forecast, in order to report reasons for variance as appropriate. Frequently organizations use roll rates (see Chapter 9) or tranche reporting, in combination with all the reports listed above, to fully understand the impact of their operational effort on actual and predicted bad debt levels.

Tranche reporting in collections works by tagging a group of accounts in a similar state at a given point in time, and monitoring subsequent performance over time. The states could include accounts:

- entering collections in a given month;

- starting enforcement action in a given month; or

- entering litigation or issued to debt collections agents in a given month.

Figure 13.3 gives a graphic example of a tranche report. It monitors the performance of debt after entering collections in terms of debt returning to order, remaining within collections or progressing on to recoveries or write-off.

Figure 13.3: Analysis of collections debt over time

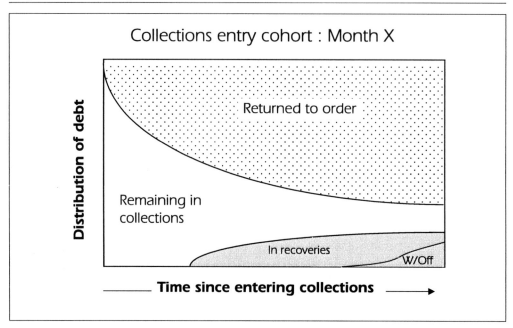

The format of these tranche reports is the same as the dynamic performance cohort matrix discussed in Chapter 8.

13.10 Organizing for Write-off

Good collections units have very specific criteria for identifying write-offs, including:

● time since the last contact was made with the customer;

● time since the last payment was received;

● number and type of actions that have taken place;

● bankruptcy papers filed; and

● fraud identification.

These criteria are also related to the outstanding balance. The higher the balance the more effort may be required before write-off is an acceptable course of action.

In some organizations, certain write-offs are processed automatically, where a given set of conditions is met. In general these apply to smaller balance cases or where a loan customer is very close to having paid off the total amount owed.

For most write-offs, the process should have two stages – proposal and sanctioning of write-off. This provides a quality control check where a more senior member of the unit sanctions the proposal of a more junior member. The more junior or inexperienced members of a unit may only have the authority to propose write-offs.

Authority to propose or sanction write off is also governed by a mandate limit, i.e. the maximum amount a given individual can write-off. The more senior or experienced individuals have the higher mandates.

14

THE USE OF AGENTS

Agents are third parties, either companies, partnerships or individuals, that are employed to represent the creditor to fulfil a specialist function. Agents usually work in areas of last resort, namely debt collection, tracing gone-aways, or picking up fraudulently used cards. Lenders almost universally prefer to resolve the issue before the need for an agent arises, or even better, prevent it occurring in the first place. However it is imperative that only bona fide agencies are employed in order to ensure that the lender's name is not sullied with any potential for adverse behaviour or publicity.

It is important to note that accounts can only be passed to agents provided that the terms and conditions of the original credit agreement allow for this. This is also true for sale of debt.

14.1   Areas of Need

Trace agencies

When a lender has failed to make contact with a customer despite all reasonable efforts over a reasonable period of time, the account may be passed to a trace agency. The agency should check a number of databases to try to establish the customer's last known whereabouts with reasonable certainty, before sending a field agent out to physically check the last known address. The agency is usually paid on a finder's fee basis (i.e. no fee is paid unless the customer is found).

Debt collection agencies (DCAs)[1]

At some point in the back-end phases of the credit cycle, it becomes cost-effective to charge-off debts and pass them over to a collection agency to pursue on the lender's behalf. This point varies for each lender depending on their collections and recoveries strategies. It is important to note that when a debt is passed on to an agency, the lender retains title to the debt. Thus all monies recovered are returned to the lender and the agency is paid on an agreed commission basis.

There are generally four types of agencies:

● high-volume, low-value portfolios. These are usually heavily automated in order to keep costs under control;

[1] Credit Extra Supplement to *Credit Today Journal*, July 1999

- general practitioners – mid-range agencies that operate competently in most areas of collections work;

- industry specific – including consumer lending; and

- geographically specific – suitable for debts focused in a localized area.

The agency works with a combination of letters and telephone calls initially, progressing to personal, door-to-door visits in cases where that would seem economically viable and feasible. They resort to litigation only after all reasonable attempts to resolve the issue have failed. In the high-volume, low-value arena (which includes a considerable amount of credit card and personal loans debt) the agency is likely to employ a standardized approach where the client (i.e. the lender) chooses letters from a standard range for the initial contacts. Telephone collections conversations are likely to be more effective because each one can be tailored to individual circumstances. After this, the agency should be left to decide, within broad parameters, the way in which it works, rather than have the lender dictating its procedures – it is this specialist skill which the lender is paying for in using an agency.

In areas of high-volume debt, the lender may chose to use more than one agency, giving the bulk of the work to a small number of preferred agencies. This allows lenders to compare their relative performance and effectiveness and react quickly where performance deteriorates. Comparisons also help when negotiating agency fees. Lenders regularly send small amounts of debt to other agencies to test their relative performance, to ensure that only the most effective agents are used.

An agency typically has 6-9 months to achieve some success once contact with the customer has been made. In this situation, the agency sends the payments back to the lender on a regular basis (either net or gross of their fees, depending on the original agreement). In order to post the full amount to the customer's account, the agent provides details of gross payments received. If the agency fails or decides early on that the chances of success are too low to warrant chasing the customer, it returns the debt to the lender as 'unrecoverable'. Prime debts are those that have gone out to an agency for the first time. Any that are returned and sent on to another agency are secondary debts.

Debt sales

There is an increasing trend towards the outright sale of tranches of debt to collection agencies. For the lender this generates immediate income and improved cash flow. The agency, on the other hand, has greater control over its collections actions, and it can probably collect over a longer period. The lender sells the debt either in 'bundles' on an occasional basis, or it supplies a regular, drip-feed of smaller numbers of cases.

One consequence of this approach is that the lender does not necessarily receive any feedback on recoveries and, on the books, the write-offs appear to have occurred in clusters. This must be taken into account when provisions are being calculated and portfolio performance is being assessed (see Chapter 9).

Card pick-up agents

In situations of bad debt or fraud, if the cardholder cannot or does not return the credit card to the issuer, an agent may be employed to call at the cardholder's residence to collect it.

Multi-function agencies

The larger agencies prefer to work in partnership with their clients, thus some of them offer multiple services as a one-stop shop:

● Trace activities may be included with collection services – known as 'trace and collect'. In these situations, the primary focus is on collection and the department may be structured with a specialist trace team operating alongside the collections teams.

● The largest companies offer a full range of services including debt counselling, trace and collect, card (and cheque book) pick-up through to credit insurance.

14.2   Setting and Controlling Standards

When selecting an agency, it is imperative to take every precaution to ensure that the agency is reputable. The basic standards required of any agency, regardless of it particular speciality include:

● being registered under the Data Protection Act and, for debt collectors, the Consumer Credit Act;

● being compliant with the Administration of Justice Act;

● being a member of an appropriate trade association; and

● having indemnity insurance cover.

In addition, the lender should:

● take up references;

● establish whether employees or sub-contractors are being used. If the latter, then establish what means of control, compliance and audit are in place;

● establish what databases are used;

● understand the agency's specific methods of working; and

● ensure adequate service-level agreements for reporting, remittance and other administrative functions.

Setting standards

Service levels should be agreed at the outset, and regularly reviewed. Items should include:

● timescales and acceptable methods for pursuing debts;

● remittance procedures;

● reporting methods and frequency.

Controlling standards

Regular auditing of the agent's methods of operation is the main way of controlling standards. The lender needs to retain the right to insist that the agency discontinues using individual collectors if they suspect that any individual is working below the agreed standards.

If the agency is given the right to sue a customer on behalf of the lender, then the lender must set the guidelines for both selecting these cases and pursuing the litigation.

14.3   Optimizing Results

The way to ensure that a lender optimizes its collection returns as a result of using an agent is to compare agency performance on a like-for-like debt basis. In time the most, and the least, efficient agencies will become apparent and only the better ones will continue being used.

Monitoring trace agents

The key measure of success is the percentage of cases with a positive trace outcome. Added to this is the dimension of timeliness. The longer an arrears case is left without any contact or collections action then the harder it becomes to collect the debt.

It is also important to monitor the number of positive trace cases that make a subsequent payment. Each positive trace outcome generates a business expense (i.e. a trace fee) and a return on this expense is needed in the form of a customer payment. Therefore two other trace success criteria are important:

● turnaround time, i.e. number of days to positive trace; and

● percentage with subsequent payment.

As with DCA monitoring, these measures should be compared across trace agents (see below) but only for comparable quality of trace cases, i.e. first or subsequent trace attempt. Geographic variations must also be taken into account.

Monitoring DCA results

The most common method of tracking a DCA's performance is to use tranche reporting. Such reports are produced routinely by all good collection agencies as a standard part of their service.

Tranche reports are an adaptation of the dynamic performance cohort matrix discussed in Chapter 8. Matrices are set up to track the repayments on debt transferred to an agency within a specific time frame, i.e. a 'tranche' of debt. Consolidation of these figures, as shown in Figure 14.1, allows the comparison of agents by monitoring the value or proportion of payments collected over time, for debt issued in a given cohort. These reports should be updated monthly or quarterly.

Figure 14.1: Tranche analysis

Analysis Cohort : Debt issued in period X							
Debt type : Prime							
Balances issued to DCAs		% Balance recovered after period:					
DCA name	Balance	1	2	3	4	5	6
DCA 1							
DCA 2							
DCA 3							
DCA 4							
Total							
Debt type : Secondary							
Balances issued to DCAs		% Balance recovered after period:					
DCA name	Balance	1	2	3	4	5	6
DCA 1							
DCA 2							
DCA 3							
DCA 4							
Total							

It is important to remember that different quality of debt will yield different results – hence the distinction in Figure 14.1 between prime and secondary debt. Tranche reports must be set up to reflect these differences. There may also be geographic influences to consider, because some agencies will have a stronger presence in some areas than others.

Reporting extensions

While 'payments collected on issued debt' is the key measure of DCA success, there are two other important criteria to monitor:

- the elapsed time before debtors make their first payment; and

- the rate at which agencies identify abortive/write-off debt (i.e. debt which is likely never to be recovered).

Tranche reporting can also be used to track these indicators.

To monitor the elapsed time-to-first payment, the matrices need to track the volume of accounts with one or more payments over time, since issued to the agent. This can then be consolidated to show comparative agency success, as shown in Figure 14.2. These reports should be updated monthly or quarterly for the first 12 months after issue.

Figure 14.2: Time-to-first payment analysis

Analysis Cohort : Debt issued in period X							
Debt type : Prime							
Cases issued to DCAs		% with 1 + payments after period:					
DCA name	Cases	1	2	3	4	5	6
DCA 1							
DCA 2							
DCA 3							
DCA 4							
Total							
Debt type : Secondary							
Cases issued to DCAs		% with 1 + payments after period:					
DCA name	Cases	1	2	3	4	5	6
DCA 1							
DCA 2							
DCA 3							
DCA 4							
Total							

The same reporting structure can be used to compare abortive debt/write-off rates by agency, reviewing performance after 6, 12, 18 and 24 months after issue. Together with time-to-first-payment analyses, these reports highlight agents that are focusing on the easiest accounts, rather than the whole portfolio of debt issued to them.

Finally the matrix report format can also be used to compare the relative performance of debt that has been subjected to different strategies, e.g. litigation or DCA's. However this comparison is only valid when equivalent groups of debt are available for comparison.

14.4 In-house or Outsourced Function

Most lenders recognize that debtors who have resisted all appeals from the lender will react more positively if they are contacted by a third party that is chasing the debt on the lender's behalf. Many lenders therefore set up an internal DCA department with a name and address that differs from the lender. This can be used as an interim measure because in-house teams are often effective with the easier cases, thereby reducing the number of accounts that are eventually sent to an outside agency.

Regardless of the chosen approach, the objective is to maximize the cost-to-income ratio. This translates into:

- containing direct costs (staff primarily); and

- enhancing, collection/trace success rates.

Specialist skills and databases are required for all types of agency work. It is usual therefore to outsource this function after a certain period of delinquency when all reasonable in-house efforts to re-establish communication with the debtor have been tried and failed.

15

LITIGATION

For any credit grantor, there are two main types of case that may go to court:

- debt recovery (where judgment is sought to enforce repayment), and
- section 75 disputes (where the credit grantor has connected lender liability).

While the larger volume of cases is debt recovery, it is likely that the potential risk to the lender may be greater with section 75 cases (see Section 15.1 below). Debt recovery cases are comparatively straightforward, and the overall exposure to the lender is easily calculated from the outstanding balances at any point in time. The process for pursuing these is discussed in Section 15.2 below.

15.1   Section 75 Cases

Under section 75 of the Consumer Credit Act 1974, the supplier and the creditor (in DCS agreements) are jointly and severally liable for faulty goods or problems with the supply of services (see Chapter 16). When the cost of the faulty goods is relatively low, the potential scale of any likely repercussion on the creditor (i.e. the company's exposure) is usually equally low. However, when a case has fraudulent or other complications then the total *potential* exposure under section 75 is almost unquantifiable. It is possible that, if one case goes to court and is awarded against the lender, it may set a legal precedent. As a result any number of similar cases may follow, with consequent financial losses as well as potential adverse publicity. For instance, the growth in e-commerce transactions could significantly increase the risk of section 75 claims. The question of whether foreign transactions are caught by section 75 remains unresolved.

15.2   The Litigation Process

Through the mid-1990s in the UK, Lord Woolf, Master of the Rolls, undertook a lengthy and major review of all civil court procedures. As a result, the litigation process for all forms of civil action has been completely redefined with effect from April 1999.

Objectives[1]

The overriding objective of the system is now to keep people out of the courts, i.e. to encourage

[1] Bootland, E. (1999) *Setting the Scene – Overriding Objectives and Proportionality,* 'Using Woolf to your Advantage' Conference, Consumer Credit Trade Association, London

the parties to make more persistent and effective efforts to settle the dispute before it gets to court. The definitive rulebook, the Civil Procedures Rules (CPR), requires all parties, including solicitors, to adopt a more open and co-operative approach. *Control* of the litigation process has shifted from the litigants and their solicitors to the court through a new set of case management procedures that encompass clearly-defined timescales and deadlines for each stage.

CPR also requires the courts to deal with all cases justly[2], which is defined as:

- ensuring that the parties are on an equal footing;

- saving expense;

- dealing with the case in ways that are proportionate:
  - to the amount of money involved;
  - to the importance of the case;
  - to the complexities of the issue;
  - to the financial position of each party.

- ensuring that it is dealt with expeditiously and fairly;

- allotting to it an appropriate share of the court's resources while taking into account the need to allot resources to other cases.

Pre-action protocols

These are the guidelines, or codes of best practice, that define the pre-action procedures. The standards set in a protocol define the 'normal and reasonable' behaviour before a claim is started. It is important to note that protocols apply only in situations where there is a dispute; most debt recovery cases are not disputed.

It is the intention that, in time, there will be specific protocols for each class of action, e.g. personal injury, repossession, debt, etc. At the time of writing, the only existing protocol is for personal injury but others are being drafted. There is currently no protocol for debt recovery, although the Law Society has a draft in hand.[3]

All protocols will aim to provide[4]:

- effective pre-action contact between the parties;

- better and earlier exchange of information;

- effective pre-action investigation by both sides;

- a basis for both parties to settle cases fairly and early without litigation; and

- a situation where proceedings can run efficiently and according to the court's timetable if litigation does become necessary.

---

[2] Lord Chancellor's Department (1999) *Civil Procedures Rules*, Lord Chancellor's Department, London
[3] The Law Society (1999) *Pre-Action Protocol for Debt Claims*, The Law Society, London
[4] Lord Chancellor's Department (1999) *Civil Procedures Rules*, Lord Chancellor's Department, London

Claims under the Consumer Credit Act 1974

The process that is described here applies to claims for the recovery of money owed under regulated agreements. There are procedural differences for claims arising under the CCA for the following specific circumstances[5]:

- to enforce an agreement relating to goods (Section 141);

- to recover protected goods (Section 90);

- to enter premises to take possession of goods (Section 92);

- for the debtor to apply for time orders (Section 129);

- under the extortionate credit provisions (Section 139); and

- for the creditor to apply for enforcement orders (Section 127).

These are likely to represent a minority of cases, and the differences are not discussed here.

Fig 15.1: Procedure for Consumer Credit Act claims[6]

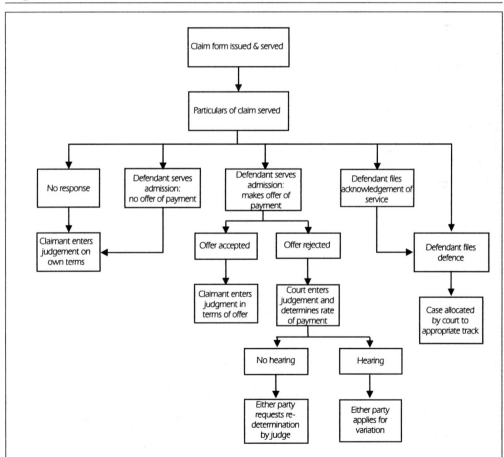

---

[5] Madge, P. (1999), *Civil Rules 2, Adviser*, No 73, pp 31-34
[6] Madge, P. (1999), *Civil Rules, Adviser*, No 72 pp 28-31

Commencement of proceedings[7]

The whole process is illustrated in Figure 15.1. Proceedings commence when the court issues a claim form at the request of the claimant. The claim form must contain:

- a concise statement of the nature of the claim; and

- where the claimant is making a claim for money, a 'statement of value'.

Statement of value

Where there is a money claim, the claimant must specify:

- the amount being claimed; and

- how much he or she expects to recover in terms of (i) not more than £5,000, or (ii) more than £5,000 but not more than £15,000, or (iii) more than £15,000.

When the expected amount recovered is less than £15,000, a claim must start in the county court; claims exceeding £15,000 must arise in the High Court. Where the claim relates to a credit agreement regulated by the Consumer Credit Act, the action must be started in the county court regardless of the amount claimed.

Particulars of claim[8]

Once issued, the claim form must be served on the defendant within four months. The claim form must either be accompanied by 'particulars of claim' or the claimant must serve these on the defendant within the following 14 days. The particulars of claim must include a concise statement of the facts on which the claimant relies and be verified by a 'statement of truth', i.e. that the facts stated in the particulars of claim are true. A copy of any written agreement must be attached.

Where the claim form includes particulars of claim, the accompanying forms must include:

- defending the claim and making a counter-claim if applicable;

- acknowledging service of the claim form; and

- admitting the claim.

Where the particulars of claim are served separately, the forms must be served with the particulars of claim and not with the claim form. This is significant because the defendant's time for responding starts from the date of service of the particulars of claim.

The defendant can respond to the particulars of claim in the following ways:

- file a defence 14 days after service of the claim form or of the particulars of claim, if later;

- file an acknowledgement of service (of the claim) within the 14-day period where he or she is unable to serve a defence within that time or wishes to dispute the court's jurisdiction;

---

[7] Madge, P. (1999), *Civil Rules, Adviser*, No 72, pp 28-31
[8] Ibid

- serve an admission on the claimant admitting the whole of the claim; or

- file an admission (and defence) at court where he or she admits only part of the claim.

There is no provision for filing an acknowledgement of service where the defendant admits the claim.

Part 36 offers[9]

Part 36 of the CPR seeks to make it easier for either party to reach a compromise so that proposals for settlement can be made. A Part 36 offer may be made at any time after proceedings have started. An offer by a defendant to settle a monetary claim in these circumstances is made by way of a Part 36 payment into the court. If the defendant has previously made an offer to settle (which complies with the provisions of Part 36) prior to the commencement of proceedings, he or she must:

- make a Part 36 payment into the court within 14 days of the service of the claim form; and

- the amount of the payment must not be less than the sum offered before the proceedings began.

The Part 36 offer must be in writing, state whether it refers to the whole or part of the claim and whether or not it includes interest.

If at trial a debtor is held to be liable for more than his or her Part 36 offer, then the court may order interest to be paid on the whole or part of any sum awarded to the creditor.

Default judgment[10]

The claimant must file a request for default judgment. If the defendant has not 'requested time to pay', the claimant may specify the terms of the judgment and judgment will be entered accordingly. If no terms are specified, judgment will be for immediate payment. An application for default judgment must be supported by evidence that:

- the particulars of claim have been served;

- either the defendant has not filed an acknowledgement of service or has not filed a defence and that, in either case, the relevant period for doing so has expired;

- the defendant has not satisfied the claim; and

- the defendant has not returned an admission to the claimant.

Default judgment cannot be entered where the defendant has filed:

- a defence;

- an acknowledgement of service; or

- served an admission together with a request for time to pay.

[9] Heath, K. (1999), *'New Court Rules in Practice'* , 'Using Woolf to your Advantage' Conference, Consumer Credit Trade Association, London
[10] Madge, P. (1999), *Civil Rules, Adviser*, No 72, pp 28-31

Admissions[11]

A defendant who wishes to admit the claim may return an admission to the claimant. The period for doing so is 14 days after service of the claim form (or of service of the particulars of claim, if later). The defendant may still return the admission to the claimant outside of this period, provided the claimant has not requested, or applied for, a default judgment. Where the defendant admits only part of the claim, the admission is filed at court and a copy sent to the claimant. A defence may also be filed, if appropriate.

Where the defendant admits all or part of the claim, he or she may make a request for time to pay, i.e. a proposal about the date of payment, or a proposal to pay by instalments at the times and rate specified in the request.

The claimant is required to file a copy of the admission and request for payment with the request for judgment. Where the defendant has requested time to pay and the claimant accepts the offer, the judgment will be for payment at the time and rate specified in the defendant's request for time to pay.

Where the claimant does not accept the defendant's proposals, he or she is required to file notice to that effect with the court, together with a copy of the admission and request for time to pay. The court then enters judgment for the amount admitted and determines the rate of payment.

Judgment can be for a specified amount of money, an amount determined by the court, delivery of goods, or a combination of these.

Determinations

Where the amount involved is £50,000 or less, the rate of payment may be determined by a court officer without a hearing. Where the amount involved is more than £50,000, the rate of payment must be decided by a judge, with or without a hearing.

The court must take into account:

- the defendant's statement of means;
- the claimant's objections; and
- any other relevant factors.

Re-determination

Where the time and rate of payment have been determined without a hearing, either party may apply for the decision to be re-determined by a judge within 14 days of service of the judgment. If the decision was made a by a court officer, the re-determination may take place without a hearing, unless one is requested in the notice of application. If a judge made the decision, the re-determination must be made at a hearing, unless the parties agree otherwise.

---

[11] Ibid.

If a party wishes to vary a decision about payment by instalments made by a judge at a hearing, they can apply for variation.

Set asides and variations[12]

Setting aside

The court must set aside a default judgment where the judgment was wrongly entered in default because the conditions for allowing a default judgment were not satisfied.

The court may set aside or vary a default judgment if:

- the defendant has a real prospect of successfully defending the claim; or

- that there is some other good reason why the judgment should be set aside/varied, or the defendant should be allowed to defend the claim.

In addition, the defendant must file a request for the judgment to be set aside or apply to the court for directions where the claimant:

- has served particulars of claim separately from the claim form; and

- has entered default judgment against the defendant; and

- subsequently has good reason to believe that the claim form did not reach the defendant before entering judgment.

However, in the meantime, the defendant may take no further step in the proceedings or the enforcement of the judgment until the judgment has been set aside or the court has disposed of the application for directions.

Varying the rate of payment

For county court judgments, either party may apply to the court to vary either the date or the rate of payment of the debt. An application should be in writing and state what order the applicant is seeking and why.

The application notice should contain a request for either a hearing or that the application be considered without a hearing. The court will then either notify the parties of the time and date of hearing or refer the matter to a district judge to decide whether the application is suitable for consideration without a hearing. Provided that the application contains a statement of truth, supporting evidence can be contained in the application itself rather than in a separate affidavit.

Enforcing a judgment

These procedures have not changed as a result of the Woolf reforms and there are several methods available to the courts:

[12] Ibid.

- *warrant of execution*: bailiffs are instructed to seize goods belonging to the defendant and sell them to pay the debt;

- *charging order*: this can be made against assets or property belonging to the defendant. If the debt is not paid, the claimant can have the assets sold to recover his or her monies;

- *attachment of earnings*: this is an order to the defendant's employer to deduct a specified sum from the defendant's salary and pay it into the court on a regular basis; and

- *enforcement and time orders*: these are provided for under the Consumer Credit Act – see Chapter 16, section 16.1.

15.3   In-house or Outsourced Function

Every credit grantor will, at some time, need to become involved in litigation with some customers. The choice is either to set up an in-house department or to outsource the whole function. There are merits to both options, and the route taken is a matter for individual companies to decide strategically.

In-house team

In the UK, most of the large lenders operate in-house teams. In some cases, this is a legacy situation. However, it should be related to the cost of running the function, the number, size and complexity of cases being handled and the amount of cash it is able to recover.

Some highly complex cases are outsourced even where there is an in-house team, when specialist skills including Counsel are required. There is a high cost for using these specialists and this is a reason for doing as much as possible in-house.

Outsourced operations

There are two main reasons why this function might be outsourced:

- A new credit grantor setting up in the UK may decide that it is easier to outsource this function. This means less operational units to establish at the outset and there will be too few cases initially to make the in-house option cost-effective.

- An in-house team may exist to undertake paperwork and the early stages, but if that team does not include a qualified solicitor, then outsourcing is more likely. The courts now expect the claimant's representative to be able to make decisions on the spot rather than just convey messages back to the organization for a decision. If a case is complex and Counsel involved, then a solicitor is the only person who can initially instruct Counsel.

15.4   Skills Requirements

An in-house litigation team is a very specialised group. There is a need for at least one person with legal training, preferably a qualified solicitor or at least para-legal training. The general skills required by all team members include:

- basic understanding of the applicable law;

- excellent interpersonal and communication skills – empathize and understand the customer's position, manage the customer to maximize the returns;

- good negotiation skills and objectivity;

- PC skills and a knowledge of the internal computer systems; and

- ability to recognize when they are out of their depth and need more specialist support.

At more senior levels, people with a broader legal background bring a wider view that enables lessons learnt in other fields to be applied to debt cases.

15.5   Systems Requirements

In many cases, litigation systems are modules that can be added onto collections/recoveries systems. These systems should include facilities for:

- prioritizing cases into queues (i.e. workflow systems);

- keeping track of the progress of cases;

- in the case of straightforward cases, automatically producing the necessary paperwork at the appropriate time;

- offering recoveries (or pre-litigation) scoring capabilities;

- interacting fully with the collections/recoveries system for moving cases back and forth as appropriate; and

- analysing the volume and value of cases at each of the stages right through to write-off.

At the time of writing, many litigation systems are not able to fulfil all the requirements of the procedures introduced in April 1999 (see Section 15.2 above) – in particular the paperwork for protocols and for Part 36 payments.

15.6   Optimizing the Litigation Process

The objective of every case is to recover the monies in the shortest time possible, with the least expense and without adverse publicity. The way to achieve this is to employ excellent staff with all the skills discussed above, together with the insight and flexibility to know when to alter the method of managing the case or dealing with the customer.

All lenders have a brand name to protect and need to be seen to be fair and reasonable. Using the court system helps to achieve this. The alternative is to use a debt collection agent where payment is purely on results but where there is less control over the collection process.

The disadvantage is that the litigation process now costs significantly more than using collections agencies. The Woolf process has introduced new stages with associated up-front costs. If internal analysis can identify the cost of an average debt recovery case, together with the relative likelihood of recovering the debt, then it should become a relatively straightforward matter to decide whether to litigate or send the case to a collections agent.

16

LEGISLATION

There are a number of consumer protection laws that are directly applicable to consumer credit and the range and depth of these is continually changing. In particular EU Directives will come into force and these may add to, or even replace, the existing legislation. The most significant of the applicable legislation is outlined here, although the broader aspects (e.g. unfair contract terms, sale of goods requirements) are not included.

16.1 Consumer Credit Act 1974[1,2]

This is the primary piece of legislation which governs most aspects of consumer credit. This Act establishes protection for the consumer in a system that licenses credit grantors and ancillary organizations. It sets up controls of traders supplying credit, or supplying goods on hire purchase/conditional sale or hire and lease, and their transactions. Only the sections that are relevant to the credit cycle are discussed here, i.e. there is no coverage of advertising regulations, securities, current accounts, hire or hire purchase/conditional sale, land-based transactions or guarantees or indemnities.

The Act itself lays down the underlying principles and a set of Regulations is the basis for its practical implementation. For example, the Act defines the concept of a cooling-off period, but it is left to the Regulations to explicitly set this period at five days.

Definition of credit

Any form of financial accommodation where goods or services are sold to a buyer without any immediate payment is defined as credit. It implies trust and confidence in the buyer's ability and intention to repay in full at some future, agreed, time. Under the Consumer Credit Act, the buyer is a non-corporate body.

Types of credit agreements

Under the Act there are two types of agreement, restricted use (RU) and unrestricted use (URU). RU applies to the acquisition of goods or services, whereas URU applies to obtaining cash loans that can then be used for any purpose.

[1] Rose, F.D. (1998) *Statutes on Commercial and Consumer Law*, Blackstones, London
[2] Patrick, P.J. (1999) 'A Day on the Law Affecting Consumer Credit' Conference, Consumer Credit Trade Association, London

Credit agreements

A consumer credit agreement is established when the creditor provides the debtor with credit. A 'regulated' agreement is any of the following, provided that the credit extended exceeds £50 and is less than £25,000. Agreements where the credit extended is outside these limits are exempt from the Act.

Debtor-creditor-supplier agreement (DCS)

This is a credit facility made available by the creditor under a pre-existing agreement between himself (or herself) and a supplier in the knowledge that the credit will be used to finance a transaction between the debtor and a particular supplier. A typical example is a credit card used at an 'acquired' merchant, or sale of goods on credit.

Running-account credit

This is one form of a DCS agreement where the debtor receives from the creditor or a third-party cash, goods and/or services to an amount or value such that the credit limit is not exceeded at any time. A credit card is a typical running-account credit agreement.

Fixed-sum credit

The debtor receives credit facilities for goods purchased from the creditor. The credit may be repaid in one or several repayments. A personal loan is an example.

Debtor-creditor agreement (DC)

This is a credit agreement that is not made under any pre-existing arrangements between the creditor and the debtor, where the credit is used to finance a transaction between the debtor and any supplier. Car finance from a third-party creditor is an example.

Exempt agreement

These are largely credit agreements where the creditor is a specific type of organization. In the UK, this includes insurance companies, friendly societies, credit unions, charities and land improvement companies.

Credit token

This is any physical document given to the debtor by a creditor to enable the debtor to acquire cash, goods or services on credit. It includes credit cards, cheques, vouchers, coupons, stamps or booklets.

Total charge for credit and APR

The total charge for credit is the total amount that the debtor is obliged to pay when taking out an agreement. It includes all interest and any explicit fees but excludes any insurance.

The annual percentage rate (APR) is this total charge expressed as a percentage. The calculation method is complex and the various formulae to be used are laid down in the Act.

Entry into credit agreements

The agreement

The Act defines the form and content of a regulated agreement. If both the debtor and the creditor do not sign the document (in its prescribed form) it is not properly executed, which means that it is unenforceable without a court order. It must include all the terms of the agreement, including any cancellation rights. A copy of the unexecuted agreement must be given to the debtor where acceptance by, or on behalf of, the creditor is not undertaken at the same time as the debtor signs the agreement.

Once the agreement has been made, a copy of the executed agreement must be sent to the debtor. Credit tokens must also be provided where this is applicable.

Cancellable agreements

The debtor has the option to cancel a regulated agreement within a short period after it is executed if any preliminary negotiations included oral representations. This predefined, short period, known as a cooling-off period, does not apply if the unexecuted agreement is signed on business premises or oral representations did not take place in any antecedent negotiations.

Recovery of monies or goods after cancellation

If the debtor exercises cancellation rights, the agreement becomes 'as if it never took place'. All monies received by the debtor under the agreement, become repayable. Any goods acquired under a DCS agreement shall be returned to the supplier. The debtor has the usual duty of care for the goods during the cooling-off period.

Matters arising throughout the duration of the agreement.

This largely covers the duties of the creditor to the debtor in terms of supplying information at various times, including regular statements and notice of any variation to the agreement.

If the debtor submits a written request, the creditor must supply a copy of the executed agreement together with a statement of the account showing its status and all monies due. This applies to both fixed-sum and running-account agreements, but does not apply to accounts with a zero balance.

Variation of agreements

Where the creditor has the right under the terms of the agreement to vary the terms, notice must be given to the debtor before the change can take effect. This usually applies to alteration in interest rates in DCS agreements.

Modifying agreements

The credit charges in a fixed-term agreement are often levied at the outset and spread across all the payments. If a debtor with a loan that is structured in this manner repays it earlier than the term of the agreement, he or she has a right to a certain level of rebate of the credit charges that have not yet become due. Regulations determine the method of calculation for this rebate. This is known as the Rule of 78.

Liability for misuse of credit facilities

The debtor is not liable for any loss arising from the misuse of the facilities, i.e. a credit card agreement. However, a debtor can be made liable for losses under a credit-token agreement up to a specified ceiling, up until the time that he or she notifies the creditor of the token's loss.

Replacement credit tokens

When credit tokens are replaced or reissued, the creditor must supply a true copy of the executed agreement with the new token. If it fails to do this, it cannot later enforce the agreement.

Joint creditor-supplier liability

This part of the Act has wide-ranging consequences. Section 75 states that the creditor is equally liable with the supplier for any breach of the contract including the unsatisfactory quality of the goods purchased using the credit. The debtor can make a claim against the creditor if the supplier is unable to fulfil its responsibilities. This usually happens when the supplier has gone out of business in the interim. It is unclear whether this liability applies to transactions that take place outside the UK.

Death of debtor

If the creditor is unable to satisfy himself that the obligations of the debtor are likely to be discharged as a result of the debtor's death, then the creditor can apply for a court order to recover the debt. A default notice cannot be issued, but steps can be taken to restrict the debt, e.g. by recovering any credit tokens.

Default and termination

The content and execution of default notices are laid down by the Act, as well as how and when they are served. The creditor must serve a written default and give the debtor a short period in which to remedy the default, before it can take any action.

The rules applicable to termination by the creditor are also set out. A creditor must give written notice of its intention to terminate an agreement and the notice must be in the prescribed form – a default, termination or enforcement notice depending on the nature of the need to terminate and the nature of the credit agreement.

Default notices are served if, as a result of a breach by the debtor, the creditor wishes to terminate the agreement, or demand earlier repayment.

Termination and enforcement notices can only be served on debtors who are not in default. They cannot be served where an agreement is of an indefinite duration, after the expiry of a fixed-term agreement.

Judicial control

Under the Act the courts are given specific powers for the enforcement of certain regulated agreements. These include Enforcement Orders and Time Orders, and the Act provides the power to impose conditions on, and vary, agreements. Extortionate credit bargains are also covered.

Enforcement orders

These are applications to the court for orders for the enforcement of improperly executed agreements. The final arbiter is the Director General of Fair Trading (DG).

Time orders

The court may grant a Time Order on application either by the creditor for an Enforcement Order, or by the debtor. The Time Order shall allow the debtor to remedy the breach within a specified time period. This may also apply to payment by instalments. The Time Order may be varied or revoked on application from the debtor or the creditor. The court may also vary or amend the terms of the original agreement, as it deems appropriate.

Extortionate credit bargains

A credit bargain is extortionate if the payments are grossly exorbitant or the agreement grossly contravenes the ordinary principles of fair dealing. If, following a submission by the debtor, a court finds that an agreement is extortionate, it may reopen the agreement in order to do justice between the parties.

Ancillary credit businesses

Under the Act the following businesses must all be licensed by the DG:

- credit brokers;
- debt adjusters;
- debt counsellors;
- debt collectors; and
- credit reference agencies.

The DG may revoke a licence if a business has contravened the boundaries of its licence.

Credit reference agencies

The Act very clearly defines the operating boundaries for credit bureaux. It defines its relationships with consumers and lenders. If a debtor applies in writing, then the creditor shall supply the name and address of any credit reference agency it used to gain information about the financial standing of the applicant before the agreement was executed.

Originally an individual had the right of access to his or her credit bureau data under the Consumer Credit Act. However, from March 2000 this protection was encompassed by the Data Protection Act 1998 – see Section 16.3. However in this context, the term 'individual' under the DPA does not include sole traders, partnerships or company directors. If anyone in these groups wishes to access his or her own data, then this is still governed by the CCA, i.e. the DPA only relates to physical individuals.

16.2   Money Laundering Regulations 1993[3]

These Regulations emanate from an EU Directive that attempts to control the processing of illicit funds (arising mainly from the illegal drugs industry) into legitimate monies. The Regulations define the requirements for verification of personal identification for new applicants for credit, and for reporting suspicious cases to the appropriate authorities.

Definition

Money laundering occurs when criminals, with funds resulting from criminal activities, attempt to conceal the true origin and ownership of these monies when entering into a new business transaction with a financial institution.

The Regulations

These apply to all:

- banks, building societies and other credit institutions that accept deposits or offer lending or leasing;

- investment businesses;

- insurance companies; and

- bureaux de change, cheque encashment facilities and money transmission centres.

All consumer and commercial transactions in excess of ECU15,000 are covered, including all forms of consumer credit, mortgages, factoring and financing of commercial transactions. These may be single or a series of linked transactions. It also applies to all running-credit agreements irrespective of credit limit (i.e. credit cards). The Regulations apply only to business that takes place within the country of the legislation and do not concern themselves with wider geographic responsibilities.

---

[3] Finance and Leasing Association (1999) *Money Laundering Guidelines*, Finance and Leasing Association, London

Requirements for financial institutions

All lenders that offer products covered by the Regulations are required to:

- establish specific internal controls and procedures for identifying potential money laundering situations;

- verify the identity of the applicant;

- retain records of this verification process for five years; and

- recognize and report any suspicious applications or transactions to the appropriate authorities.

Internal controls

An appropriate person (a Money Laundering Officer) must be appointed as the person responsible for deciding whether a transaction is suspicious and he or she is also the central point of contact for the law enforcement agencies. There is also a requirement to set up procedures and systems for the above functions. Company directors can be held personally liable for any breaches.

Verification of identity

An individual's identity is defined as his or her name(s), the address (including postcode) at which they can be found, and the date of birth. Verification must take place within a reasonable timescale and be appropriate to the circumstances. At least two separate forms of verification should be used, one each for the name and the address.

Face-to-face applications

The name and address should be independently verified from one of a wide range of documents or sources (including driving licence, credit or debit cards, passport or utility bill) which can be inspected at the point of sale. Credit reference checks against the voters roll should also be undertaken. If the applicant is an existing customer and the computer systems enable existing relationships to be accessed, this should provide an adequate means of independent verification.

Non-face-to-face applications

These include applications received by post, telephone, fax or the Internet. The requirements are exactly the same as face-to-face applications, but the process may be undertaken in stages, i.e. make an initial assessment of whether the business is an acceptable proposition, and if it is, take a credit reference and then go back to the applicant for other verification documents.

Record keeping

Financial institutions are required to keep precise and detailed audit trails of the identity evidence for at least five years from the date that the business was transacted irrespective of when and how the relationship may end. These records may be in electronic or paper form.

Recognition and reporting of suspicious transactions

There is a statutory obligation on all staff to report any suspicious application or financial transaction to the Money Laundering Officer in line with internal procedures.

Accounts and payments systems need to be able to identify all credits/deposits that are greater than a pre-defined amount (which may be less than the legal limit to allow for linked transactions). These must be investigated to determine the source of the funds and the purpose of the credit.

There is also a statutory requirement to implement appropriate training to make staff aware of the policies and procedures as well as the legal requirements.

16.3   Data Protection Acts 1984 and 1998[4,5]

The 1984 Act was designed to protect against the misuse of computerized personal data. The 1998 Act has extended the scope of the original to include manual filing systems.

Definitions

- *Data* is any information recorded in a form that can be processed either manually or automatically by a computer, and information that is manually recorded with the intention of processing it on a computer.

- *Personal data* is any data that relates to a living individual who can be identified but excludes sole traders, partnerships and company directors.

- *Sensitive data* is data covering race, religion, political issues, health and sex, and criminal, or allegedly criminal, offences.

- A *data controller* is any person (or company) who holds data.

- A *data subject* is the person to whom the data relates.

- *Processing* data means obtaining, amending, augmenting, deleting, rearranging or extracting data.

Registration

All data controllers and computer bureaux must register with the Data Protection Commissioner (the government official responsible for enforcing the Act). This includes credit bureaux.

---

[4] Patrick, P. J. (1999) *'A Day on the Law Affecting Consumer Credit'* Conference, Consumer Credit Trade Association, London

[5] Sharp, A. (1999) *'Legislative Compliance Update'*, ICM 6th Annual Conference on Credit Scoring, Leeds

Data protection principles

There are eight principles for handling personal data. This data shall:

- be obtained and processed fairly and lawfully;
- be obtained and processed only for specified and lawful purposes;
- be adequate, relevant and not excessive;
- be accurate and kept up to date;
- not be kept for longer than is necessary for its original purpose(s);
- be processed in accordance with the rights of the data subject;
- be subject to appropriate security measures to prevent unauthorized access, usage, accidental loss or damage; and
- not be transferred to countries that do not have adequate data protection legislation.

Processing

The Act covers all forms of computer-based processing and telephone monitoring systems.

Subject access provisions

Any consumer can ask any data controller whether he or she holds personal data about them, and, if so, to supply a copy of it and to provide any necessary explanations. The data subject also has the right to have any inaccuracies corrected and to give details of any relevant data processing that may be applied to the data. The data controller must supply information about the enquirer only. If individuals can prove that they have suffered damage as a result of inaccurate data being held (or loss of the data) then they are entitled to compensation.

Individuals can also specifically require a data controller not to process their data for the purposes of direct marketing.

A data controller must obtain the data subject's consent to make enquiries of, and subsequently record information at any credit bureau. (Subject access to personal data held or processed by credit bureaux was originally provided for under the Consumer Credit Act, but this right was transferred to the Data Protection Act 1998 with effect from 1 March 2000.)

Automated decision making

Where a decision about a customer is made wholly by automated means, the customer has the right to be informed of the logic behind the decision but this explanation need not involve the disclosure of trade secrets. If the data subject is dissatisfied with the decision he or she can require that the decision be reviewed manually. Manual decision making is not covered by the Act.

Arbiter

The final arbiter under the Act is the Data Protection Commissioner.

16.4 Other Relevant Legislation

Discrimination laws[6]

Under these various Acts, it is an offence to isolate any person for non-standard treatment (at any stage of the credit cycle) because of ethnic group, religion, sex, marital status, geography, nationality or disability. This extends to the development of scorecards where the inclusion of any of these items as individual characteristics in either the analysis or the finished predictive model is disallowed. The geographic limitation is a localized one in that a small local cluster of houses or a suburb or village cannot be isolated for individual attention. This practice is known as red-lining. (The name derives from the original practice of physically drawing a red line on a map around the affected area.)

The Acts involved are the Sex Discrimination Act 1975, the Race Relations Act 1976 and the Disability Discrimination Act 1995.

Theft Acts 1968 and 1978[6, 7]

A person who uses any form of deception to obtain:

- property (including money) belonging to another with the intention of permanently depriving him of it; or

- services from another on the understanding that they will be paid for;

is committing a theft.

Of particular interest to creditors is *evasion of liability by deception*. This occurs if a person dishonestly secures the discharge of the whole or part of any existing liability or does so with the intent to make that default a permanent situation. It is also an offence if a debtor, by deception, persuades a creditor to wait for, or forego, payment, or dishonestly obtains any exemption from the liability to pay. A person who persuades a creditor to accept a cheque that bounces, with the intent of creating a permanent default with it, also commits an offence.

Forgery and Counterfeiting Act 1981[8]

This Act covers making a 'false instrument' with the intent of using it to induce someone to accept it as genuine, thereby inducing him to commit an act to his own (or someone else's) detriment. It is also an offence to copy, use or possess machinery/goods for making false instruments. The Act explicitly includes cheque cards and credit cards.

---

[6] HMSO (1968) *Public General Acts and Measures 1968*, Chapter 60, HMSO, London
[7] HMSO (1978) *Public General Acts and Measures 1978*, Part 1, Chapter 31, HMSO, London
[8] HMSO (1981) *Public General Acts and Measures 1981*, Part 1, Chapter 45, HMSO, London

Fraud and Deception Bill[9]

This is a new bill intended to cover the deficiencies in existing legislation in the criminal areas of fraud and deception. Although most of it is not applicable to consumer credit, there are two relevant areas:

- *Constructive deception*:

  - a person commits an offence if he or she intentionally or recklessly causes a legal liability to pay money to be imposed on another, knowing that the other does not consent to his or her doing so and that he or she has no right to do so; and

  - the other should not be regarded as consenting to the imposition of the liability if his or her consent is procured by deception; but

  - a person should not commit the offence if, at the time of causing the liability to be imposed, he or she believes that the other would have consented to his or her doing so if the other had known all the material circumstances.

- *Misuse ('deception') of machines* – in particular, the Internet. If fraudulent conduct exists in connection with accessing or using a service on the Internet, this is considered as an extension of theft, i.e. theft of services.

Electronic Communications Bill[10]

The main purpose of this bill is to help to build confidence in electronic commerce and the technology underlying it. This bill proposes the formal recognition of electronic signatures and electronic data storage. It provides for:

- a statutory approvals scheme for businesses and other organizations providing cryptography services (such as electronic signature services) and confidentiality services;

- the legal recognition of electronic signatures;

- the use of electronic communications or electronic storage of information, as an alternative to traditional methods; and

- the removal of obstacles in other existing legislation to the use of electronic communication or data storage.

---

[9] www.gtnet.gov.uk/lawcomm/library
[10] www.dti.gov.uk/cii/elec/ecbill_3.html

17

REGULATORY AND VOLUNTARY BODIES

Most industries can be broken down into two broad sectors, namely the practitioners (in this case, credit grantors) and 'overseers' (government or semi-governmental bodies that impose the rules within which the practitioners operate). Practitioners are by far the larger group, but overseers are likely to be the more influential. In the consumer credit industry, overseer organizations include:

● government departments that exist for the purposes of generating, monitoring and enforcing the relevant legislation (e.g. OFT, DTI);

● practitioner-based bodies whose purpose is to support, and speak on behalf of, suppliers (e.g. trade associations); and

● mutual self-help practitioner organizations (e.g. CIFAS, GAIN).

In the consumer credit world, there is also another group that operates alongside these: voluntary bodies that work mainly in the area of consumer advice and debt counselling.

17.1   Government Bodies

In the UK, three government departments are responsible for upholding the main aspects of consumer credit legislation. These are the Department of Trade and Industry (DTI), Office of Fair Trading (OFT) and the Office of the Data Protection Commissioner (DPC). There are other support organizations, some of which are local government functions.

Department of Trade and Industry (Consumer Affairs Division)[1]

The DTI's overall aim is to increase UK competitiveness and scientific excellence in order to generate higher levels of sustainable growth and productivity in a modern economy. Within this, the Consumer Affairs Division states that it aims to:

● help consumers to make well-informed purchases which encourages innovation and competitiveness; and

● protect them from unsafe products and unfair business practices.

---

[1] www.dti.gov

Office of Fair Trading[2]

The Office of Fair Trading plays an important role in protecting the economic welfare of consumers, and in enforcing UK competition policy. The OFT is a non-ministerial department of government with a range of legal responsibilities and is the principal UK fair trading authority.

The OFT's quoted roles are to:

- identify and correct trading practices that are against the consumer's interests;

- regulate the provision of consumer credit;

- act directly on the activities of industry and commerce by investigating and remedying anti-competitive practices and abuses of market power; and

- bring about market structures that encourage competitive behaviour.

Data Protection Commissioner[3]

The Office of the Data Protection Commissioner is an independent body established to control the use of personal data held on, or processed by, computers. The Queen appoints the Commissioner as an independent officer who reports directly to Parliament. The duties of the Commissioner are set down in the Data Protection Act and include:

- maintaining a register of data users and computer bureaux and making it publicly available;

- disseminating information on the Act and how it works;

- promoting compliance with the Data Protection Principles;

- encouraging the development of Codes of Practice to help data users comply with the principles;

- considering complaints about breaches of the Principles or the Act; and

- prosecuting offenders, or serving notices on those contravening the Principles.

This latter objective includes consumer protection from malpractising credit-related organizations. Enforcement of the applicable legislation is the responsibility of the local Trading Standards Associations.

Trading Standards Offices[4]

These are the UK's local government law enforcement agencies for consumer-related statutes, as well as providers of advice and assistance to consumers and businesses. (There is a wealth of sources/advice on their excellent website.)

---

[2] www.oft.gov.uk
[3] www.dpr.gov.uk
[4] www.xodesign.co.uk/tsnet

National Consumer Council

This government quango undertakes consumer-focused research, and feeds ideas for consumer protection back to the government. It does not provide support directly to the consumer. At the time of writing, its role is under review in a government White Paper which proposes widening its remit[5].

17.2   Trade Associations

These are organizations whose members are mainly companies trading in the same sector or industry. Their purpose is to support, advise and help their members as well as represent their members' interests by lobbying government on their behalf. A good trade association provides the following functions[6]:

● operates an effective mechanism for consulting members and understanding their views;

● monitors and anticipates the legislative and regulatory process; ensures that its views on matters that significantly affects its members are taken into account at the earliest opportunity;

● shapes polices and initiatives proactively;

● puts forward well-researched, cogently-argued cases to government;

● behaves as a credible and authoritative advocate for its sector;

● forms and presents a view on issues where there may be conflicting interests among members;

● represents the sector's interests effectively in the European Union (EU);

● liaises with counterparts in the EU at both national and European level and takes joint action with them; and

● understands the workings of EU institutions, including the Commission and Parliament.

17.3   Self-regulation

Codes of practice

Every reputable credit grantor wishes to apply policies and procedures that are within the law, and represent current best practice. However, there is often considerable room for interpretation of the relevant legislation – particularly if it is relatively new and untested in the courts. Therefore, bodies such as trade associations often establish codes of practice which are a form of self-regulation. These serve to set minimum standards for operating practice, and they are more easily adjusted should new circumstances or needs arise. The

---

[5] Department of Trade and Industry (1999), *modern markets: confident consumers*, Department of Trade and Industry, London

[6] Boleat, M. (1996) *Trade Association Strategy and Management*, Association of British Insurers, London

alternative is usually legislation which is much more rigid, often inappropriate, slower to be introduced and considerably more time-consuming and expensive to monitor or amend.

In the UK, all the consumer credit-related trade associations operate codes of practice, with which members are obliged to conform. Membership of some trade associations is seen as a sign of high professional standards and behaviour. Therefore, for a company to be expelled from membership because it has contravened the code of practice could lead to its going out of business.

The main code for the consumer credit industry is the Banking Code[7]. This was devised jointly by the British Bankers Association, the Building Societies Association and the Association for Payment Clearing Services in the mid-1990s. It is a 'voluntary code followed by all banks and building societies in their relations with personal customers in the United Kingdom'. Although this is primarily aimed at branch banking and current accounts in particular, there are guidelines covering plastic cards, lending procedures and notification and responsibilities for lost or stolen cards. Copies are available from any branch of banks or building societies.

Occasionally there are particularly adverse circumstances in the industry, which prompt several bodies to collectively set up new codes, which then apply to the whole industry. The rapid growth in credit card and cheque fraud in the 1980s is an excellent example of this. In 1987, a speaker at a Consumer Credit Trade Association conference suggested that the credit industry had a wider responsibility to protect the consumer from the rapidly expanding fraud 'industry' and they should work together, non-competitively, to set up some industry-based preventative measure. Consequently, the CCTA set up a working party with a group of retail lenders and a year later the Credit Industry Fraud Avoidance Scheme (CIFAS) system was launched. (Ten years on, more than 160 members in the industry support CIFAS and it has become the industry-standard, fraud-prevention tool.)

Areas covered by codes of practice[8, 9]

These are guidelines applicable to both the association and its members in terms of professional conduct. These usually cover what would be deemed commonsense, best practice for running any business legally, ethically and prudently.

General conditions applicable to most associations include:

a. On the part of the member:

- terms and conditions of doing business;

- customer confidentiality;

- guarantees and securities; and

- complaints and conciliation.

[7] BBA Enterprises Ltd (1998), *The Banking Code*, BBA Enterprises Ltd, London
[8] Finance and Leasing Association (1992) *Code of Practice*, Finance and Leasing Association, London
[9] Credit Services Association (1999) *Code of Practice*, Credit Services Association, Norwich

b. On the part of the Association:

- monitor member's compliance with the Code, report regularly on that compliance, and take disciplinary action in any cases of non-compliance.

Specific terms are also included to cover the details of the particular activity of members. For example, the Credit Services Association's members are all consumer debt collectors. Its code of practice lays down clear guidelines for professional conduct when collecting debts.

Guide to Credit Scoring[10,11]

This is another important example of industry-driven self-regulation. In the early 1980s, credit scoring was increasingly being used as the main credit-assessment tool. It was little understood by the general public and the OFT was concerned about the potential for its misuse. As a result, four trade bodies collaborated and in 1983 produced the *Guide to Credit Scoring*. It was endorsed by the OFT and set out best practice for users of credit scoring. A year later, the *Guide* was reviewed by the OFT, which basically confirmed the content of the original edition.

The *Guide* covers:

- principles of design;
- principles of implementation;
- principles of operation;
- principles of decision making; and
- information to consumers; and
- review of declines.

This *Guide* remained the basis for operating credit-scoring systems for the next 10 years. Over that period, the use of scoring techniques became much more widespread and there was a plethora of new technical developments. In 1992 the OFT again reviewed it but apart from some specific new recommendations the previous edition was largely endorsed.

The 1992 review recommended two significant changes, namely that:

- consumers be informed that credit-scoring techniques were being used, and
- under certain circumstances, reasons for refusing the credit should be given to the applicant.

Other than these, the OFT concluded that 'the existing legislation, supplemented by the *Guide to Credit Scoring* provides ample [consumer] protection'.

In 1999, the OFT together with an industry working party, reviewed the *Guide* again and a new edition of the Code is to be published in 2000. New guidelines are expected which

---

[10] Sharp, A. (1999), *'Legislative/Compliance Update'*, ICM 6th Annual Conference on Credit Scoring, Leeds
[11] Office of Fair Trading (1992) *Credit Scoring*, Office of Fair Trading, London

will bring the *Guide* into line with the Data Protection Act 1998 in regard to automated decisions (see Chapter 16).

This *Guide* is probably the best example of self-regulation and collaborative effort seen in the industry in many years. That it has survived with only minimal changes for more than 15 years despite enormous growth in the use of credit-scoring tools, techniques and areas of application is a tribute to the industry and those trade bodies that devised it originally.

Standing Committee on Reciprocity (SCOR)[12]

SCOR is a body of consumer credit trade association and credit bureaux representatives which exists to oversee the principles and practice of data sharing, in particular CAIS and Insight. (These schemes share credit data among members to prevent over-commitment, bad debt, fraud and money laundering.) SCOR aims to impose a 'like for like' basis for contributing and accessing data, i.e. 'what you give is what you get'. It provides advice and guidance, recommends changes to the trade associations, monitors compliance and reviews best practice.

17.4   Voluntary Organizations

These all primarily provide services directly for, and to, the consumer. They may influence government on behalf of the consumer by direct lobbying, through the media or seeking the active involvement of government bodies in their activities.

Debt counselling bodies

Money Advice Trust[13]

This is a charity that works across the UK with seven partner agencies. It and its partners (all charities) aim to provide effective money advice directly to anyone with debt problems anywhere in the UK. The members are:

- Birmingham Settlement (the UK's first money advice centre);
- Citizens Advice Scotland;
- Federation of Independent Advice Centres;
- Money Advice Association*;
- Money Advice Scotland*;
- National Association of Citizens Advice Bureaux; and
- Northern Ireland Association of Citizens Advice Bureaux.

(*These organizations are associations whose members are individual money advisors rather than institutions that supply services directly to the consumer.)

[12] Coe, C. (1999) *'Standing Committee on Reciprocity – An Update'*, ICM 6th Annual Conference on Credit Scoring, Leeds
[13] Ruddock, J. (1999) *'Learning Opportunities'*, Adviser No 75, pp 32-36

Consumer Credit Counselling Service

This is also a charity, set up in the mid-1990s, offering a service based on a US model to provide a free debt counselling service to consumers. The creditor to whom the debt is due pays a small percentage of any monies recovered to the CCCS; the service is free to consumers. For funding reasons, the CCCS prefers to assist debtors who still have some realizable assets (whereas debtors using CAB offices – or other money advisory centres – often have little or no income or assets). It has a number of branches and offers a telephone helpline service to consumers.

Money Advice Liaison Group

This is a non-policy-making discussion forum for any organization involved in consumer lending or consumer debt. It was set up in 1987 to establish a liaison forum and encourage good working practice. Its members include representatives from trade associations, relevant government departments and all the partners in the Money Advice Trust. It does not offer services directly to the public.

Consumers Association

This is an independent commercial organization operating in the area of consumer protection, including financial services issues. Its members are individual consumers to whom it provides a variety of services including regular publications; it does not offer debt counselling. It also fulfils a watchdog and lobbying role in any area of consumer protection.

18

GLOSSARY OF TERMS

A

Acceptance rate: The percentage of the total applications that are accepted.

Accepts: Those applications that pass the credit review process.

Account management: Wide-ranging operational function dealing with customers during the active life of their account(s), i.e. while their account(s) are in order.

Account management scorecard: A statistically-derived behavioural scorecard(s) developed for predicting the future risk on accounts that are currently in order; generally used for setting credit, shadow and target limits, and for authorizations decisions.

Acquirer: An organization that recruits a retailer who then accepts credit card transactions. Usually a bank.

Actuary percentage: The proportion of the outstanding balance of a product that the lender expects will not be repaid. Used in provision estimation.

Application data: The information available about an applicant that is taken from the application form.

Application processing: Operational function dedicated to the timely processing of new applications in line with company lending policies.

Application processing system: A computer system or software, which automates all stages of the credit review process. It can include validation checks, policy rules and on-line credit referencing. It may be run on a mainframe or on personal computers (either singly or networked).

Application score: The score calculated at the time of application. Some organizations use this term for the score based on the application data alone (i.e. excluding scorecard characteristics that use credit bureau data).

Application scoring: A statistically-derived model that predicts the credit risk for applications if they are accepted. It comprises a scorecard and a set of associated statistics for interpreting score in terms of risk. The traditional term for this was *credit scoring*.

Attribute: An item of information about an applicant or an account holder. A range or set of these items is interrelated to form a characteristic. For example, 'tenant' is one attribute of the characteristic 'residential status'.

Attribute strength: The measure of an individual attribute's ability to discriminate between any two outcomes (usually good and bad).

Attrition: Accounts that become inactive, dormant or close.

Attrition scoring: A form of behaviour scoring in which the predicted outcome is the likelihood of an account becoming dormant or closing in the near future. Used by marketing departments to retain good customers.

Authorizations: The process whereby the credit card issuer permits, or declines to permit, a new cardholder transaction.

B

Bad rate: The percentage of accounts that perform in an unsatisfactory manner as defined by the good/bad definition that was used in the scorecard development.

Bads: Accounts with unacceptable repayment behaviour. The credit grantor is unlikely to transact any future business with these account holders.

Behavioural scoring: A statistically derived model for predicting a specific dimension of future behaviour on an existing account. Models can be designed to predict, for example, risk, attrition, churn, propensity, response and revenue. The score is recalculated regularly (typically monthly) and can be used to make decisions on marketing, authorizations, limit setting and debt collection/recoveries activities.

Benchmarking consortium: Industry group that seeks to set benchmarks of best practice/ performance for a given industry/sector.

Break-even odds: The ratio of the number of good accounts needed to balance the losses generated by one bad account.

C

CAB: Citizens Advice Bureau.

CAIS: A UK proprietary payment history system used for sharing financial account information. The acronym stands for 'Credit Account Information Sharing'.

Can't pays: Debtors who have defaulted on payments because of their financial inability rather than any intent not to pay.

CCJs: County Court Judgments – a court order to a debtor in serious default that he or she must repay the debt. An English term whose equivalent elsewhere is Judgments, or in Scotland is Decree.

Champion/challenger strategies: An experimental set of two or more competing strategies designed to determine the extent to which a new strategy (challenger) can improve an outcome or performance, when it is tested against the existing (champion) strategy. The experimental strategy is applied in a single decision area, e.g. collections, and can be repeated any number of times with new challengers.

Characteristic: Any data item that could appear in a scorecard. These can be derived from the application form, internal files or credit references. For example, applicant's age or type of vehicle being purchased.

Characteristic analysis: A regular statistical report that compares the current attribute distribution of a particular characteristic with its corresponding distribution in the development sample. It shows changes in applicant profiles over time. It can also be used for non-scored characteristics.

Characteristic strength: A measure of a characteristic's ability to discriminate between two outcomes (usually good and bad). This is the maximum contribution that the characteristic can make to the scorecard.

Charge-off: A point in the delinquency cycle at which an account in arrears is moved from the main accounts system (i.e. charged-off) to a recoveries system/function.

Churn: The propensity for, and the rate at which, account holders leave one lender to take up a better offer with a competitor.

Classing: Analysis of the predictive strength of a characteristic.

CIFAS: Credit Industry Fraud Avoidance Scheme. A non-competitive, industry-wide shared information scheme for identifying fraudulent applications.

Claimant: The party instigating a court action, usually the lender/creditor.

Cohort: A group of items sharing a common quality, e.g. all accounts opened in the same month. Also known as a *tranche*.

Collections: Operational function dedicated to the process of managing accounts in the early stages of arrears/non-payment, or in excess.

Collections scorecard: A statistically derived behavioural scorecard for predicting future risk for accounts in the early stages of collections.

Consolidation: A loan offered as a means of amalgamating a number of other, smaller loans (usually from multiple lenders), particularly where the customer may be in arrears. The loan principal is generally paid out to the other lenders.

Correlation: The overlap in the predictive content of two or more data items. For example, the ownership of a home telephone and the ownership of a telephone directory are two characteristics that have nearly 100% correlation. Neither data item contributes any additional information about the applicant that is not already known from just one of them. Also known as *interaction*.

CPR: Civil Procedures Rules. The definitive book on court procedures.

Credit bureau: A commercial organization that collects and supplies credit-related information about individuals and companies. Also known as Credit Reference Agency.

Credit bureau score: The total number of points gained when characteristics only available from a credit reference are scored. This can be generated in-house as part of the credit scoring process or it can be a generic score that has been generated by a bureau based on all the information it holds on a customer.

Credit insurance: A specialist form of insurance which covers losses from bad debts.

Credit reference agency: See *credit bureau*.

Credit reference information: The information resulting from an enquiry on a credit bureau's files. In the UK this includes judgments, voters roll, previous search and shared financial/non-financial account information.

Credit scoring: The traditional term for a statistically derived model for predicting credit risk. It comprises a scorecard and a set of associated statistics for interpreting score in terms of risk.

Credit strategy: Alternative name for *risk management*.

Customer scoring: Developing and applying scorecards at the customer level instead of at an individual product/account level. It takes into account all the products held by the customer, and is used to set an overall credit limit that can be apportioned between different products.

Cut-off score: The score that represents the boundary between accepted and rejected applications, i.e. the lowest acceptable score. This figure is determined by the credit grantor and is adjustable.

Cut-off strategy: A plan that determines the cut-off score. This is usually decided on the basis of volume of accepted accounts required, or acceptable bad rate, or a combination of these. It varies for different products, different scorecards and over time.

Cycle time or point: A four-weekly or monthly date at which accounts are updated with financial transactions – payments, fees, interest, purchases, cash advances. For credit cards, statements are produced at this point.

D

Data: The raw ingredients (usually facts or figures) that, when processed, produce information or scorecards or management information reports.

Data capture: The process of collecting data from application forms or other paper-based sources, and transferring it to computer media. This may involve keying or scanning.

Declared limit: The credit limit that is notified, i.e. declared, to the customer.

Declines: Those applicants who fail the credit review process. Also known as *rejects*.

Decree: The Scottish equivalent of the English County Court Judgment.

Default data: Accounts that are three months or more in arrears.

Default notice: A notice that must be sent to customers in arrears before litigation or other recoveries actions can be taken to recover the debt. Once the notice has been served the lender has the right to demand repayment of the full balance outstanding rather than only the arrears outstanding.

Defendant: The party responding to a court action, usually the debtor.

Delinquent data: Accounts that are so far in arrears that the relationship between lender and debtor has broken down.

Development sample: A set of applications/accounts used to develop a scorecard.

Discrimination: The ability of a scorecard to differentiate between two polarized outcomes (or two potential outcomes) – usually goods and bads.

Distribution: The pattern of observed values in a dataset. For example, score distribution is the number of occurrences of each score in a sample.

Divergence: The extent to which a scorecard can discriminate between potentially good and bad accounts based on average scores of goods and bads, taking into account the variance around the average scores.

Dormants: Credit or charge card accounts that are rarely or never used by the cardholder.

Dynamic delinquency report: A regular report that monitors delinquency levels by score for a set of accounts which have been open for approximately the same length of time (i.e. they have the same exposure period). The reports are typically produced monthly (sometimes quarterly). It provides the source data for the *dynamic performance cohort matrix.*

Dynamic performance cohort matrix: A report that is regularly updated to monitor the growth in the delinquency levels for a set of accounts which have been open for approximately the same length of time (i.e. they have the same exposure period). The reports are typically updated monthly (sometimes quarterly).

E

Electoral roll: See *voters roll.*

Encryption: A computerized fraud prevention technique in which data transmitted over a network is scrambled before transmission and unscrambled on receipt.

Excess: Credit card accounts where the current balance exceeds the declared limit. Also called *over-limit.*

Exclusions: Applications/accounts that are not included in a development sample because either the applicant or the account behaviour patterns are atypical, or because there is no intention to score such applications in the future. Examples include staff, VIP, deceased, stolen, or fraudulent applications/accounts.

Extended credit: When the balance on a credit card is only partly repaid each month, the cardholder has taken extended credit.

F

Final score: A credit score that includes application data and all other, internal or external, data.

Final score report: A statistical report that relates the final score distribution for a particular set of applications to the accept/reject decision.

Floor limit: A financial ceiling, allocated by the merchant acquirer, given to retailers who accept credit cards; all transactions above this limit must be authorized. It is a credit and fraud control measure.

Fraud: Deception for the purposes of obtaining credit.

Fraud scoring system: Uses a scorecard(s) to identify potentially fraudulent credit card transactions and/or applications.

Full payers: Credit cardholders who pay their balance off in full each month, thereby incurring no interest.

G

GAIN: Gone Away Information Network. A non-competitive, industry-wide shared information scheme for identifying and tracing absconders who are in arrears.

Generated characteristic: A new characteristic created from two or more characteristics. For instance, 'loan-to-value' is a mortgage scorecard characteristic generated from the property value and the amount of the loan requested.

Generic scorecard: These are generalized risk models, developed and sold by outside vendors, based on information held by the vendor. The information used in such models is generally bureau-based and includes public records, shared-account information, bureau searches and geo-demographic indicators.

Geo-demographic systems: Classification of personal data based on various demographic criteria, e.g. census, voters roll, financial or neighbourhood data.

Gini coefficient and curve: A statistical measure of the efficiency of a scorecard.

Good/bad definition: Precise commercial definitions of good and bad accounts. This includes definitions for indeterminates and exclusions.

Good/bad odds: The ratio of good to bad accounts.

Goods: Accounts with acceptable repayment behaviour patterns. The credit grantor would wish to transact future business with these account-holders.

Grouping: Attributes of similar strength are amalgamated into larger groups. This reduces the total number of attributes and ensures that the sample count for each one is large enough to be statistically sound.

I-K

Indeterminates: Those accounts that fall between the definitions of good and bad. They may have a mildly delinquent history or not have sufficient maturity to be clearly classified. Ideally these should be no more than 5% of the development sample.

Information: The result of processing large quantities of raw data into meaningful outputs.

Insight: A UK proprietary payment history system used for sharing financial account information.

Issuer: An organization that recruits cardholders and issues the plastic card. Usually but not always a financial institution.

Interactions: See *correlations.*

Interval statistics: A table of scoring results that shows, for each score, the percentage of applicants which can be expected to achieve any particular score, together with the bad rate and marginal bad rate.

Judgment: A legally binding decision handed down by a court of law requiring a debtor to pay the creditor and the means by which this is to be achieved. Abbreviated as CCJ.

K-S (Kolmogorov-Smirnov) curve: A statistical measure of the efficiency of a scorecard.

M-N

Markov Chain model: A statistical method that can be used for estimating provision levels based on generalized roll rates.

Model: Representation of the future based on past experience, generally derived through statistical analysis.

Money laundering: The illegal process of passing illicit funds through an account (or several accounts) to disguise the original source of the funds.

Monitoring: The business function of producing regular management reports in order to control the scorecard(s) and the lending functions. Industry-standard reports are population stability, characteristic analysis, override analysis, final score report and dynamic delinquency reports. Also known as *tracking.*

Neural network: Modelling technique based on artificial intelligence or the network of nerve cell connections in the brain.

O

OCR: Optical Character Recognition – software that scanners use to convert images into characters or digital files.

Odds: The probability that a specific event will occur expressed as a ratio of one event to another, e.g. good/bad odds.

Over-limit: Credit card accounts where the current balance exceeds the declared limit. Also called *excess*.

Override analysis: A regular statistical report that relates, by score-bands, the number of overrides occurring.

Overrides: A decision that contradicts the scored recommendation, e.g. an accept below the cut-off or a reject above the cut-off.

P

Payments Systems Organizations: Organizations (such as Visa and MasterCard) that provide international payment networks for the benefit of members. Companies that issue credit cards and recruit merchants who accept credit cards are the members. Abbreviated as PSOs.

Performance scoring: See *behaviour scoring*.

Points: The values assigned to each attribute in a scorecard.

Policy rule: Any rule that is applied in addition to the scoring process in order to arrive at an accept/reject decision, e.g. decline all applicants aged under 18.

Population: All the applicants who have applied for a particular credit product, irrespective of whether they are ultimately accepted or rejected.

Population stability report: A statistical report that reflects changes in a population by score-band.

Portfolio: A collection of accounts held by a credit grantor for a given product.

Positive data: Accounts that are up to date and in order.

Power dialler: Telecommunications equipment that stores future outbound telephoning requirements and automatically dials telephone numbers.

Pre-screening: The process of cleaning a mailing list by removing any entries that do not meet a predefined set of conditions, e.g. the existence of CCJs.

Pre-screening scorecard: A scorecard used to identify accounts that are likely to be most suitable for a mailshot.

Principal sets: The two groups used in a two-outcome statistical modelling process, e.g. good/bad or active/inactive.

Probability: The likelihood of a certain event occurring in a pre-defined time scale.

Promises: Offers made by customers whose accounts are in arrears to repay some or all of the debt by an agreed date and in agreed instalments.

Propensity scorecard: Marketing scorecard that predicts the likelihood (or propensity) of an existing customer taking more credit/another loan, etc.

Provision: An accounting measure for the amount of outstanding balances that a lender expects will not be repaid.

PSOs: Payments Systems Organizations.

R

Rank order: To put any group of like items in either ascending or descending order.

Recoveries: Operations function dedicated to the collection of debts remaining after charge-off.

Red lining: The illegal practice of declining an applicant for credit solely on the basis of his or her address.

Reissued plastic: A credit card that has been routinely produced to replace an expired card. See also *replacement plastic*.

Reject inference: The process of deducing how a rejected applicant would have behaved had he or she been granted the credit. The resultant data is then included in the scorecard modelling process.

Rejects: See *declines*.

Replacement plastic: A credit card that has been issued as a one-off event to cover the loss or theft of an existing card. See also *reissued plastic*.

Response scoring: The process of using a scorecard to predict the likelihood of targets responding to a mailshot. If the likelihood is too low, they are removed from the list before mailing.

Revolvers: Card account-holders who do not pay off the full balance each month. See also *Transacters*.

Risk-based pricing: A strategy in which the interest rate or other terms are set in line with the perceived risk.

Risk management: Strategic function responsible for optimizing credit losses versus business development. Sometimes known as *credit strategy*.

Roll rates: The percentage of accounts at any level of arrears that progresses, or rolls on, to the next (worse) level of arrears.

S

Sample: Statistically representative sub-set of the total population.

Score: A one-dimensional summary of a particular aspect of customer behaviour, based on the information known about that customer at a specific point in time.

Scorecard: A set of questions, called characteristics, with a set of answers, called attributes. Each attribute has a different score value. For any given customer, the attribute scores are summed to give a total score that is interpreted using the scorecard statistics.

Search: Enquiry made at a credit bureau.

Shadow limit: An undeclared credit limit, which is usually greater than the declared limit, to which the lender will extend credit on a particular product.

Short settlement: An agreed amount, which is less than the full amount due, that the debtor will pay, and the creditor will accept, in full repayment of the debt.

Sub-population: Any sub-group within the main population that is sufficiently different from the rest of the population to justify being identified separately.

Strategy manager systems: Proprietary systems for implementing account management strategy design and testing for application or behavioural scoring.

Swap set: Those applications that would have been accepted under the previous decision process, but would be rejected by the implementation of a new scorecard, and vice-versa.

T

Target limit: The maximum amount that a lender is prepared to extend to a customer across all his or her product holdings. There is no tolerance in this limit.

Time-line model: A means of illustrating where different activities occur in relation to each other over time.

Through-the-door population: All the applicants for any particular credit or financial product irrespective of the final accept/reject decision. Sometimes abbreviated to TTD population.

Trace: Operational function dedicated to finding debtors who have absconded without leaving a forwarding address or contact point.

Tracking: See *monitoring*.

Transacters: Card account-holders who pay off the full balance each month. See also *Revolvers*.

Tranche: A group of accounts opened in the same period. Alternatively known as a *cohort.*

Transition matrix: Gives the likelihood of an account in any one state at one point in time moving into any other state at a second point in time.

TTD population: Through-the-door population.

U-W

Underwriting: The process of assessing the risk of any request for credit and reaching an accept or decline decision based on that assessment.

Validation: The process of testing the final scorecard before delivery. The supplier undertakes this before delivery, and the user should repeat the process before the scorecard is implemented.

Validation sample: A small percentage of a scorecard development sample (typically 20%) which is excluded from the scorecard modelling process so that it can be used to test the final scorecard.

Voters roll (VR): A government list of all the adults who have registered their eligibility to vote in national or regional elections. Also known as *electoral roll.*

VR see *Voters roll.*

Won't pays: Debtors who have defaulted on payments and deliberately choose not to pay for whatever reason. They usually have the ability to pay but not the intent.

Write-off: Any debt that is considered totally unrecoverable. Could be caused by fraud or bad debt.

Index